Authors

Leslie W. Crawford, Ed.D.
Georgia College & State University

Rebecca Bowers Sipe, Ed.D.
Eastern Michigan University

Zaner-Bloser

Educational Consultants

Barbara Ann Marinak, Ph.D.
Assistant Professor
Millersville University

Catherine C. Thome, Ed.D.
English/Language Arts and Assessment Coordinator
Educational Services Division
Lake County Regional Office of Education
Grayslake, IL

Science Content Reviewer

Michael Grote, Ed.D.
Math and Science Education
Columbus Public Schools
Columbus, OH

Teacher Reviewers

Janice Andrus, Chanhassen, MN
Shannon Basner, Hollis, NY
Teressa D. Bell, Nashville, TN
Victoria B. Casady, Ferguson, MO
Kristin Cashman, Mechanicsburg, PA
Jeanie Denaro, Brooklyn, NY
Susan H. Friedman, Ph.D., Sharon, PA
Katherine Harrington, Mechanicsburg, PA
Dianna L. Hinderer, Ypsilanti, MI
Eleanor Kane, Stow, OH
Jean Kochevar, Minneapolis, MN
Diane L. Nicholson, Pittsburgh, PA
Susan Peery, San Antonio, TX
David Philpot, San Francisco, CA
Jodi Ramos, San Antonio, TX
Jacqueline Sullivan, Sunnyvale, CA
Rita Warden-Short, Brentwood, TN
Roberta M. Wykoff, Stow, OH

Cover Concept: Holcomb Gallagher Adams

Cover Illustration: The Artifact Group

Design: Trent Marx, MarxVisual

Photography: Cover model, George C. Anderson; Interior models, Tom Dubanowich; Stopwatch image © Royalty-Free/Corbis; p. 7 © Wes Thompson/Corbis; p. 99 © Cathy Melloan/PhotoEdit; p. 199 © Detroit Opera House; p. 309 © David Muench/Corbis; p. 345 George C. Anderson

Art Credits: pp. 8, 28, 30, 50, 52, 74, 100, 124, 126, 152, 154, 174, 200, 222, 224, 256, 258, 284, 310, 332, 334, 362, 364, 386 Illustrated Alaskan Moose Studio; pp. 129, 130, 134, 142, 150, 225, 261, 262, 263, 348, 349, 359, 360, 361 Marilyn Rodgers Bahney Paselsky; pp. 273, 275, 282, 283 Pat Dewitt Grush

ISBN13: 978-0-7367-6106-2
ISBN10: 0-7367-6106-3

Zaner-Bloser, Inc., P.O. Box 16764, Columbus, Ohio 43216-6764

1-800-421-3018, www.zaner-bloser.com

Printed in the United States of America   08 09 10 11 12 (13880) 5 4 3 2 1

Authors

Leslie W. Crawford, Ed.D.
Georgia College & State University

Rebecca Bowers Sipe, Ed.D.
Eastern Michigan University

Zaner-Bloser

Table of Contents

NARRATIVE writing

Unit Opener 6

Memoir
Memoir Traits .10
Memoir Model. 11
Memoir Rubric 12
Prewriting: Gather Information 16
Prewriting: Organize Ideas 17
Drafting: Write a Draft. 18
Revising: Extend Writing 20
Revising: Clarify Writing 21
Editing: Check Sentences 22
Editing: Proofread Writing. 23
Grammar/Mechanics Practice 24
Publishing: Share Writing 26

Historical Episode
Historical Episode Traits. 32
Historical Episode Model 33
Historical Episode Rubric 34
Prewriting: Gather Information 38
Prewriting: Organize Ideas 39
Drafting: Write a Draft. 40
Revising: Extend Writing 42
Revising: Clarify Writing 43
Editing: Check Sentences 44
Editing: Proofread Writing. 45
Grammar/Mechanics Practice 46
Publishing: Share Writing 48

Biography
Biography Traits 54
Biography Model. 55
Biography Rubric 56
Prewriting: Gather Information 60
Prewriting: Organize Ideas 61
Drafting: Write a Draft. 62
Revising: Extend Writing 64
Revising: Clarify Writing 65
Editing: Check Sentences 66
Editing: Proofread Writing. 67
Grammar/Mechanics Practice 68
Publishing: Share Writing 70

Narrative Test
Read the Prompt 76
Writing Traits in the Scoring Guide 78
Narrative Test Response Model 79
Planning My Time. 83
Study the Writing Prompt 84
Prewriting: Gather Information 86
Prewriting: Organize Ideas 87
Prewriting: Check the Scoring Guide . . .88
Drafting: Write a Draft. 90
Revising: Extend Writing 92
Revising: Clarify Writing 93
Editing: Check Sentences 94
Editing: Proofread Writing. 95
Test Tips 97

DESCRIPTIVE writing

Unit Opener. **98**

Business Letter

Business Letter Traits. 102
Business Letter Model 103
Business Letter Rubric 106
Prewriting: Gather Information 110
Prewriting: Organize Ideas. 111
Drafting: Write a Draft. 112
Revising: Extend Writing 114
Revising: Clarify Writing 115
Editing: Check Sentences 116
Editing: Proofread Writing. 117
Grammar/Mechanics Practice 118
Publishing: Share Writing 120

Scientific Observation

Scientific Observation Traits. 128
Scientific Observation Model 129
Scientific Observation Rubric 132
Prewriting: Gather Information 136
Prewriting: Organize Ideas. 137
Drafting: Write a Draft. 138
Revising: Extend Writing 142
Revising: Clarify Writing 143
Editing: Check Sentences 144
Editing: Proofread Writing. 145
Grammar/Mechanics Practice 146
Publishing: Share Writing 148

Descriptive Vignette

Descriptive Vignette Traits 156
Descriptive Vignette Model. 157
Descriptive Vignette Rubric 158
Prewriting: Gather Information 162
Prewriting: Organize Ideas. 163
Drafting: Write a Draft. 164
Revising: Extend Writing 166
Revising: Clarify Writing 167
Editing: Check Sentences 168
Editing: Proofread Writing. 169
Grammar/Mechanics Practice 170
Publishing: Share Writing 172

Descriptive Test

Read the Prompt 176
Writing Traits in the Scoring Guide. . . .178
Descriptive Test Response Model 179
Planning My Time. 183
Study the Writing Prompt 184
Prewriting: Gather Information 186
Prewriting: Organize Ideas. 187
Prewriting: Check the Scoring Guide . .188
Drafting: Write a Draft. 190
Revising: Extend Writing 192
Revising: Clarify Writing 193
Editing: Check Sentences 194
Editing: Proofread Writing. 195
Test Tips 197

Table of Contents

EXPOSITORY writing

Unit Opener **198**

Book Report: Response to Literature
Book Report Traits 202
Book Report Model 203
Book Report Rubric 204
Prewriting: Gather Information 208
Prewriting: Organize Ideas 209
Drafting: Write a Draft 210
Revising: Extend Writing 212
Revising: Clarify Writing 213
Editing: Check Sentences 214
Editing: Proofread Writing 215
Grammar/Mechanics Practice 216
Publishing: Share Writing 218

Research Report
Research Report Traits 226
Research Report Model 227
Research Report Rubric 230
Prewriting: Gather Information 234
Prewriting: Organize Ideas 237
Drafting: Write a Draft 240
Revising: Extend Writing 244
Revising: Clarify Writing 246
Editing: Check Sentences 248
Editing: Proofread Writing 249
Grammar/Mechanics Practice 250
Publishing: Share Writing 252

How-To Guide: Instructional Text
How-To Guide Traits 260
How-To Guide Model 261
How-To Guide Rubric 264
Prewriting: Gather Information 268
Prewriting: Organize Ideas 269
Drafting: Write a Draft 270
Revising: Extend Writing 272
Revising: Clarify Writing 274
Editing: Check Sentences 276
Editing: Proofread Writing 277
Grammar/Mechanics Practice 278
Publishing: Share Writing 280

Expository Test
Read the Prompt 286
Writing Traits in the Scoring Guide 288
Expository Test Response Model 289
Planning My Time 293
Study the Writing Prompt 294
Prewriting: Gather Information 296
Prewriting: Organize Ideas 297
Prewriting: Check the Scoring Guide . .298
Drafting: Write a Draft 300
Revising: Extend Writing 302
Revising: Clarify Writing 303
Editing: Check Sentences 304
Editing: Proofread Writing 305
Test Tips 307

PERSUASIVE writing

Unit Opener 308

Editorial

Editorial Traits. 312
Editorial Model 313
Editorial Rubric. 314
Prewriting: Gather Information 318
Prewriting: Organize Ideas 320
Drafting: Write a Draft. 322
Revising: Extend Writing 324
Revising: Clarify Writing 325
Editing: Check Sentences 326
Editing: Proofread Writing. 327
Grammar/Mechanics Practice 328
Publishing: Share Writing 330

TV Commercial Script

TV Commercial Script Traits. 336
TV Commercial Script Model 337
TV Commercial Script Rubric 340
Prewriting: Gather Information 344
Prewriting: Organize Ideas 346
Drafting: Write a Draft. 350
Revising: Extend Writing 352
Revising: Clarify Writing 353
Editing: Check Sentences 354
Editing: Proofread Writing. 355
Grammar/Mechanics Practice 356
Publishing: Share Writing 358

Persuasive Speech

Persuasive Speech Traits. 366
Persuasive Speech Model 367
Persuasive Speech Rubric. 368
Prewriting: Gather Information 372
Prewriting: Organize Ideas 373
Drafting: Write a Draft. 374
Revising: Extend Writing 376
Revising: Clarify Writing 377
Editing: Check Sentences 378
Editing: Proofread Writing. 379
Grammar/Mechanics Practice 380
Publishing: Share Writing 382

Persuasive Test

Read the Prompt 388
Writing Traits in the Scoring Guide 390
Persuasive Test Response Model 391
Planning My Time. 395
Study the Writing Prompt 396
Prewriting: Gather Information 398
Prewriting: Organize Ideas 399
Prewriting: Check the Scoring Guide . .400
Drafting: Write a Draft. 402
Revising: Extend Writing 404
Revising: Clarify Writing 405
Editing: Check Sentences 406
Editing: Proofread Writing. 407
Test Tips 409

NARRATIVE
writing tells a story to the audience.

Hi, I'm Ashley. I'm studying narrative writing in school, and I think it's going to be one of my favorite types of writing. I love telling stories, so I'm looking forward to sharing them in print, too!

IN THIS UNIT

1. **Memoir**
2. **Historical Episode**
3. **Biography**
4. **Writing for a Test**

Name: Ashley
Home: Kansas
Interests: history, spending time
with family and friends,
volunteering for
community projects
Favorite Book: *Thief of Hearts*
by Laurence Yep

What's a Memoir?

It's a description of an important experience in the author's life. I'll need to figure out which of my experiences will make an interesting memoir.

What's in a Memoir?

Narrator
Because the narrator is the person writing the memoir, the story is told in the first-person point of view, using the word *I*.

Reflective Tone
This is how I want my memoir to sound. I'll use a reflective, or thoughtful, tone so the reader will understand how I feel. I can create a reflective tone by asking questions and/or drawing conclusions.

Voice? I totally thought voice was just used for talking.

Voice
The writer uses voice to express his or her unique style. In other words, my writing should sound like me. To create voice in my writing, I can include phrases and words that I often use.

Sequence
This is the order in which I'll describe my story's events. I can include flashbacks that interrupt the chronological order, and I can use transition words to help readers follow the sequence of my story.

Why write a Memoir?

There are tons of reasons for writing a memoir. I jotted some down to help me think about why I want to write.

Entertainment

I've done some interesting stuff, and even if I didn't see the humor at the time, things have happened to me that could make readers laugh. Entertaining the reader is one reason to write a memoir.

Personal Reflection

Writing about an experience can help me reflect on why it was important or what I learned. The reader might be able to connect to my experience and learn from it as well.

Education

Some events or experiences can be educational. If I describe what I've learned from my experiences, maybe my readers will learn something, too.

Relay a Message

The experiences I remember best are ones that have affected me in serious ways. They have taught me something about myself or about life in general. Relaying these messages to the reader is another reason to write a memoir.

Memoir Writing Traits

I know that there are six traits of good writing, so I'll use them to help me as I write. Here are the traits of a good memoir.

Trait	Description
Information/Organization	The memoir is focused on one major life experience. The memoir is well sequenced.
Voice/Audience	A reflective tone conveys meaning and insight to the reader.
Content/Ideas	Details bring the story to life.
Word Choice/Clarity	Word choice is varied.
Sentence Fluency	Well-chosen questions build suspense throughout.
Grammar/Mechanics	Spelling, punctuation, and capitalization are correct. Simple and perfect tense are used correctly.

I can use Manny's memoir on the next page as a model for my own writing. Later, we'll check out how he used the traits to help him write.

Summer Surprise
by Manny Reyes

Narrator

Voice

Sequence

Reflective Tone

If someone had told me in June that the most surprising event of the summer wouldn't happen until the beginning of September, I would have laughed.

But right before school began, my best friend, Kenny, invited me to spend Labor Day weekend with his family. I thought it was going to be awesome. But when Kenny told me this year's destination, my jaw dropped. "Camping?" I asked. "You're kidding—right?"

"Nope," said Kenny. "Mom and Dad want to try something totally new."

I really wasn't sure whether to accept the invitation. Me? Camping? I am a city kid through and through. Then, I thought about how Kenny and I always have a great time no matter what we do. So reluctantly, I said yes.

But when that fateful Friday afternoon arrived, all I wanted to do was hole myself up under my bedcovers and disappear. My heart was filled with dread, and my backpack was stuffed with city comforts. If the bathroom sink had fit, I totally would've crammed it in!

Eventually, the Millers pulled up in their SUV. Gear was tied on top and piled in the seats, along with Kenny and his annoying sister, Grace. Everyone was so chirpy that I really hoped they wouldn't notice my gloomy mood.

We cruised for about two hours, the signs of civilization disappearing as we approached the campsite. Finally, Mr. Miller parked the car, and we unpacked all the stuff. Twilight was descending. "Better start setting up these tents," said Kenny's dad.

A question popped into my head: "Could I make it back to the city on foot?" But I was quickly distracted as Mrs. Miller called out directions while we fumbled around with poles and pegs. It was pitch black by the time we finished. Mr. Miller built a campfire, and Kenny and I checked out our tent. It was pretty big inside. I thought, "Maybe this won't be so bad after all!"

As we sat by the fire, we toasted marshmallows and sang campfire songs. It was then that I noticed the knot in my stomach had loosened. I was actually beginning to enjoy this! Bug spray kept away the mosquitoes, and there were bathrooms right down the hill. There was even a lake on the way in, which we were planning on swimming in the next day. "Check it out," said Kenny, pointing up. The sight took my breath away. A sea of stars lit up the sky.

The next day, I woke early. I was excited about eating an outdoor breakfast, and I was a little amazed, too, at how life can surprise you!

Memoir Rubric

The traits of a good memoir from page 10 have been used to make the rubric below. By using 1, 2, 3, or 4 check marks to judge each trait, you can decide how well any memoir was written.

	Excelling ✓✓✓✓	Achieving ✓✓✓	Developing ✓✓	Beginning ✓
Information/Organization	The memoir is focused on one experience and is well sequenced.	The memoir is mainly focused on one experience and is mostly sequential.	Some of the memoir is focused on one experience and is somewhat sequential.	The memoir needs to be well sequenced and focused on one experience.
Voice/Audience	A reflective tone consistently conveys meaning and insight.	A reflective tone conveys meaning and insight in many areas.	A reflective tone conveys meaning and insight in some areas.	The tone needs to be more reflective throughout.
Content/Ideas	Many details bring the story to life.	Some details are included.	A few details are included.	More details are needed to bring the story to life.
Word Choice/Clarity	Word choice is varied.	Word choice is varied in some areas.	Word choice is varied in a few areas.	Word choice should be more varied.
Sentence Fluency	Well-chosen questions build suspense throughout.	Some questions build suspense in some areas.	A few questions build suspense in a few areas.	Well-chosen questions should be used to build suspense throughout.
Grammar/Mechanics	Spelling, grammar, and the use of simple/perfect tense are correct.	There are a few errors in spelling, grammar, and simple/perfect tense usage.	There are several errors in spelling, grammar, and simple/perfect tense usage.	There are many errors in spelling, grammar, and simple/perfect tense usage.

Using the Memoir Rubric to Study the Model

Let's use the rubric to check Manny Reyes's memoir, "Summer Surprise." How many check marks would you give Manny for each trait?

 Information/Organization

- **The memoir is focused on one major life experience.**
- **The memoir is well sequenced.**

Manny focuses his memoir on a specific experience—his first time camping. I like the way he introduces his topic while also explaining how he feels. His writing is also easy for the reader to understand.

[from the writing model]

But right before school began, my best friend, Kenny, invited me to spend Labor Day weekend with his family. I thought it was going to be awesome. But when Kenny told me this year's destination, my jaw dropped. "Camping?" I asked. "You're kidding—right?"

 Voice/Audience

- **A reflective tone conveys meaning and insight to the reader.**

Manny uses a reflective tone to express his current views on a past experience. In the passage below, notice how he uses an "if" clause to reflect on the views he had at the beginning of the summer.

[from the writing model]

If someone had told me in June that the most surprising event of the summer wouldn't happen until the beginning of September, I would have laughed.

Content/Ideas

• **Details bring the story to life.**

Manny makes his story interesting by using specific details to describe his experience. In this paragraph, he not only tells his readers that he was waiting for the Millers, he also shows them. He uses specific images and details to express his fear and nervousness.

[from the writing model]

But when that fateful Friday afternoon arrived, all I wanted to do was hole myself up under my bedcovers and disappear. My heart was filled with dread, and my backpack was stuffed with city comforts. If the bathroom sink had fit, I totally would've crammed it in!

Word Choice/Clarity

• **Word choice is varied.**

Manny uses a wide variety of words so that he doesn't bore his reader with repetitive language. In this passage, he could have written *It was getting dark.* But I like what he chose much better.

[from the writing model]

Finally, Mr. Miller parked the car, and we unpacked all the stuff. Twilight was descending.

Sentence Fluency

• Well-chosen questions build suspense throughout.

There are plenty of ways to keep the action moving and build suspense in a story. Sometimes it helps to use a question, which can act as a cliff-hanger. This leaves the reader wondering what will happen next. In the passage below, Manny uses a question to make the reader wonder if he will really try and walk back to the city.

[from the writing model]

A question popped into my head: "Could I make it back to the city on foot?"

Grammar/Mechanics

• Spelling, punctuation, and capitalization are correct. Simple and perfect tense are used correctly.

When describing a series of events, it's important to use the correct verb tense so that readers can tell when things really happened. Manny begins this paragraph in the simple past tense, but then he uses the past perfect tense *had loosened* to show how his stomach settled before he began enjoying himself.

[from the writing model]

As we sat by the fire, we toasted marshmallows and sang campfire songs. It was then that I noticed the knot in my stomach had loosened. I was actually beginning to enjoy this!

I'm going to write a memoir about an important experience in my own life. I'll make sure to follow the rubric and use good writing strategies. Keep reading to see how I do it!

Prewriting Gather Information

Information/Organization

The memoir is focused on one major life experience.

Writing Strategy

Jot down notes about a major life experience.

When I found out I'd be writing a memoir, I realized there are a bunch of ideas to choose from. I could write about the first time I saw a major league baseball game or about the time I helped build houses for the homeless. But those are memories from a while ago. I think I'll write about a recent rainy weekend at my family's lake house instead. At the time, I had no idea the experience would turn out to be so memorable. And since my classmates are my audience, I think they'll appreciate the unexpected message of my memoir. I'll begin by brainstorming some notes.

My Notes About the Lake House

✔ family goes there on weekends and vacations

✔ usually swim, canoe, relax on beach, barbecue

✔ disappointing rainy weather—boredom and bickering

✔ did puzzles, read, wrote

✔ found an old photo album

✔ pictures included woman in red dress, grandparents' wedding, lake house

Practice!

Now it's your turn. Choose an experience to write about. Jot down notes about the things you remember the most.

Prewriting Organize Ideas

Writer's Term

Story Frame

Use a **Story Frame** to sequence important story elements such as setting, introduction, rising/falling action, climax, and resolution.

The rubric says my memoir should be well sequenced. I'll use a Story Frame to help me organize ideas. As I write, it will serve as an outline of events.

Story Frame

Setting:	My family's lake house
Introduction:	My family needed a getaway; we went to the lake house to relax.
Rising Action (Event 1):	It rains.
Rising Action (Event 2):	I'm disappointed, but I keep busy by writing in my journal, doing a puzzle, and reading.
Rising Action (Event 3):	The next day brings more rain.
Climax:	I find an old photo album.
Falling Action (Event 1):	My family enjoys viewing photos together.
Resolution:	I realize that the rain has caused us to reconnect and enjoy each other's company.

Practice!

Now it's your turn. Use a Story Frame to sequence the events of your memoir.

Reflect

Is my topic interesting? Will my Story Frame help me sequence events as I write?

Drafting Write a Draft

Voice/Audience

A reflective tone conveys meaning and insight to the reader.

Writing Strategy

Use a reflective tone to convey meaning and insight to the reader.

Writer's Term

Tone

Tone reflects the author's attitude or manner of expression. It's how the writing sounds. Tone can be funny, sarcastic, or even sad, but it should match the writer's purpose. A writer can use a **reflective tone** to express meaning and insight.

Now I'll use my Story Frame to help me write. The rubric says I should use a reflective tone to express meaning, so I'll try to be thoughtful about the experience I'm describing.

I'll do my best with spelling and grammar. However, I plan to concentrate more on the big picture and worry about mistakes later. I can always fix those when I revise. Read the beginning of my draft on the next page.

[DRAFT]

Rained In

by Ashley

It had been a long, hectic September, so I was thrilled when I heard we would be spending the weekend at our lake house. I couldn't wait to relax on the beach, go canoeing, and eat barbeque. But when we arrived it was raining.

This was a big drag. But I tried not to let it get me down. I spent the day writing in my journal and putting together a 300-piece dinosaur puzzle. When I snapped at my little brother, Steve, Mom asked me what was wrong.

[used a reflective tone]

"Hello! It's raining!"

"Don't worry, Ashley. There's always tomorrow," said Mom.

Practice!

Now it's your turn. Use a reflective tone so that your readers understand how you feel.

Reflect

Is my tone thoughtful enough? Will it help my readers understand how I feel?

Revising Extend Writing

Content/Ideas

Details bring the story to life.

Writing Strategy   Add details to bring the story to life.

Writer's Term

Details

Details are the specific words used to describe a person, place, idea, or thing. For effective writing, choose details that are clear, colorful, and appealing.

After I finished my draft, I checked the rubric again. It said that I should use details to bring my story to life. Here's a passage where I added details to help my readers feel as if they were at the lake house with me.

[DRAFT]

[added details]

I supposed Mom was right. With a sigh, I staked out a position
in the comfy chair by the porch,
where I could listen to the rain. But Steve, who had used up all
's rhythmic beat
his patience by lunchtime, would not leave me alone. By dinner,
(the non-barbecue kind)

everyone's nerves were fried.

Practice!

Now it's your turn. Add details to bring your memoir to life.

Revising Clarify Writing

Word Choice/ Clarity

Word choice is varied.

Writing Strategy

Use a thesaurus to help me vary my word choice.

✏️ Writer's Term

Thesaurus

A **thesaurus** is a book or an on-line reference that contains words and their synonyms (words with similar meanings) and antonyms (words with opposite meanings).

The rubric says my word choice should be varied, so I used a thesaurus to help me find synonyms for dull words that I found in my draft. Take a look at how I replaced some common words with more interesting, descriptive ones.

[DRAFT]

[varied word choice]

But in the morning, the rain was ~~coming~~ *pounding* down in sheets. At breakfast, Mom passed around French toast as she ~~talked~~ *chirped* in an upbeat tone that was obviously put on for our benefit. No one was buying it. "This weekend is officially a bust," I ~~said~~ *complained*.

Practice!

Now it's your turn. Use a thesaurus to help vary word choice in your draft.

Reflect

Have I used enough details to help readers visualize my experience? Have my revisions made my memoir clearer?

Editing Check Sentences

Sentence Fluency

Well-chosen questions build suspense throughout.

Writing Strategy

Use questions to build suspense.

Now I have to edit my writing. The rubric says I should use well-chosen questions to build suspense. At first, I was confused about how to do this, but then I remembered a mystery novel I once read. Each time the author used a question at the end of a paragraph or a chapter, it made me want to read on to find out the answer. Now that I think about it, I can use a question to help build suspense right before the climax of my memoir.

[DRAFT]

[used a question to build suspense]

How was I going to get through another soggy day? ~~I couldn't make it through another day.~~ I plopped on the floor next to the bookcase and looked for something to read.

Practice!

Now it's your turn. Use questions to make your reader wonder what will happen next.

Editing Proofread Writing

Grammar/Mechanics Spelling, punctuation, and capitalization are correct. Simple and perfect tense are used correctly.

Writing Strategy Make sure that simple and perfect tense are used correctly.

Writer's Term

Simple Tense/Perfect Tense
The **simple tense** tells what happens in the present, what happened in the past, and what will happen in the future. The **perfect tense** tells what started in the past and is still happening, what began in the past and was completed, and what will begin and end in the future.

Now I'll check for errors in grammar and mechanics. Also, the rubric says I should make sure that simple and perfect tense are used correctly. When I reviewed my draft, I found some errors, so I think I'll fix them now.

[DRAFT]

photo

[corrected past perfect tense] ⟶ had

"I see you found the ~~foto~~ album," said Mom. She seen me take

out a thick, leather-bound book.

[changed past perfect to simple past tense] ⟶ fell

As I leafed through the pictures, my eyes ~~had fallen~~ on a

striking girl in a red dress. "Who's this, Mom? She's beautiful."

Practice!

Now it's your turn. Edit for errors in grammar and mechanics, making sure that simple and perfect tense are also used correctly.

Grammar/Mechanics

For more practice with simple and perfect tense, use the exercises on the next two pages.

Reflect

I added a question to build suspense. Did it work? Do my edits make sense?

Simple and Perfect Tense

KNOW the RULE

- The **simple present tense** tells what happens now.
  Example: Beth and her dog **walk** to the river.
- The **simple past tense** tells what happened in the past. In most cases, add *–ed* to the end of a simple present tense verb.
  Example: Beth **walked** to the river yesterday.
- The **simple future tense** tells what will happen in the future. Add the helping verb *will* to a simple present tense verb.
  Example: Beth **will walk** to the river tomorrow.
- The **present perfect tense** tells what began in the past and may still be happening. Add the helping verb *has or have* to a simple past tense verb.
  Example: Beth **has walked** to the river many times.
- The **past perfect tense** tells what began in the past and was completed. Add the helping verb *had* to a simple past tense verb.
  Example: Beth **had walked** to the river many times.
- The **future perfect tense** tells what will begin in the future and end in the future. Add the helping verb *will* to a present perfect tense verb.
  Example: Beth **will have walked** many times by the week's end.

Practice the Rule

On a separate sheet of paper, write the verb in parentheses that correctly completes each sentence.

1. Yesterday, Mom (need/needed) almost a dozen eggs to make breakfast.
2. If the rain (stopped/had stopped), we could have gone swimming.
3. Viewing photos (has made/will have made) my family closer.
4. We (have vacationed/vacation) at the lake house many times.
5. By the week's end, we (have learned/had learned) the value of family.

Apply the Rule

Read the following memoir, looking for simple/perfect tense errors. Then, rewrite the story correctly on another sheet of paper.

Dog Business

My mom suggested that I start my own dog-walking business, so I posted over a hundred flyers around town and waited for a call.

Then, Mrs. Gould call and ask me to walk her little dog, Lucy. By the time we hung up, Mrs. Gould and I agree on a fee. We also have discussed where I should walk Lucy.

I was really happy with my job, so it was great to hear from Joey Danes. He will have owned two 100-pound golden retrievers. I would have to walk three dogs at once, but I knew I could do it.

The next day, Lucy and I pick up Rover and Arnold, and I immediately realized what I have gotten myself into. Each dog wanted to go a different route. As we were entering the park, a family of ducks came by, stealing the attention of both Rover and Arnold. Holding on for dear life, I had picked up Lucy and tried desperately to keep up with the retrievers, but they sprint after the ducks. Unfortunately, we were headed straight for the pond. Before I could control the situation, we were all soak!

Now, I know they say you can't teach an old dog new tricks, but by the time I get this business up and running, I'm sure I will learn all kinds of old tricks from new dogs!

Publishing **Share Writing**

Publish my memoir in a class journal.

Now that I've finished my memoir, I need to think about how to publish it. I could post my story on a Web page or read it to a classmate, but I'd really like to publish it in our class journal. That way, all of my classmates can read it. First, I'll read through it one last time to make sure it includes all of the items on my checklist.

My Checklist

✔ The memoir focuses on one experience.

✔ It has a clear sequence of events.

✔ A reflective tone adds meaning.

✔ Details make the memoir lively.

✔ Word choice is varied.

✔ Spelling, capitalization, and punctuation are correct. Simple and perfect tense verbs are used correctly.

Practice!

Now it's your turn. Make a checklist to check your memoir. Then, make a final draft to publish.

Rained In

by Ashley

It had been a long, hectic September, so I was thrilled when I heard we would be spending the weekend at our lake house. I couldn't wait to relax on the beach, go canoeing, and eat barbecue. But when we arrived, it was raining.

This was a big drag. But I tried not to let it get me down. I spent the day writing in my journal and putting together a 300-piece dinosaur puzzle. When I snapped at my little brother, Steve, Mom asked me what was wrong.

"Hello! It's raining!"

"Don't worry, Ashley. There's always tomorrow," said Mom.

I supposed Mom was right. With a sigh, I staked out a position in the comfy chair by the porch, where I could listen to the rain's rhythmic beat. But Steve, who had used up all his patience by lunchtime, would not leave me alone. By dinner (the non-barbecue kind), everyone's nerves were fried. As I tucked myself into bed, I hoped for clear skies the next day.

But in the morning, the rain was pounding down in sheets. At breakfast, Mom passed around French toast as she chirped in an upbeat tone that was obviously put on for our benefit. No one was buying it. "This weekend is officially a bust," I complained. How was I going to get through another soggy day? I plopped on the floor next to the bookcase and looked for something to read.

"I see you found the photo album," said Mom. She had seen me take out a thick, leather-bound book.

As I leafed through the pictures, my eyes fell on a striking girl in a red dress. "Who's this, Mom? She's beautiful."

My mother laughed, "Well thank you, dear. That's me."

"Get out of town!" I said in disbelief. But it was Mom, posing in her prom dress. She told me she had shopped for weeks without finding anything she liked. Then, my grandmother brought down the red dress from the attic—and it was perfect.

We settled on the couch, and soon, we were joined by Dad and Steve. Slowly, we flipped through the album, savoring each page. Each photograph held a story, a piece of our family's past. Finally, peace settled over us, and we were able to enjoy the rest of the day inside, in each other's company.

As we drove home that night, I realized we not only went to the lake house to discover the open space of the outdoors, we also went to discover each other.

Reflect

Did I use all of the traits of a good memoir? Check it against the rubric, and don't forget to use the rubric to check your own memoir, too.

Ways to Publish a
Memoir

You might find that you want to share your memoir with others. But before you do, you should think about how to publish it. Here are some ideas.

 Read your memoir aloud to a classmate. Then, discuss his or her reaction.

 Submit your story to a literary magazine that publishes student work.

✓ Post your work on a Web site that focuses on autobiographical works.

✓ Include your memoir in an art display containing pictures that enhance the writing.

✓ Take your story home and share it with your family.

Writing Across the Content Areas
Memoir

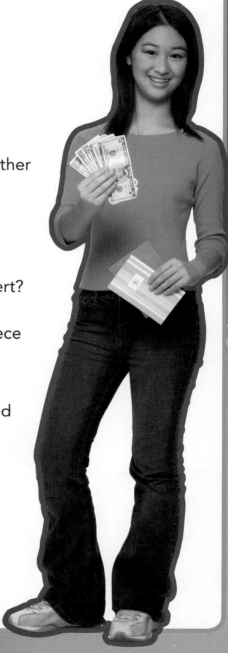

Your school subjects can be a great source of writing ideas. Choose a subject and see what topics you can come up with. Here are some examples.

Science

- Write about a memorable nature hike or other outdoor activity.

- Describe a time when violent weather affected you in some way.

Art and/or Music

- Have you ever attended a live music concert? Share your experience.

- Write about a time when you created a piece of art or wrote a piece of music.

Math

- Describe what you would do if you received a gift of money.

- Write about a time when you studied particularly hard for a math test and it paid off.

What's a Historical Episode?

It's a story that combines historical settings, characters, and events with fictional story elements. I think this will be fun because I can learn about history as I write.

What's in a Historical Episode?

Setting
This is the time and place in which a story happens. When I write my historical episode, I'll choose the setting first because it will give me ideas about characters and plot.

Characters
The characters are the people in the story. They can be fictional or based on real-life people. Either way, my characters will have to act in a way that's true to the setting.

Dialogue
This is the characters' actual words. If I use historical characters, I probably won't know what they really said, but I can imagine the way they spoke at the time. This is one of the ways that I can make my historical episode seem realistic.

Theme
This is the story's message about life. Because I'm setting my episode in the past, I have to be careful to include issues that are still important to people in modern-day times.

Dearest Ellen,
Mother simply does not understand me.

Dear Ellie,
Mom just doesn't get me.

Why write a Historical Episode?

There are many different reasons for writing a historical episode. I'll list some here. Maybe this will help me figure out why I want to write.

Entertainment
Reading a historical episode can be fun. Entertaining the reader is a good reason to write.

Information
I can gather historical information from a textbook and use it in my historical episode. Then, readers can learn from my writing.

Make Connections
I know that some people don't like to read about history because they think it has nothing to do with current issues. But a good historical episode connects people across the ages because it tells a story that is timeless.

Historical Episode Writing Traits

I know that there are six traits of good writing. But what makes a good historical episode? I'll use this list to help me write.

Information/ Organization	The story focuses on one historical event. Story elements are well organized.
Voice/ Audience	The setting and theme are clearly described for the reader.
Content/ Ideas	Historical details are included throughout.
Word Choice/ Clarity	Dialogue reflects the time and place in which the characters live.
Sentence Fluency	Sentence length is varied throughout.
Grammar/ Mechanics	Spelling, punctuation, and capitalization are correct. Dialogue punctuation is also correct.

I can use Carrie Taylor's historical episode on the next page as a model for my own writing. Later, we'll check out how Carrie used the traits to help her write.

Edie's Other Engagement

by Carrie Taylor

Characters — *Setting*

Theme

"Edie, you must be dreaming!" cried Hank. "This is America in 1943! No matter what you want, they'll never let women fly planes in this war. No, Edie, I won't allow it. No fiancée of mine is going to be a World War II Fly Girl."

"Well, Hank," said Edie, "I agree with you on two things. First, I *am* dreaming. I'm dreaming of the day that I graduate from Women Airforce Service Pilot training and get my pilot's wings. And second, you're right: No fiancée of yours is going to be a pilot in the war. If you're not going to support me in this, I'll just have to do it alone."

Dialogue

"Then I guess this is it, Edie," Hank said slowly. "I'm very sorry. But I want my wife at home, not on a plane!"

"Then this is good-bye," sighed Edie. "I leave tomorrow for flight school. I'll always remember you, Hank. I hope you'll understand someday."

It's hard to believe that was almost six months ago. Poor Hank. I miss him sometimes. But I wasn't about to let him tell me that I couldn't follow my dream. And now, can you believe it? I've finished my WASP training, and I'm graduating. Today—December 17, 1943—I will finally get my wings.

I always dreamed I would fly someday. And now I'll have the chance. My mission now is to join other women in ferrying planes to bases across the United States so that our male pilots, who are badly needed at the front, will be released from ferrying duties. Just imagine my excitement!

When I applied to be a Woman Airforce Service Pilot, I thought I didn't stand a chance. Thank goodness my parents didn't feel the same way as Hank. No, Mother and Dad were right there behind me, cheering me on. And now it is graduation day. If only Hank were here to see me now. But wait a minute—there he is!

"Edie, I'm so proud of you," cried Hank. "Now, how about putting this engagement ring back on? It goes perfectly with your new wings."

"No, Hank," said Edie. "I'm afraid that my only engagement right now is with the U.S. Air Force. It's too bad you couldn't be with me when I really needed your support. I think I'll fly solo for a while."

Historical Episode

Rubric

The traits of a good historical episode from page 32 have been used to make the rubric below. By using 1, 2, 3, or 4 check marks to judge each trait, you can decide how well any historical episode was written.

	Excelling ✓✓✓✓	Achieving ✓✓✓	Developing ✓✓	Beginning ✓
Information/ Organization	The story focuses on one event and is well organized throughout.	Most of the story focuses on one event and is mostly organized.	The story focuses on several events and is loosely organized.	The story should focus on one event and should be better organized.
Voice/ Audience	The setting and theme are clear to the reader.	The setting and theme are mostly clear to the reader.	The setting and theme are clear in a few places.	The setting and theme need to be clearer.
Content/ Ideas	Historical details are included throughout.	Many historical details are included.	Some historical details are included.	More historical details are needed throughout.
Word Choice/ Clarity	All of the dialogue is true to the setting.	Most of the dialogue is true to the setting.	Some of the dialogue is true to the setting.	The dialogue needs to be more true to the setting.
Sentence Fluency	Sentence length is varied throughout.	Sentence length is varied in some areas.	Sentence length is varied in a few areas.	Sentence length should be varied throughout.
Grammar/ Mechanics	Spelling, grammar, and dialogue punctuation are correct.	There are a few errors in spelling, grammar, and dialogue punctuation.	There are several errors in spelling, grammar, and dialogue punctuation.	There are many errors in spelling, grammar, and dialogue punctuation.

Historical Episode
Using the Rubric to Study the Model

Now, let's use the rubric to check Carrie Taylor's historical episode, "Edie's Other Engagement." How many check marks would you give Carrie for each trait?

Information/Organization

- **The story focuses on one historical event.**
- **Story elements are well organized.**

Carrie introduces the major story event—Edie's decision to become an air force pilot—in the opening paragraph. This decision causes conflict with her fiancé and leads to other story events.

[from the writing model]

". . . No, Edie, I won't allow it. No fiancée of mine is going to be a World War II Fly Girl."

Voice/Audience

- **The setting and theme are clearly described for the reader.**

Carrie lets the reader know the theme and setting of the story right at the start. Notice how Hank's opening dialogue names the setting (America in 1943) and hints at the theme (women's place on the front lines).

[from the writing model]

"Edie, you must be dreaming!" cried Hank. "This is America in 1943! No matter what you want, they'll never let women fly planes in this war. . . ."

• **Historical details are included throughout.**

Carrie includes a lot of historical details that make the reader believe the story really happened. Although it's fiction, the reader learns these real-life details along the way: World War II was going on in 1943, and women pilots were called Fly Girls, WASPs, or Woman Airforce Service Pilots. At graduation, they were given wing-shaped pins.

[from the writing model]

I've finished my WASP training, and I'm graduating. Today—December 17, 1943—I will finally get my wings.

• **Dialogue reflects the time and place in which the characters live.**

Carrie's characters sound real because they talk like people who lived during World War II. Americans probably didn't speak much differently in 1943 than they do today. But if you read Hank's words below, you'll see how they reflect an old-fashioned attitude.

[from the writing model]

"Then I guess this is it, Edie," Hank said slowly. "I'm very sorry. But I want my wife at home, not on a plane!"

Sentence Fluency

- **Sentence length is varied throughout.**

I like how Carrie's sentences aren't all the same length. Check out the paragraph below. It begins with two short sentences, and a long sentence follows. Then, Carrie ends with another short sentence. This variety makes her writing more interesting to read.

> **[from the writing model]**
>
> I always dreamed I would fly someday. And now I'll have the chance. My mission now is to join other women in ferrying planes to bases across the United States so that our male pilots, who are badly needed at the front, will be released from ferrying duties. Just imagine my excitement!

Grammar/Mechanics

- **Spelling, punctuation, and capitalization are correct. Dialogue punctuation is also correct.**

In her story, Carrie includes both the narrator's thoughts and characters' exact words. Sometimes Edie and Hank speak to each other, and sometimes Edie speaks to the reader. Because the dialogue is always enclosed in quotes, I can easily tell who's speaking to whom.

> **[from the writing model]**
>
> "Then I guess this is it, Edie," Hank said slowly. "I'm very sorry. But I want my wife at home, not on a plane!"
>
> "Then this is good-bye," sighed Edie. "I leave tomorrow for flight school. I'll always remember you, Hank. I hope you'll understand someday."

I'm going to write a historical episode set during an interesting time period. I'll follow the rubric and use good writing strategies. Read on to see how I do it!

Prewriting **Gather Information**

Information/Organization

The story focuses on one historical event.

Writing Strategy

Choose a historical event and gather information from several resources, including the Internet and primary sources.

Last year, my family moved to Kansas from New York. So when I was asked to write a historical episode, I decided to write about a family that settles in Kansas in the late 1870s. To gather information, I read a few articles and a book about sod houses. I also got some information from the Internet, including a primary source: a letter written by a guy who lived in a sod house. Here are some of my notes.

My Notes on Sod Houses

✔ hardly any trees, so couldn't build log cabins
✔ used blocks of prairie sod to build "soddies"
✔ cheap to build and didn't burn down in prairie fires
✔ dirt roofs leaked
✔ mice, snakes, and bugs—frequent "guests"

Writer's Term

Primary Source
A **primary source** is the person or book that is closest to the information. For example, a primary source about the Revolutionary War would be the journal, diary, or letter of a person who lived through the war.

Practice!

Now it's your turn. Choose a historical period in which to set your story. Then, think of a story idea. Gather information from a variety of resources.

Prewriting Organize Ideas

Information/Organization Story elements are well organized.

Writing Strategy Make a Story Map to organize story elements.

✏️ **Writer's Term____**

Story Map
Use a **Story Map** to organize story elements such as setting, characters, theme, conflict, and resolution.

The rubric says to organize my story elements, so I'll include these on a Story Map. Then, I'll use the Story Map to keep me focused as I write.

Story Map

Setting: Abilene, Kansas, 1876

Major Character(s): The narrator, Jeremy Thompson
Minor Character(s): Jeremy's sister, Lulu

Theme: Adjusting to a new place is often difficult.
Conflict: Jeremy doesn't like his new home in Kansas.

Plot		
Event 1	Event 2	Event 3
When the Thompsons arrive in Kansas, Jeremy hates it and wants to go back home.	After the neighbors help the Thompsons build a soddie, Jeremy discovers some of its pitfalls.	Jeremy gets a good laugh while teasing Lulu about her method of picking up cow chips.

Resolution: Jeremy realizes that teasing Lulu makes him feel more "at home."

Practice!

Now it's your turn. Organize story elements by using your notes to make a Story Map.

Reflect

How did I do? Do you think my Story Map will help me as I write?

Drafting Write a Draft

Voice/Audience

The setting and theme are clearly described for the reader.

Writing Strategy

Clearly describe the setting and theme for the reader.

Writer's Term _____

Setting/Theme

The **setting** is the time and place of the story. Let the audience know the setting as soon as possible to help them understand what's happening. The **theme** is a message about life that the author wants to express in the story.

Now I'll use my Story Map to help me write my draft. According to the rubric, I need to be really clear about the setting and theme. That's because the setting has a big effect on both the plot and the theme. If I don't describe these elements right away, my reader may not understand what's going on or why the characters act in certain ways. See how I included the setting and theme in my first two paragraphs on the next page?

Proofreading Marks

⌐ Indent	ℓ Take out something
≡ Make a capital	⊙ Add a period
/ Make a small letter	SP Spelling error
∧ Add something	¶ New paragraph

[DRAFT]

Home, Sod Home

Looks like we made it in time to celebrate the Fourth of July.

In a few weeks, our fair nation will be 100 years old. Abilene,

[setting]

Kansas, is an abominable place! Ma says, "Don't worry, Jeremy.

It'll grow on you." But I doubt it. So far, the only things that have

grown on me are the bumps from my bug bites.

This place is nothing like the home we left in Kentucky. There's

barely a tree in this place. People on these plains build their

homes out of dirt. They call it sod, and they call their houses

soddies. I think it's all disgusting. I want to go back to Kentucky.

[theme]

Practice!

Now it's your turn. Write a draft using details from your Story Map to introduce the setting and theme to your readers.

Reflect

What do you think? Will my details help readers understand the story's setting and theme?

Revising Extend Writing

Content/Ideas

Historical details are included throughout.

Writing Strategy

Add historical details.

✏ Writer's Term_____

Historical Details

Historical details are facts and information about an actual time, place, or event in history. They help the reader understand the time period being described.

After I wrote my draft, something dawned on me: My reader probably doesn't know much about life on the Great Plains in 1876. According to the rubric, I need to use plenty of historical details, so I decided to add some information to help my readers understand what it was like to live in a sod house.

[DRAFT]

I still don't like this place. When it's dry out, the dust is unbearable. I swear, I don't know which is worse.

Dirt drifts down from the ceiling of our soddy and adds an unwelcome flavor to our food. It crumbles from the walls and gets stirred up under our feet until there's a coating of dust over everything. When it rains, the roof leaks for days.

[added historical details]

Practice!

Now it's your turn. Add some historical details to help your readers picture life in the past.

Revising Clarify Writing

Word Choice/Clarity

Dialogue reflects the time and place in which the characters live.

Writing Strategy

Make sure dialogue reflects the time and place in which the characters live.

The rubric says that I should make my characters sound realistic—like people who could have lived during the time in which I set my story. When I reread my draft, I realized that I could make it sound more authentic. In my research, I came across different words that people used during pioneer times, so I replaced some of my original words with ones that I found. I also corrected an error in verb tense, since I noticed it while adding dialogue.

[DRAFT]

[corrected verb tense] → had

The only good laugh that I have in the last two months was when

"Girl,
my little sister was picking up cow chips. What in the world are ← tarnation

you doing?" I asked. "Are you trying to pick up those cow chips

'em
or eat them?"

[used dialogue that reflects the setting]

Practice!

Now it's your turn. Revise dialogue that sounds unrealistic by using words and speech patterns that fit the historical setting.

Reflect

What do you think of my revisions? Are they true to the setting?

Editing Check Sentences

 Sentence Fluency

Sentence length is varied throughout.

Writing Strategy

Vary sentence length.

OK, now I'll edit my writing. The rubric says to vary the length of my sentences. I know it's boring to read sentences that are all the same length, so I'll look over my draft to see if I can create some sentence variety.

[created sentence variety]

[DRAFT]

Home! Heck, we don't even have one. Nor do we have any logs to build one. This place is nothing like the home we left in Kentucky. There's barely a tree in this place. People on these plains build their

Practice!

Now it's your turn. Vary sentence length to make your writing more interesting.

Editing Proofread Writing

 Grammar/ Mechanics Spelling, punctuation, and capitalization are correct. Dialogue punctuation is also correct.

Writing Strategy Make sure that I have punctuated dialogue correctly.

Writer's Term

Dialogue

Dialogue, a conversation between characters, is always enclosed in quotation marks.

Now it's time to check for errors in spelling, punctuation, and capitalization. The rubric says that I should make sure I've punctuated dialogue correctly, so I'll focus on that, too. Here are some of the edits I made to my draft.

[DRAFT]

I had tears rolling down my cheeks. "So after you're done stabbing them with that fork," I said slowly, "are you planning to use it at supper?"

[added end mark before closing quote]

[enclosed a quotation]

Practice!

Now it's your turn. Edit your draft for spelling, punctuation, and capitalization. Make sure that you have punctuated dialogue correctly.

 Grammar/ Mechanics

For more practice with punctuating dialogue, use the exercises on the next two pages.

Reflect

I worked hard to edit my draft. Have my edits made my writing clearer and more interesting?

Punctuating Dialogue

- **Dialogue,** a conversation between characters, is always enclosed in **quotation marks.**
- Use **opening quotes** at the beginning of dialogue.
- Use **closing quotes** at the end of dialogue.
- Begin dialogue with a **capital letter,** unless it has been interrupted by an expression such as *she said.* Add **end punctuation** (period, question mark, exclamation point, or comma in place of a period) before the closing quotes. Also, add end punctuation, if necessary, at the end of the sentence containing the dialogue.
- Always begin a new paragraph when the speaker changes.
  Examples:
  "Hey, Jeremy! Why don't you help your sister pick up those cow chips?" asked Pa.
  "Sure thing, Pa," I grinned. "Just let me grab my fork."

Practice the Rule

Number a separate sheet of paper 1–5. Rewrite each sentence, adding quotation marks, commas, and end punctuation in the appropriate places. Use capitalization where needed.

1. Did you know that my great-great-grandfather was a homesteader I asked
2. I didn't Sarah replied tell me about it
3. Well I began his name was Albert, and he moved from Virginia to Nevada in 1861
4. How did he like Nevada Sarah asked
5. They say he liked it quite a bit I said he was, apparently, pretty content.

Apply the Rule

Read the historical episode, looking for errors in dialogue punctuation. Then, rewrite the story correctly on another sheet of paper.

Off From Independence

Betsy's father had told her not to fret. "Don't think about the length of the journey, girl he'd warned. We'll just take it step by step." But amid the crunch of travelers camped on the prairie just outside Independence, Missouri, Betsy could not get her mind off the trek that would take them along the Oregon Trail.

Betsy! Finally, I've found you!" Betsy's older brother, Sam, came running through the crowd. Mama's going to be mad, Betsy told him. "we've been looking for you all over the place"

"Well, I'm back now said Sam. Where's Pa? Sam then ran toward their wagon, with Betsy kicking up dust behind him.

I saw them, Pa" Sam shouted. "Up by the river junction—all heading out at the same time! No one could move. we need to get ready. I don't want to be stuck in the back with the other greenhorns"

"Watch your mouth, Sam," said Mama "Don't be ashamed to come from the city"! "Sorry," said Sam. But listen! The trail boss was making some folks throw things off their wagons. You should see it—cast iron skillets, sacks of flour—just piles of stuff along the road"!

"That's because they overpacked," said Pa "we're lucky your cousins made the journey first. Now we know not to pack house and home!"

Publishing Share Writing

Dramatize my story.

My historical episode is finished! Now I can think about how to publish it. I could add it to a class anthology, or I could submit it to a history-themed magazine that publishes student writing. But I really like the idea of turning my story into a play. I can get a few classmates to help me perform it—and then my story will really come to life! First though, I want to read through it one last time to make sure it includes all of the items on my checklist.

My Checklist

✔ The story focuses on one historical event and is well organized.

✔ The setting and theme are clear.

✔ Historical details appear throughout.

✔ Dialogue is true to the setting.

✔ Sentence length is varied.

✔ Spelling, capitalization, and punctuation, including dialogue punctuation, are correct.

Practice!

Now it's your turn. Make a checklist and check your historical episode. Then, make a final draft to publish.

Home, Sod Home

by Ashley

Looks like we made it in time to celebrate the Fourth of July. In a few weeks, our fair nation will be 100 years old. Abilene, Kansas, is an abominable place! Ma says, "Don't worry, Jeremy. It'll grow on you." But I doubt it. So far, the only things that have grown on me are the bumps from my bug bites.

This place is nothing like the home we left in Kentucky. Home! Heck, we don't even have one. Nor do we have any logs to build one. There's barely a tree in this place. People on these plains build their homes out of dirt. They call it sod, and they call their houses soddies. I think it's all disgusting. I want to go back to Kentucky.

With help from the neighbors, who are turning out to be a kind and generous bunch, we got our soddy built in pretty good time. Home, sod home. I still don't like this place. When it's dry out, the dust is unbearable. Dirt drifts down from the ceiling of our soddy and adds an unwelcome flavor to our food. It crumbles from the walls and gets stirred up under our feet until there's a coating of dust over everything. When it rains, the roof leaks for days. I swear, I don't know which is worse.

And then there's the matter of fueling the place. Seems we homesteaders must use what we have most of—cow chips. The only good laugh that I have had in the last two months was when my little sister was picking up cow chips. "Girl, what in tarnation are you doing?" I asked. "Are you trying to pick up those cow chips or eat 'em?"

Seems Lulu found the whole chip-picking ordeal distasteful. As she stabbed delicately at each chip with a fork, she said, "I refuse to touch these things. They're foul and dirty and smelly."

I had tears rolling down my cheeks. "So after you're done stabbing them with that fork," I said slowly, "are you planning to use it at supper?"

Lulu glared at me. Then, she glared at her fork. A cow chip was poised on the end. "I'm never eating again!" she cried. "And it's all your fault!" She threw down her fork and stomped off. A cloud of dust danced merrily in her wake.

Well, my sister and I were at it again. At least something was starting to feel like home.

Reflect

Did I use all the traits of a good historical episode in my writing? Check it against the rubric, and don't forget to use the rubric to check your own historical episode.

Ways to Publish a
Historical Episode

As you decide how to publish your work, think about who will be reading it. Then, pick the best way to share it. Here are some ideas for publishing your historical episode.

✓ **Check the Internet for sites that focus on different historical eras. Then, post your story.**

✓ **Include your work as part of a multimedia presentation.**

✓ **Submit your story to a magazine that publishes student work.**

✓ **Take your paper home and share it with your family.**

✓ **Include your historical episode as part of a class anthology of historical fiction.**

Writing Across the Content Areas
Historical Episode

Choose a school subject and see how many related writing topics you can brainstorm. Check out these examples.

Science
- Choose a famous inventor and write a fictional story about an actual discovery.
- Write about a historical weather-related disaster.

Social Studies
- Write a fictional story based on a major national event.
- Fictionalize an event in the life of a famous historical figure.

Art and/or Music
- Research a specific painting or sculpture. Make up a story about how it was created.
- Fictionalize a day in the life of a famous Renaissance artist.

What's a Biography?

It's a story about a real person's life. I'm looking forward to writing a biography because there's a world of people I can write about. I can choose someone who really interests me—and become a biographer!

What's in a Biography?

Third-Person Narrator
The writer of a biography narrates the story but is not involved in the action. I'll use the third-person point of view to narrate and objectively present my biography.

Characters
These are the important people in my subject's life. They are often more than story characters: They can also function as great sources of information about the subject of a biography.

Logical Sequence
It makes perfect sense for a writer to start a biography at the beginning of a subject's life and move through it in chronological order. But as long as the sequence is logical, a writer can also flash back and flash forward between key moments in the subject's life.

Direct Quotations
I can include direct quotations from important people in my subject's life. This will help bring my biography to life.

Why write a Biography?

There are many reasons for writing a biography. As I made this list, I realized my purpose for writing will probably depend on the subject of my biography.

Entertainment
Reading a biography can be fun. If I make sure I focus on what's most interesting about my subject, I'll be sure to entertain my readers.

Lessons
Some people have played important roles in history, or have lived their lives as examples for others. If this applies to my subject, my biography can teach valuable lessons to my readers.

Connections
A good biography should tell a story about a real person—someone who is probably like other people in many ways. As I write, I'll remember to think about what my readers might have in common with my subject. That way, my audience can connect with the story.

Information
There are many people I've heard of, but don't know much about. The purpose of my biography could be to inform my readers with details about a familiar face or name. Or I could inform my audience about a lesser-known person.

Biography Writing Traits

I know that there are six traits of good writing. Here's a list of what makes a good biography. I'll use it to help me write.

Information/ Organization	The writer focuses on one person. The biography is logically sequenced.
Voice/ Audience	An interesting event grabs the reader's attention in the introduction.
Content/ Ideas	Direct quotations bring the biography to life.
Word Choice/ Clarity	Words are used correctly.
Sentence Fluency	Sentences and paragraphs are logically placed.
Grammar/ Mechanics	Spelling, punctuation, and capitalization are correct. There are no sentence fragments or run-ons.

I can use Stewart Chase's biography on the next page as a model for my own writing. Later, we'll check out how he used the traits to help him write.

GILBERT CHASE: A MAN ON THE MOVE

by Stewart Chase

Characters

On the day my Great-Grandpa Gilbert was born, fate was in the mood for practical jokes. You see, Gilbert Chase was born breech on April Fools' Day, 1905. My mother told me that his mother always used to say, "Baby Gil was born breech 'cause he wanted to hit the ground running."

Logical Sequence

Third-Person Narrator

And run he did! It seemed his friends and family could never keep up with him. All through school he was the fastest boy in any race, and his grades were better than everyone else's, too. After he graduated from high school in 1923, he was accepted into the University of Illinois. Four years later, he graduated at the top of his class. In 1928, Gil opened a chain of stores that sold all kinds of electrical appliances. By that time, about two thirds of the country had electricity, and people were buying things on credit. Gil made tons of money.

His first major purchase, a Model T Ford sedan, cost him $295 right off the assembly line. Great-Grandpa Gil loved his new Model T. He drove it all over town. His friends would see him coming, and he'd pick them up for rides. Often, he'd stop at the ice cream parlor and treat them to their favorite flavors. "He's generous to a fault, that Gil," his friend Bruce would always say.

And Gil would always reply, "Brucie! What's the fun of having money if you can't share it with your friends?"

Direct Quotation

Those trips to the ice cream parlor paid off because that's where Gil met his future wife. Her name was Alice Smith, and according to Gil, "She was the most beautiful gal I had ever seen." Gil married her, and their wedding took place on July 19, 1929—exactly six months from the day they met.

Gil and Alice lived a very good life, though things got a bit lean during the Great Depression. They had two children—Scott, born in 1931, and Fay, born in 1934—and gave them the best of everything.

On his 40th birthday, Gil's friends and family threw him a huge surprise party at the country club. Gil was so shocked that he sat in a chair and cried.

He said he felt wonderful after the party, but Great-Grandma Alice said he didn't look right. She took him home and put him to bed. When she checked on him just before midnight, Great-Grandpa Gil was dead.

The doctor said that Gil had had a stroke and died in his sleep. My mom says that her Grandpa Gil was just in a hurry to meet his maker.

Biography
Rubric

The traits of a good biography from page 54 have been used to make the rubric below. By using 1, 2, 3, or 4 check marks to judge each trait, you can decide how well any biography was written.

	Excelling ✓✓✓✓	Achieving ✓✓✓	Developing ✓✓	Beginning ✓
Information/ Organization	The biography is logically sequenced and focused on one person.	Most of the biography is logically sequenced and focused on one person.	Some of the biography is logically sequenced and focused on one person.	The biography should be logically sequenced and focused on one person.
Voice/ Audience	An interesting event grabs the reader's attention in the introduction.	An interesting event is included in the introduction.	An event is included in the introduction, but it could be more interesting.	An interesting event should grab the reader's attention in the introduction.
Content/ Ideas	Direct quotations bring the biography to life.	Many direct quotations are included.	A few direct quotations are included.	Direct quotations should bring the biography to life.
Word Choice/ Clarity	All words are used correctly.	Most words are used correctly.	Some words are used correctly.	All words should be used correctly.
Sentence Fluency	Sentences and paragraphs are logically placed.	Most sentences and paragraphs are logically placed.	Some sentences and paragraphs are logically placed.	Sentences and paragraphs should be logically placed.
Grammar/ Mechanics	There are no run-ons, sentence fragments, spelling, or grammar errors.	There are a few run-ons, sentence fragments, spelling, and grammar errors.	There are several run-ons, sentence fragments, spelling, and grammar errors.	There are many run-ons, sentence fragments, spelling, and grammar errors.

Using the Rubric to Study the Model

Biography

Let's use the rubric to check Stewart Chase's biography, "Gilbert Chase: A Man on the Move." How many check marks would you give Stewart for each trait?

Information/Organization

- **The writer focuses on one person.**
- **The biography is logically sequenced.**

Stewart focuses his biography on Gilbert Chase, telling the key events of his subject's life in logical order. He even uses transitional phrases (underlined in the passage below) to tell how much time passed between one key event and the next.

[from the writing model]

<u>After he graduated</u> from high school in 1923, he was accepted into the University of Illinois. <u>Four years later</u>, he graduated at the top of his class. <u>In 1928</u>, Gil opened a chain of stores that sold all kinds of electrical appliances.

Voice/Audience

- **An interesting event grabs the reader's attention in the introduction.**

Stewart introduces his great-grandfather by describing his unusual birth on April Fools' Day. This is great because the reader immediately knows that the biography is going to be unique in some way.

[from the writing model]

On the day my Great-Grandpa Gilbert was born, fate was in the mood for practical jokes. You see, Gilbert Chase was born breech on April Fools' Day, 1905. My mother told me that his mother always used to say, "Baby Gil was born breech 'cause he wanted to hit the ground running."

Content/Ideas

- **Direct quotations bring the biography to life.**

I like how Stewart includes direct quotes to help the reader understand what Gilbert Chase was really like. Some of the quotes are from people who knew him, and some are from Gilbert himself. Look at this example.

[from the writing model]

"He's generous to a fault, that Gil," his friend Bruce would always say.

And Gil would always reply, "Brucie! What's the fun of having money if you can't share it with your friends?"

Word Choice/Clarity

- **Words are used correctly.**

Stewart's writing is easy to read because he uses words correctly. In this next passage, Stewart uses the word *lean*. This word has several different meanings (incline, rest against, thin, lacking in fullness), but Stewart uses it to express the idea that Gilbert's family had to do without many things.

[from the writing model]

Gil and Alice lived a very good life, though things got a bit lean during the Great Depression. They had two children—Scott, born in 1931, and Fay, born in 1934—and gave them the best of everything.

• Sentences and paragraphs are logically placed.

The paragraphs in Stewart's biography are well placed. Also, the sentences within each paragraph flow from one to the next in a way that makes sense. This makes the biography easy to follow.

[from the writing model]

Those trips to the ice cream parlor paid off because that's where Gil met his future wife. Her name was Alice Smith, and according to Gil, "She was the most beautiful gal I had ever seen." Gil married her, and their wedding took place on July 19, 1929—exactly six months from the day they met.

 • Spelling, punctuation, and capitalization are correct. There are no sentence fragments or run-ons.

If Stewart's biography ever contained any sentence fragments or run-ons, he made sure to correct them before publishing his work. You can tell Stewart's sentences are complete because each one contains both a subject and a predicate.

[from the writing model]

The doctor said that Gil had had a stroke and died in his sleep. My mom says that her Grandpa Gil was just in a hurry to meet his maker.

My Turn!

I'm going to write a biography about someone I'd like to know more about. I'll follow the rubric and use good writing strategies. Read on to see how I do it!

Prewriting Gather Information

Information/Organization

The writer focuses on one person.

Writing Strategy

Choose a person as the focus of my biography. Then, write interview questions and conduct an interview.

When my teacher said to write a biography, the first thing I did was choose a subject. I chose my grandmother because everyone says I look and act a lot like her. Then, I wanted to do some research about her. Because she died before I was born, I decided to interview her children: my father and my aunt. Finally, I wrote some interview questions.

My Interview Questions

✔ What do you remember most about my grandma, Mai Chaw?

✔ What would you like other people to know about her?

✔ What memories do you have of Mai Chaw and of leaving Laos?

✔ Do you have any memories of Mai Chaw in the refugee camp?

Practice!

Now it's your turn. Choose a person to be the focus of your biography. Gather information by writing interview questions and conducting an interview.

Prewriting Organize Ideas

Information/Organization

The biography is logically sequenced.

Writing Strategy Plot important events on a Timeline.

✏️ **Writer's Term**

Timeline
A **Timeline** can help you sequence key events in chronological order, the order in which they happened.

I know from the rubric that organization is important in a biography. If I don't describe the key events of Grandma Mai's life in order, my reader could get confused. After I conducted my interviews, I took all the information I gathered and plotted the most important events on a Timeline.

Timeline

Mai born in Laos on Jan. 9

Mai marries Bon Chaw

Mai gives birth to Huy

Family gets news of trip to America

| 1949 | 1966 | 1967 | 1968 | 1970 | 1975 | 1977 | 1978 |

Mai meets Bon Chaw

Mai gives birth to Pang

Family escapes to Thailand

Mai dies on Jan. 5

Practice!

Now it's your turn. Organize your biography by plotting the most important events on a Timeline.

Reflect

Do you think my interview questions were helpful? Will my Timeline help me stay focused as I write?

Drafting Write a Draft

Voice/Audience

An interesting event grabs the reader's attention in the introduction.

Writing Strategy

Grab the reader's attention with an interesting event in the introduction.

OK, now I'm ready to begin writing. The rubric says that I should introduce Grandma Mai in an interesting way. I'll start with the family's escape to Thailand and then flash forward, telling the story in chronological order from that point on. I won't worry too much about punctuation and spelling errors. The important thing is to get my ideas down.

After I started writing though, I noticed that I used simple and perfect tense verbs correctly. Verb tense has given me trouble in the past, so I'm happy to see that's not the case anymore.

The Courage of Mai Chaw

by Ashley

"Still, children, stay very still!" said Mai Chaw. "We must keep the raft nice and steady." Her desperate voice repeated those words until she could no longer speak. She and her children were running for their lives, and their lives depended on keeping that raft afloat and unnoticed. As they glided across the Mekong River, away from Laos, Mai wondered if they'd make it to Thailand.

[attention-grabbing event]

She was num with fear, but she had to go on. Only hours before, she

[correct use of past perfect tense]

had seen her husband dragged away by communist soldiers. Though it was 1975, and the fighting in Vietnam had ended, Mai's battle was only beginning. She was in for the fight of her life. She had to protect herself and her children from the communist soldiers. They would face certain death if they were found.

My father told us that our mother was very strong.

[correct use of simple past tense]

Practice!

Now it's your turn. Write a draft using a key event from your Timeline to grab your readers' attention.

Reflect

What do you think? Is the event that I used to begin my biography interesting enough to hook my readers?

Revising Extend Writing

 Content/Ideas   Direct quotations bring the biography to life.

Writing Strategy   Add direct quotations to bring the biography to life.

✏️ **Writer's Term**___

Direct Quotations

Direct quotations are the exact words that someone says. They are enclosed in quotation marks, just like dialogue.

After I drew my audience into Grandma Mai's story, I decided to go back and describe her. Instead of using my own words, I decided to use some direct quotations from my interviews. I guess I was right on track because the rubric says quotations will bring my biography to life. I had to be careful, though. I know quotations are similar to dialogue, and I've had trouble with dialogue punctuation before. That's why I added a quotation mark as soon as I saw that it was missing!

[DRAFT]

[added a direct quote]

"Our mother survived the journey because she was a very strong person," said my father, Huy Chaw.

~~My father told us that our mother was very strong.~~

"Yes, she was very strong," agreed his sister (my aunt) Pang, "and she was the bravest person I've ever known."

[corrected dialogue punctuation]

Practice!

Now it's your turn. Add some direct quotations to bring your biography to life.

Revising Clarify Writing

Word Choice/Clarity

Words are used correctly.

Writing Strategy

Use a dictionary to make sure I have used words correctly.

I had my teacher look over my draft. She said my story was interesting, but she reminded me to check what the rubric says about using words correctly. It's a good thing, too, because I spotted some errors.

[DRAFT]

— [corrected word usage] —

Mai arrived in the world on January 9, 1949. She was born in Laos, a small country in Southeast Asia. As soon as she ~~aged~~ **was old enough**, she began working in the rice paddies with her family. They farmed their paddies from sunup until sundown. Planting and harvesting rice was **backbreaking** ~~complicated~~ work that left them exhausted. But Mai was strong. And happy.

Practice!

Now it's your turn. Replace words that are used incorrectly with words that better fit the ideas you want to get across.

Reflect

Have my revisions created a clearer picture of my story?

Editing Check Sentences

Sentence Fluency Sentences and paragraphs are logically placed.

Writing Strategy Reorder awkwardly placed sentences and paragraphs.

After I finished revising, I read my paper to a friend. He said that part of my biography was hard to follow because some sentences seemed out of order. I know from the rubric that I should think about sentence placement, so I reread the section that seemed unclear. Then, I moved one of my sentences and placed it where it made better sense.

[DRAFT]

[reordered an awkwardly placed sentence]

~~After a year of preparation, Mai and Bon were married.~~ Mai met
After a year of preparation, Mai and Bon were married.
Bon Chaw when they were both seventeen. Soon, they fell in love. A

year after that, Mai had my Aunt Pang; two years after that, she had

my father, Huy.

Practice!

Now it's your turn. Reorder sentences and paragraphs that are out of sequence.

Editing Proofread Writing

 Grammar/Mechanics Spelling, punctuation, and capitalization are correct. There are no sentence fragments or run-ons.

Writing Strategy Correct sentence fragments and run-ons.

Writer's Term

Sentence Fragments/Run-on Sentences

A **sentence fragment** is not a complete thought. It is missing either a subject or a predicate. A **run-on sentence** is a compound sentence that is joined incorrectly.

My final step is to check for errors in spelling, punctuation, and capitalization. Also, the rubric says I should correct any sentence fragments or run-on sentences. I'll do that now!

[DRAFT]

[formed a complete sentence]

Things went well for Bon and Mai's ~~and their~~ family until they got
                                    Bon
involved in the Vietnam War. Fought against communism. Guiding
                                                        by
American soldiers to safety when their planes were shot down in the

jungles of Laos.

Practice!

Now it's your turn. Edit your draft for spelling, punctuation, and capitalization. Also, correct sentence fragments and run-ons.

 Grammar/Mechanics

For more practice correcting sentence fragments and run-ons, use the exercises on the next two pages.

Reflect

Have my edits helped my writing? Are my ideas clearer now?

Sentence Fragments and Run-ons

KNOW the RULE

A group of words that is missing a subject or a predicate is a **sentence fragment**. Correct a fragment by adding the missing subject or predicate.

> **Fragment:** Born in Laos. (subject missing)
> **Correct:** Mai Chaw was born in Laos.

Fragment: The fighting in Vietnam. (predicate missing)
Correct: The fighting in Vietnam had ended.

A **run-on sentence** is a compound sentence that is joined incorrectly. Correct a run-on sentence by adding a semicolon or a comma and a conjunction. You may also break it into two sentences.

> **Run-on:** The United States said they would help they never did.
> **Correct:** The United States said they would help; they never did.
> **Correct:** The United States said they would help, but they never did.
> **Correct:** The United States said they would help. They never did.

Practice the Rule

Number a separate sheet of paper 1–5. Then, read each item below. Write *F* if the item is a fragment or *R* if the item is a run-on. Then, rewrite each item correctly.

1. Some people think that Laos is located in Africa it is actually in Southeast Asia.
2. Laos is bordered by China to the north the western border lies along the Mekong River.
3. Governed by a single party.
4. More than fifty ethnic groups live in Laos they are officially divided into three categories.
5. Rugged mountains in northern Laos.

Apply the Rule

Read the biography, looking for sentence fragments and run-ons. Then, rewrite the story correctly on another sheet of paper.

Helie Lee: Author or Adventurer?

In 1996, when Scribner published <u>Still Life With Rice: A Young American Woman Discovers the Life and Legacy of Her Korean Grandmother</u>, Helie Lee saw a dream fulfilled: understanding her Korean legacy. As it turned out, however, the dream came at great price her book's international popularity put the lives of North Korean relatives in danger.

Lee was born in 1964 in Seoul, South Korea originally, her family had lived in North Korea. In 1953, many people fled the North. When the communists took power after the Korean War, Lee's uncle did not make it to the South.

<u>Still Life With Rice</u> ends with Lee's grandmother's dearest wish: to see her son again. She would get her wish, but only after Lee, by naming her uncle in her book, unwittingly made him and other North Korean relatives targets of the repressive government. Living in Los Angeles at the time, Lee could only think of one thing to do: rescue her uncle. She and other relatives. Embarked on a dangerous mission. And in December 1997, the family was united in South Korea.

Publishing Share Writing

Submit my biography to a Web site.

Now that I've finished my biography, I want to publish it. I could add it to a class anthology or I could see if a magazine would publish it. I really want people to know my grandmother's story because it's so much like the stories of other Hmong refugees in America. So I think I'll publish it on a Web site about the Hmong people. First though, I want to read through it one last time to make sure it includes all of the items on my checklist.

My Checklist

✔ The story focuses on one person and is logically sequenced.

✔ An interesting event draws the reader in.

✔ Direct quotations add life to the biography.

✔ Words are used correctly.

✔ Sentences and paragraphs are well placed.

✔ Spelling, capitalization, and punctuation are all correct. There are no run-ons or fragments.

Practice!

Now it's your turn. Make a checklist and check your biography. Then, make a final draft to publish.

The Courage of Mai Chaw
by Ashley

"Still, children, stay very still!" said Mai Chaw. "We must keep
the raft nice and steady." Her desperate voice repeated those words
until she could no longer speak. She and her children were running
for their lives, and their lives depended on keeping that raft afloat and
unnoticed. As they glided across the Mekong River, away from Laos,
Mai wondered if they'd make it to Thailand.

She was numb with fear, but she had to go on. Only hours before,
she had seen her husband dragged away by communist soldiers.
Though it was 1975, and the fighting in Vietnam had ended, Mai's
battle was only beginning. She was in for the fight of her life. She had
to protect herself and her children from the communist soldiers. They
would face certain death if they were found.

"Our mother survived the journey because she was a very strong
person," said my father, Huy Chaw.

"Yes, she was very strong," agreed his sister (my aunt) Pang, "and
she was the bravest person I've ever known." That's how Mai Chaw's
children describe her. They say she had been that way from the day
she was born.

Mai arrived in the world on January 9, 1949. She was born in Laos,
a small country in Southeast Asia. As soon as she was old enough,
she began working in the rice paddies with her family. They farmed

their paddies from sunup until sundown. Planting and harvesting rice was backbreaking work that left them exhausted. But Mai was strong and happy. She was always smiling, and she never complained about hard work.

Mai met Bon Chaw when they were both seventeen. Soon, they fell in love. After a year of preparation, Mai and Bon were married. A year after that, Mai had my Aunt Pang; two years after that, she had my father, Huy.

Things went well for Bon and Mai's family until they got involved in the Vietnam War. Bon fought against communism by guiding American soldiers to safety when their planes were shot down in the jungles of Laos. Bon and several of his countrymen helped save many American soldiers' lives. The United States said they would help

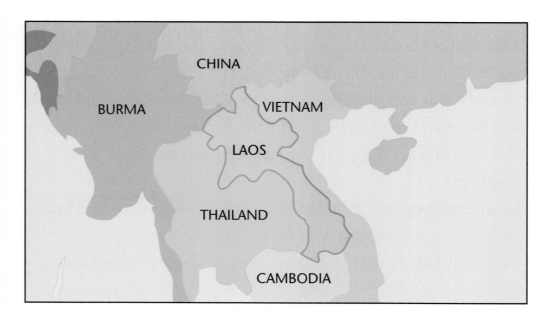

the Laotians in return, but they never did. Instead, they pulled out of Vietnam in 1975 and left the Hmongs to suffer the consequences of having fought against the communists. Many villages were destroyed, and the communists killed anyone who they thought had helped the Americans. Bon, who had helped American soldiers, was labeled a traitor. The communists tied him up and took him away, leaving Mai to protect their children.

Taking what she could, Mai soon found herself on a raft escaping to Thailand with her children. They were all frightened, but Mai stayed brave through it all. It took weeks, but she finally got herself and the children to a refugee camp.

Mai spent the next two years at the refugee camp, waiting to see if she and her family would be relocated to the United States. On December 29, 1977, word finally came; they would soon be leaving for America. She and her children would be safe! One week later, though, Mai had a heart attack and died.

Mai never saw the United States, but her children and grandchildren definitely benefited from her courageous act.

Reflect

What do you think? Did I use all the traits of a good biography in my writing? Check it against the rubric. Don't forget to use the rubric to check your own biography.

Ways to Publish a Biography

As you decide how to publish your work, think about who will be reading it. Then, you can pick the best way to share it. Here are some ideas for publishing your biography.

 Read your biography aloud to the class.

 Include your biography as part of a multimedia presentation on famous people or family roots.

 Submit your story to a magazine that publishes student work.

 Include your biography as part of a class anthology.

 Take your biography home and share it with your family.

Writing Across the Content Areas
Biography

School subjects can be great sources for writing ideas. Choose a subject and see how many related topics you can brainstorm. Check out these examples.

Science

- Choose a fascinating science career. Then, write a biography about a person in this field.

- Who made the most significant discovery or developed the most important invention of our time? Write his or her biography.

Language Arts

- Write about the life of your favorite author.

- Tell the story of someone who has impacted the world of Web content. Possibilities include search engine innovators, famous bloggers, and people who have launched Internet forums or networks.

Art and/or Music

- Write about an artist or musician whose style appeals to you.

- How did your favorite artist or musician make it big? Tell his or her story.

NARRATIVE test writing

Read the Writing Prompt

I know that every writing test starts with a writing prompt. Most writing prompts have three parts:

Setup This part of the writing prompt gives you the background information you need to get ready to write.

Task This part of the writing prompt tells you exactly what you are supposed to write: a personal memoir.

Scoring Guide This section tells how your writing will be scored. To do well on the test, you should include everything on the list.

Remember the rubrics you've been using? When you take a writing test, you don't always have all of the information that's on a rubric. But the scoring guide is a lot like a rubric. It lists everything you need to think about to write a good paper. Like the rubrics you've used, many scoring guides are based on the six important traits of writing:

 Information/Organization

 Content/Ideas

 Sentence Fluency

 Voice/Audience

 Word Choice/Clarity

 Grammar/Mechanics

Think about a time when you helped another person or people in some way.

Write a personal memoir about that experience.

Be sure your writing

- is well organized. The sequence of events should be clear and easy to follow.

- includes details to make the story interesting.

- contains dialogue that makes the account interesting and complete.

- has clear, concrete words.

- includes prepositional phrases for sentence variety.

- contains correct grammar, punctuation, capitalization, and spelling.

Writing Traits
in the Scoring Guide

Look back at the scoring guide in the writing prompt on page 77. Not every writing prompt will include each of the six writing traits, but this one does. You can use the following chart to help you better understand the connection between the scoring guide and the writing traits in the rubrics you've been using.

- **Be sure your writing is well organized. The sequence of events should be clear and easy to follow.**

- **Be sure your writing includes details to make the story interesting.**

- **Be sure your writing contains dialogue that makes the account interesting and complete.**

- **Be sure your writing has clear, concrete words.**

- **Be sure your writing includes prepositional phrases for sentence variety.**

- **Be sure your writing contains correct grammar, punctuation, capitalization, and spelling.**

Look at Eric Weismann's story on the next page. Did he follow the scoring guide?

A New Face

by Eric Weismann

"Students, I'd like to introduce you to Andrew Mancini," said our teacher, Ms. Kennedy, one morning as we began class.

It was midway through my eighth grade year at South Lincoln, and it seemed weird to me that we were getting a new student at this time of year. I wondered how Andrew felt. He was a tall, gangly kid, with a thick mop of brown hair that fell across his eyes. He wore clothes that were too small, showing his sharp wrists and bony ankles. His sneakers looked like they came straight from a garage sale. When Ms. Kennedy introduced him, he half smiled and looked down at his desk.

That first day at school, I noticed that Andrew was really quiet and wasn't very happy. He kept chewing on his pencil and looking out the window. At lunchtime, he sat all by himself. I felt really bad for him. Did he want to be by himself, or did he think that no one wanted to hang out with him? I wanted to say something, but I wasn't sure how to approach him.

That night, I told my parents about Andrew. "It has to be hard to start all over again in a new school, making friends and finding your way around," my mom said, "especially when everyone around you already knows one another."

My dad suggested that I introduce Andrew to some of my friends. "Just start out by saying hello to him," he said. "Ask him if he likes to play basketball."

The next day, I made a point of saying hello to Andrew first thing in the morning. "Did you and your family just move to the area?" I asked him.

Andrew perked up a bit. "Yeah, my dad got transferred here from California."

"Well, I think you'll like it here," I told him. "You want to meet my friends?"

"Yeah!" he said.

At lunch, he sat with my friends and me. We all found out that we had a lot in common.

"Hey," he said, "do you guys like to play basketball?"

"Of course," I said.

He laughed. "You know, maybe this new school isn't so bad after all."

Using the Scoring Guide to Study the Model

Let's use the scoring guide to check Eric's writing test, "A New Face." How well does his essay meet each of the six writing traits?

Information/ Organization

- **The story is well organized. The sequence of events should be clear and easy to follow.**

Eric tells the story in a logical order. He uses transitional phrases (underlined below) to tell the reader how much time passes between one event and the next. Here is an example.

<u>That first day at school</u>, I noticed that Andrew was really quiet and wasn't very happy. He kept chewing on his pencil and looking out the window. <u>At lunchtime</u>, he sat all by himself. I felt really bad for him. Did he want to be by himself, or did he think that no one wanted to hang out with him? I wanted to say something, but I wasn't sure how to approach him.

Voice/ Audience

- **The writing includes details that make the story interesting.**

Eric gets me interested with details about Andrew. I can visualize what Andrew looked like and how he must have felt.

He was a tall, gangly kid, with a thick mop of brown hair that fell across his eyes. He wore clothes that were too small, showing his sharp wrists and bony ankles. His sneakers looked like they came straight from a garage sale. When Ms. Kennedy introduced him, he half smiled and looked down at his desk.

Content/Ideas

- The writing contains dialogue that makes the account interesting and complete.

Eric uses dialogue in his memoir. This makes the story more interesting, and it tells me exactly how he got to know Andrew. Here's an example.

"Did you and your family just move to the area?" I asked him.

Andrew perked up a bit. "Yeah, my dad got transferred here from California."

"Well, I think you'll like it here," I told him. "You want to meet my friends?"

Word Choice/Clarity

- The writing has clear, concrete words.

Eric uses appropriate language to tell his story. His words are really clear and concrete, and this makes his description vivid and interesting.

He was a tall, gangly kid, with a thick mop of brown hair that fell across his eyes. He wore clothes that were too small, showing his sharp wrists and bony ankles. His sneakers looked like they came straight from a garage sale. When Ms. Kennedy introduced him, he half smiled and looked down at his desk.

Using the Scoring Guide to Study the Model

- **The writing includes prepositional phrases for sentence variety.**

Eric uses a variety of sentence patterns. He avoids repetition by starting some of his sentences with a prepositional phrase. He also includes complex sentences. Here's an example.

At lunch, he sat with my friends and me. We all found out that we had a lot in common.

- **The writing contains correct grammar, punctuation, capitalization, and spelling.**

It looks like Eric spelled correctly and used the right punctuation. Don't forget to check for mistakes in your own work. For example, if you know you often forget to capitalize proper nouns, you should pay close attention to capitalization. Editing for grammar and mechanics at every step of the writing process will help you avoid errors on your final test.

Planning My Time

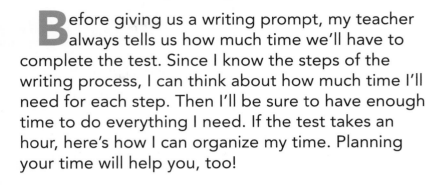

Before giving us a writing prompt, my teacher always tells us how much time we'll have to complete the test. Since I know the steps of the writing process, I can think about how much time I'll need for each step. Then I'll be sure to have enough time to do everything I need. If the test takes an hour, here's how I can organize my time. Planning your time will help you, too!

Step 4:
Editing
10 minutes

Step 1:
Prewriting
25 minutes

Step 3:
Revising
10 minutes

Step 2:
Drafting
15 minutes

Prewriting Study the Writing Prompt

Writing Strategy Study the writing prompt to be sure I know what to do.

The first thing I do is study my writing prompt so I'll know exactly what I'm supposed to do. Usually, a writing prompt has three parts, but the parts aren't always labeled. Look for the setup, task, and scoring guide on your writing prompt, just like I did on mine below. Then, label each part and circle key words in the setup and the task that tell what kind of writing you need to do and who your audience will be. I circled my topic in purple, and what kind of writing I'll be doing (a memoir) in red. The writing prompt doesn't say who the audience is, so I'll write for my teacher.

My Writing Test Prompt

Setup — Have you ever had an experience where the outcome was not what you expected it to be?

Task — Write a memoir about an experience that turned out differently than you expected.

Scoring Guide — Be sure your writing

- is well organized. The sequence of events should be clear and easy to follow.

- includes details to make the story interesting.

- contains dialogue that makes the account interesting and complete.

- has clear, concrete words.

- includes prepositional phrases for sentence variety.

- contains correct grammar, punctuation, capitalization, and spelling.

Think about how the scoring guide relates to the six writing traits in the rubrics you've studied. Not all of the traits will be included in every scoring guide, but you need to remember them all to write a good essay.

- **Be sure your writing is well organized. The sequence of events should be clear and easy to follow.**

I want my reader to be able to follow the story, so organization is important.

- **Be sure your writing includes details to make the story interesting.**

I want to grab the reader's interest right away, so I'll be sure to include plenty of colorful details.

- **Be sure your writing contains dialogue that makes the account interesting and complete.**

I have to remember to use dialogue throughout my story. That'll make it more interesting.

- **Be sure your writing has clear, concrete words.**

I need to be sure that my words are clear and easy to understand.

- **Be sure your writing includes prepositional phrases for sentence variety.**

I can add life to my writing by using different kinds of sentences. Prepositional phrases will help make my sentences flow.

- **Be sure your writing contains correct grammar, punctuation, capitalization, and spelling.**

I should always remember to check my grammar and mechanics anytime I write.

Prewriting Gather Information

Information/Organization

Writing Strategy Respond to the task.

Writers always gather information before they begin writing. When you write to take a test, you can find a lot of information in the writing prompt. Let's take another look at the task, since this is the part of the writing prompt that explains what I'm supposed to write. Remember, there's not much time! That's why it's really important to think about how you'll respond before you begin to write.

I see that first I have to come up with a time when an experience turned out differently than I expected. I recently took a surprising visit to a nursing home, so I'll jot down some notes about it.

Task ——— ⎡ Write a (memoir) about an experience that turned out differently than you expected.

Notes

 I went to Green Oaks Retirement Home.

 I did crafts with the residents.

Remember! Think about how you'll respond to the task part of your writing prompt before you begin to write. Then, jot down some notes to help you gather information.

Prewriting Organize Ideas

I don't have a lot of time, so I'll begin organizing my ideas right away. I'll start by choosing a graphic organizer. I'm writing my memoir in chronological order, so I'll use a Story Frame to help me record story events.

Setting:	Green Oaks Retirement Home, a local nursing home
Introduction:	supposed to do a community service project at Green Oaks and wasn't happy about it
Rising Action (Event 1):	director took me to room; people waiting seemed bored
Rising Action (Event 2):	director introduced me
Rising Action (Event 3):	residents started making necklaces
Climax:	residents started having a good time
Falling Action (Event 1):	helped Mrs. Fields find pretty beads
Falling Action (Event 2):	Rose did great job
Falling Action (Event 3):	residents were pleased; probably lonely and enjoyed the company
Falling Action (Event 4):	residents thanked me and invited me back
Resolution:	visit Green Oaks once a month

Reflect

Did I include enough details on my graphic organizer?

Remember! Choose a graphic organizer that's appropriate for the type of essay you are writing.

Prewriting Check the Scoring Guide

Information/Organization

Writing Strategy Check my graphic organizer against the scoring guide.

In a test, there's usually not much time to revise, so that makes prewriting more important than ever! Before I get started, I'll check my Story Frame against the scoring guide in the writing prompt.

Setting:	Green Oaks Retirement Home, a local nursing home
Introduction:	supposed to do a community service project at Green Oaks and wasn't happy about it
Rising Action (Event 1):	director took me to room; people waiting seemed bored
Rising Action (Event 2):	director introduced me
Rising Action (Event 3):	residents started making necklaces
Climax:	residents started having a good time
Falling Action (Event 1):	helped Mrs. Fields find pretty beads
Falling Action (Event 2):	Rose did great job
Falling Action (Event 3):	residents were pleased; probably lonely and enjoyed the company
Falling Action (Event 4):	residents thanked me and invited me back
Resolution:	visit Green Oaks once a month

- Be sure your writing is well organized. The sequence of events should be clear and easy to follow.

I'll use the introduction from my Story Frame. Then, I'll include the details from the other boxes, since they're already in chronological order.

- Be sure your writing includes details to make the story interesting.

I included a bunch of details on my Story Frame.

- Be sure your writing contains dialogue that makes the account interesting and complete.

I didn't use any dialogue in my Story Frame, so I'll make sure to include some when I write.

- Be sure your writing has clear, concrete words.

I'll be sure to use clear words as I explain the events that are listed on my Story Frame.

- Be sure your writing includes prepositional phrases for sentence variety.

I'll need to remember to do this as I write.

- Be sure your writing contains correct grammar, punctuation, capitalization, and spelling.

I'll check for proper grammar and mechanics when I edit my draft.

Remember! Before you start to write, reread the scoring guide in the writing prompt to be sure you know what to do.

Reflect

My Story Frame doesn't include every point in the scoring guide, but I think it covers most of them. Is there anything else that I'm forgetting?

Drafting Write a Draft

Writing Strategy Engage the reader with interesting details.

My Story Frame already includes some interesting information that will help make my memoir exciting. But I checked it one more time to see if there were any more details that I wanted to add to my draft. I thought of some things I'd like to include while writing, so I'll begin now.

[DRAFT]

Getting Crafty

by Ashley

[interesting details]

Doing crafts at a nursery home was not how I wanted to spend my Saturday but I had made a committment to visit the Green Oaks Retirement Home as part of my school community service project. And I wasn't too happy about it!

When I arrived, the director, Ms. Hill, led me into a room where some of the ederly residents were sitting. Almost all of them were women in wheelchairs, and they seemed pretty bored, too!

Ms. Hill introduced me.

One lady told me I had a pretty name and I thanked her.

Ms. Hill said the lady, Rose, could no longer see. I wondered how she'd be able to do a craft. I thought I was wasting my time!

    I told the ladies we were going to be making beaded necklaces. I tied the ends for them and set them out in front of them. I told them it was easy and showed them how to get started. I could tell they started to have a good time.

    One woman, Mrs. Fields, asked, "Ashley, which do you think would look prettiest? I showed her a few beads that I thought would look good on her necklace.   **[interesting details]**

    I noticed that even Rose was doing a great job using her hands to feel for beads and string them on.

    When we finished, some of the residents were pretty pleased with their necklaces. Everyone seemed to be in a much better mood than when I had first arrived—even me! I realized that they were probably lonely there. Liked to have people come and visit.

    They told me thanks and asked if I'd come again. I was happy to have brightened their day, and I promised I'd be back soon.

    Now, I visit the green oaks retirement home once a month, and I always look forward to going!

Remember! Include details and personal observations to make your story stand out.

Reflect

What do you think? Are my details colorful enough to hold the reader's interest?

Revising **Extend Writing**

Content/ Ideas

Writing Strategy Add dialogue to strengthen characterization.

Now that I have written my draft, I'll read it to myself to see if anything is missing. The scoring guide says to use dialogue to strengthen characterization. When I reread my draft, I saw that there were some areas where I could add some interesting dialogue to help the reader get a better idea of what my experience was like.

[DRAFT]

[added dialogue]

Ms. Hill introduced me. "Ashley," said one lady. "What a pretty name." "Thanks," I mumbled.

~~One lady told me I had a pretty name and I thanked her.~~

Remember! Instead of explaining what someone said, write it as dialogue.

Word Choice/ Clarity

Writing Strategy Use clear, concrete words.

I'll read my paper again to see if any parts could be clearer. The scoring guide says that I should use clear, concrete words to explain my story, and I see some places where I can do this.

The paragraph about beading the necklaces seems a little confusing. I'll change some words to make it better.

[DRAFT]

— [used clear, concrete words] —

I told the ladies we were going to be making beaded necklaces.

I tied the ends ~~for them~~ of each of the residents' strings and set ~~them out~~ out beads in front of them. I told

them it was easy and showed them how to get started. I could tell

they started to have a good time.

Reflect

What do you think of my revisions? Have they helped clarify and add interest to my writing?

Remember! Replace vague words with clear, concrete vocabulary.

Editing Check Sentences

Writing Strategy Use prepositional phrases to add sentence variety.

The scoring guide says I should include prepositional phrases for sentence variety. I read my story again and decided to start some sentences with prepositional phrases because I don't want my writing to be boring to the reader. Here's one example.

[DRAFT]

[added a prepositional phrase]

Before I left,

They told me thanks and asked if I'd come again. I was happy to have brightened their day, and I promised I'd be back soon.

> **Remember!** Use different types of sentences in your writing to keep your reader interested. Adding prepositional phrases will help your sentences flow.

Writing Strategy Check my grammar, punctuation, capitalization, and spelling.

There's just one last step! The scoring guide says to use correct grammar and mechanics. I always leave plenty of time to check for errors in these important areas!

Getting Crafty

by Ashley

Doing crafts at a nursing home was not how I wanted to spend

my Saturday, but I had made a ~~committment~~ commitment to visit the Green

Oaks Retirement Home as part of my school community service

project. And I wasn't too happy about it!

When I arrived, the director, Ms. Hill, led me into a room where

some of the ~~ederly~~ elderly residents were sitting. Almost all of them were

women in wheelchairs, and they seemed pretty bored, too!

Ms. Hill introduced me. "Ashley," said one lady. "What a pretty name."
"Thanks," I mumbled.

~~One lady told me I had a pretty name and I thanked her.~~

Ms. Hill said the lady, Rose, could no longer see. I wondered how

she'd be able to do a craft. I thought I was wasting my time!

Remember! Check your grammar, punctuation, capitalization, and spelling every time you write for a test.

I told the ladies we were going to be making beaded necklaces.
of each of the residents' strings   out beads
I tied the ends ~~for them~~ and set ~~them out~~ in front of them. I told

them it was easy and showed them how to get started. I could tell

they started to have a good time.

One woman, Mrs. Fields, asked, "Ashley, which do you think

would look prettiest?" I showed her a few beads that I thought

would look good on her necklace.

I noticed that even Rose was doing a great job using her hands

to feel for beads and string them on.

When we finished, some of the residents were pretty pleased

with their necklaces. Everyone seemed to be in a much better

mood than when I had first arrived—even me! I realized that they
                                                              and
were probably lonely there, Liked to have people come and visit.
Before I left,
      They told me thanks and asked if I'd come again. I was happy

to have brightened their day, and I promised I'd be back soon.

Now, I visit the green oaks retirement home once a month, and

I always look forward to going!

Reflect

Is my writing missing anything? Check it against the scoring guide. Remember to use your writing prompt's scoring guide to check your writing anytime you take a test!

I'm finished! You just have to remember to use the writing process when you take a writing test. The process is a little different for a test, but you'll do fine as long as you remember these important tips.

TEST TIPS

1. **Study the writing prompt before you start to write.** Most writing prompts have three parts: the setup, the task, and the scoring guide. The parts probably won't be labeled. You'll have to figure them out for yourself!

2. **Make sure you understand the task before you start to write.**

   • Read all three parts of the writing prompt carefully.

   • Circle key words in the task part of the writing prompt that tell what kind of writing you need to do. The task might also identify your audience.

   • Make sure you know how you'll be graded.

   • Say the assignment in your own words to yourself.

3. **Keep an eye on the clock.** Decide how much time you will spend on each part of the writing process and try to stick to your schedule. Don't spend so much time on prewriting that you don't have enough time left to write.

4. **Reread your writing. Check it against the scoring guide at least twice.** Remember the rubrics you've used? A scoring guide on a writing test is like a rubric. It can help you keep what's important in mind.

5. **Plan, plan, plan!** You don't get much time to revise during a test, so planning is more important than ever.

6. **Write neatly.** Remember, if the people who score your test can't read your writing, it doesn't matter how good your essay is!

DESCRIPTIVE
writing describes something to the reader.

i, I'm Josh. I'm learning about descriptive writing in school, and I really think I'm going to have fun with it. I like sharing with my friends and family all the things that happen to me, and now I'll learn some strategies to turn those experiences into full-length pieces of descriptive writing.

IN THIS UNIT

1. **Business Letter**
2. **Scientific Observation**
3. **Descriptive Vignette**
4. **Writing for a Test**

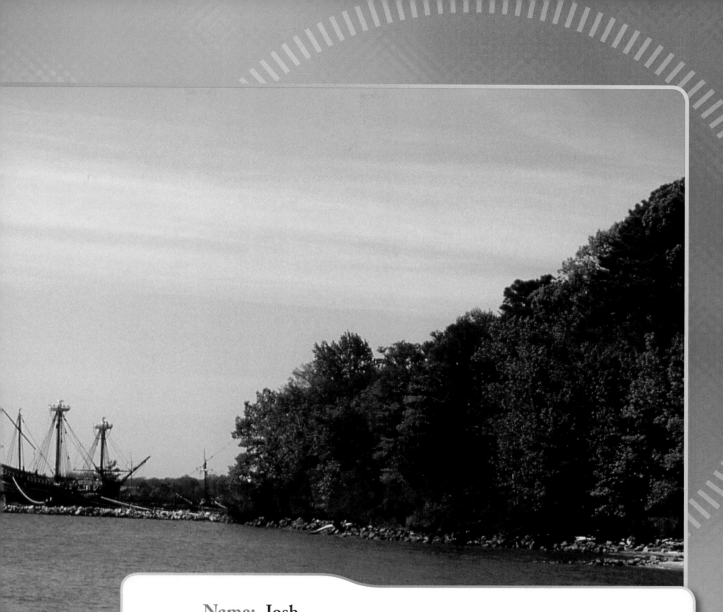

Name: Josh
Home: Virginia
Hobbies: going to the movies,
playing baseball,
spending time at
the beach
Favorite Movie: *Star Wars*

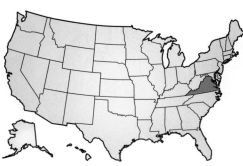

What's a Business Letter?

It's a formal letter written to a person or a company. Knowing how to write a good business letter is an important skill that will help me communicate with the world beyond friends and family.

What's in a Business Letter?

Purpose
This is why I'm writing the letter in the first place. The purpose of my letter will help guide what I write, so I'll keep this in mind as I draft.

Supporting Facts
I should think about my main idea or topic and back it up with facts that support it. I plan to build each paragraph around one supporting fact.

Tone
This is how I want my letter to sound. My tone has to suit my audience and my purpose, so I'll have to think about who will be reading the letter and why I'm writing it. This is a business letter, so I'll avoid slang and use a formal, respectful tone.

Vivid Details
My letter should include vivid details that enhance description. But I also need to remember that details should be relevant to my ideas and purpose, too!

Why write a Business Letter?

There are all kinds of reasons for writing a business letter. I gave it some thought, and I came up with this list of ideas.

Information

Keeping people informed about a product or a service is a great reason for writing a business letter. For example, I might want to present details about a school club or team and ask a company to be our sponsor. Or I could let a business know I'd like some information about its products or store locations.

Request an Action

A business letter is a good format to use when you want to persuade a company to donate to a cause, make a new product, or take some other kind of action.

Response to an Issue

If I buy a game that doesn't work, or the school committee decides to cut music classes, I can respond by writing a letter. This way, I can describe my reaction in a calm, professional way.

Business Letter Writing Traits

What goes into a good business letter? I can answer this question by focusing on the six traits of good writing. I'll use the list below when I write my letter.

Information/ Organization	The letter focuses on one main idea or topic. The letter has many facts to support the main idea.
Voice/ Audience	The letter format is correct, and the tone is appropriate.
Content/ Ideas	Vivid details enhance the description.
Word Choice/ Clarity	The letter contains no irrelevant details.
Sentence Fluency	Concise sentences help the writing flow.
Grammar/ Mechanics	Spelling, punctuation, and capitalization are correct. All subjects and verbs agree.

I can use Denny McCabe's business letter on the next three pages as a model for my own writing. Later, I'll analyze how Denny used the traits to help him write.

1045 Stonegate Drive
Westmont, IL 60559
August 3, 20--

Mr. Ronald Richards, General Manager
Woodcreek Theaters
1 South Mall Drive
Clarendon Hills, IL 60514

Dear Mr. Richards:

Purpose ⤵

I am writing to tell you about the unpleasant experience that I had at your new theater complex this evening. I was expecting an exciting evening, especially after all the publicity about the twelve new screens with plush seating and state-of-the-art sound systems. It was at one of these screens—Theater 6, to be exact—that I arrived to see *Exploring Space*. My experience was disappointing, considering everything that happened tonight.

Supporting Fact ↙

Three problems made it impossible to enjoy the movie. The first relates to the lack of service in the lobby area. A large cinema complex should have more than one concession stand, and this one did. Two circular, glass-topped counters displayed a tempting array of candies, sodas, popcorn, and hot snacks such as nachos. ← Vivid Details

Although the lobby was packed with moviegoers, only one counter was open because only two ushers were available to work. The lines were so long that people started pushing and shoving to get to the front. Some particularly impatient people even shouted out their orders before those in front of them could say what they wanted. After someone complained, the second concession stand was opened. This might have eased the problem, if the manager hadn't taken one of the ushers from the first counter to staff it. Now, two stands were functioning, but with only one staffer apiece. After waiting 15 minutes for popcorn, I left empty-handed, only to stand in another disgruntled, slow-moving crowd to get to my film on time.

Supporting Fact

When I finally took my seat, I was immediately confronted with a second problem: the conditions inside Theater 6. For starters, the theater was freezing cold. Before the coming attractions even began, several people asked the manager to adjust the thermostat. She said she would take care of it, but the temperature never changed. Consequently, several people sitting around me got up and left about halfway through the movie. Other people opted to stay, fidgeting endlessly by shrugging on their coats and squirming in their seats, as if keeping in constant motion might keep them warm.

Vivid Details

Supporting Fact

In addition, Theater 6 looked and felt as if it had never been cleaned. In my row, empty containers littered the floor, topped with a layer of discarded popcorn puffs stuck to a coating of spilled soda. This was a multi-sensory nightmare. Aside from the horrible sight of it, there was the sticky feel of jelly candies plastered to the back of my chair, and the sucking sound my sneakers made each time I lifted them off the floor. I assume that this problem stemmed from the same cause as the situation in the lobby: understaffing. Perhaps the lack of ushers made it impossible to keep up with between-show cleanings.

Supporting Fact

The third problem was the presentation of the movie itself. First, there was the sound. Although we could barely hear our own movie, we could clearly hear the one in Theater 5. As soon as *Exploring Space* began, people started asking for the volume to be adjusted. Even so, we couldn't really hear it until the film's final half hour. Then, the film suddenly stopped right at the high point of the movie! The technician got it started again pretty quickly, but it was too late. Along with everything else that had gone wrong, the interruption ruined any enjoyment I was getting out of the movie. At that point, I gave up and left.

Considering the events of this evening, I may not return to the new Woodcreek Theaters. I hope you consider this feedback because, without certain improvements, the new cinema complex might have an extremely short run.

↰ **Tone**

Sincerely,

Denny McCabe

Denny McCabe

Business Letter

Rubric

The traits of a good business letter from page 102 have been used to make the rubric below. By using 1, 2, 3, or 4 check marks to judge each trait, you can decide how well any business letter was written.

	Excelling ✓✓✓✓	Achieving ✓✓✓	Developing ✓✓	Beginning ✓
Information/ Organization	The letter focuses on one topic and has many facts for support.	The letter mostly focuses on one topic and has some facts for support.	The letter sometimes focuses on one topic and has a few facts for support.	The letter should focus on one topic and contain many facts for support.
Voice/ Audience	The letter format is correct, and the tone is appropriate.	The letter format is mostly correct, and the tone is usually appropriate.	A few parts of the letter are missing, and the tone is inappropriate in some areas.	The letter format should be correct, and the tone should be appropriate.
Content/ Ideas	Many vivid details enhance the description.	Some vivid details enhance the description.	A few vivid details enhance the description.	More vivid details are needed to enhance the description.
Word Choice/ Clarity	The letter contains no irrelevant details.	The letter contains very few irrelevant details.	The letter contains several irrelevant details.	The letter should not contain any irrelevant details.
Sentence Fluency	Concise sentences help the writing flow throughout.	Concise sentences are used in some areas.	Concise sentences are used in a few areas.	More concise sentences are needed to help the writing flow throughout.
Grammar/ Mechanics	Spelling, grammar, and subject-verb agreement are correct.	There are very few errors in spelling, grammar, and subject-verb agreement.	There are several errors in spelling, grammar, and subject-verb agreement.	There are many errors in spelling, grammar, and subject-verb agreement.

Business Letter

Using the Rubric to Study the Model

Let's use the rubric to check Denny McCabe's business letter. How many check marks would you give Denny for each trait?

 Information/Organization

- **The letter focuses on one main idea or topic.**
- **The letter has many facts to support the main idea.**

Denny organizes his letter well. He first explains that there were three problems at the movie theater. Then, he goes on to describe the order in which they happened, using each problem as a topic sentence to support his overall disappointment.

[from the writing model]

Three problems made it impossible to enjoy the movie. The first relates to the lack of service in the lobby area.

 Voice/Audience

- **The letter format is correct, and the tone is appropriate.**

Denny's business-letter format is correct. He includes all six letter parts (heading, inside address, greeting, body, closing, and signature), and his polite tone matches his choice of genre. In his conclusion, Denny lets Mr. Richards know that he is concerned about the welfare of the theater.

[from the writing model]

I hope you consider this feedback because, without certain improvements, the new cinema complex might have an extremely short run.

Business Letter

 Content/ Ideas

• **Vivid details enhance the description.**

Denny states the problems he encountered and describes his experience in detail. Because the details he uses are specific and colorful, they really help him get his point across.

[from the writing model]

In my row, empty containers littered the floor, topped with a layer of discarded popcorn puffs stuck to a coating of spilled soda. This was a multi-sensory nightmare. Aside from the horrible sight of it, there was the sticky feel of jelly candies plastered to the back of my chair, and the sucking sound my sneakers made each time I lifted them off the floor.

 Word Choice/ Clarity

• **The letter contains no irrelevant details.**

Denny's main idea is that his experience at the new theater complex was really unpleasant. He explains why by describing how each problem affected him and the other moviegoers. All these details relate to his purpose, and I didn't read anything that seemed off point. In this section, all the details were necessary to describe how understaffing led to chaos.

[from the writing model]

Although the lobby was packed with moviegoers, only one counter was open because only two ushers were available to work. The lines were so long that people started pushing and shoving to get to the front. Some particularly impatient people even shouted out their orders before those in front of them could say what they wanted.

Sentence Fluency

• Concise sentences help the writing flow.

I enjoyed reading Denny's writing. His sentences aren't choppy, and he doesn't ramble. He gives the reader specific details but not in an overwhelming way. Notice how the sentences below offer just the right amount of information to make the writing flow.

[from the writing model]

For starters, the theater was freezing cold. Before the coming attractions even began, several people asked the manager to adjust the thermostat. She said she would take care of it, but the temperature never changed.

Grammar/Mechanics

• Spelling, punctuation, and capitalization are correct. All subjects and verbs agree.

Denny also does the little things well—like putting commas and periods in the right places, and checking his spelling. All his subjects and verbs agree, too. I don't see any errors in his writing, do you?

[from the writing model]

The third problem was the presentation of the movie itself. First, there was the sound. Although we could barely hear our own movie, we could clearly hear the one in Theater 5. As soon as *Exploring Space* began, people started asking for the volume to be adjusted. Even so, we couldn't really hear it until the film's final half hour.

My Turn!

Now I'm going to write a business letter, but I'll focus on a positive experience. I'll use the rubric, along with good writing strategies, to help me write a detailed letter. Read along to see how I do it.

Prewriting Gather Information

 Information/Organization

The letter focuses on one main idea or topic.

Writing Strategy

List my main idea or topic. Then, list details that support it.

I enjoy going to the movies, too. So when I read Denny's letter, I understood how he felt. I also remembered an experience at the movie theater that could have been horrible if not for some quick thinking by the theater manager. I knew this would make a great topic for a business letter, so I jotted down the idea. Then, I listed some supporting details.

Main Idea: To thank the manager of my local theater for how she handled a tough situation

Supporting Details:

- Biggest blockbuster of the summer; a lot of people; manager had us form different lines

- Temperature over 90°; many waited outside; manager passed out free water

- Film scheduled to start, and people still filing in; manager held up start time

- Not everyone got into the last show; manager gave free tickets to everyone in line and told them to come back the next day

Practice!

Now it's your turn. Choose a topic for a business letter. Then, write down your main idea and supporting details.

Prewriting Organize Ideas

Information/Organization

The letter has many facts to support the main idea.

Writing Strategy

Make a Main-Idea Table to organize my information.

Writer's Term

Main-Idea Table

A **Main-Idea Table** can help you structure a piece of writing by organizing your main idea and supporting details in a logical way. Write your main idea or topic at the top of the table. Then, fill in the "legs" with supporting facts, details, and examples.

According to the rubric, it's important that every fact in my letter supports my main idea. I've already listed some details. Now, I'll organize them in a Main-Idea Table. I'm going to write about how the manager solved problems, so I'll label these details "Problem" and "Solution."

Main-Idea Table

Main Idea: I want to thank the manager of the York Street Theater for how she handled a tough situation.

Problem: When <u>Voyage to Mars</u> opened, the theater was swamped with people. **Solution:** To let the crowd in faster, the manager had us form different lines.	**Problem:** The temperature was over 90°, and many people had to wait outside. **Solution:** The manager had some employees walk down the lines and pass out free ice water.	**Problem:** When the film was scheduled to start, people were still filing into the theater. **Solution:** The manager held up the start time until every seat was filled.	**Problem:** Not everyone in line got into the last show of the night. **Solution:** The manager gave free tickets to everyone still in line and invited them back.

Practice!

Now it's your turn. Organize your main idea and supporting details into a Main-Idea Table.

Reflect

Do you think I included enough details to get started?

Drafting Write a Draft

Voice/Audience The letter format is correct, and the tone is appropriate.

Writing Strategy Make sure my letter format is correct and my tone is appropriate.

Now I'm ready to start writing my business letter. The rubric reminds me that I need to include the six parts of a letter: heading, inside address, greeting, body, closing, and signature. It also says I should use an appropriate tone. Because I'm writing a business letter, I'll make sure that my tone sounds friendly and polite but businesslike.

Right now, I'm just going to focus on getting my ideas down. I'll do my best with spelling and grammar, but I know I can always go back and check for errors later. You can see most of my draft on the next page.

Proofreading Marks

⌐ Indent	ℓ Take out something
≡ Make a capital	⊙ Add a period
/ Make a small letter	(SP) Spelling error
∧ Add something	¶ New paragraph

[DRAFT]

[heading]
8301 Bell Avenue
Ivor, VA 23866
August 30, 20—

[inside address]
Mrs. Paula Locascio, Manager
Main Street Theater
2 Main Street
Ivor, VA 23866

Dear Mrs. Locascio: ← [greeting]

[body]

I am writing to thank you for the way you handled a really tough situation on the night of August 5. As I'm sure you and your staff recalls, that was the opening nite of the summer's biggest blockbuster, <u>Voyage to Mars</u>. The theater was filled with people, but thanks to your quick thinking, we didn't have to wait long.

The high heat and humidity also contributed to people's discomfort, but again, You prevented what could have been an unbearable situation. Everyone standing—and wilting—outside thought your idea of passing out free ice water was fantastic! You made the wait as comfortable as possible, and the crowd really appreciated it.

[appropriate tone]

Practice!

Now it's your turn. Write a draft using the notes from your Main-Idea Table. Remember to use an appropriate tone and to include all six parts of a business letter.

Reflect

What do you think? Did I forget to include any letter parts? Is my tone appropriate?

Revising Extend Writing

Content/Ideas   Vivid details enhance the description.

Writing Strategy   Look for places to add vivid details.

Now that I've written my draft, I think I'll check the rubric again. It says description is important, so I'll look for places to add details that will bring my letter to life. I think my third paragraph could use some work in this area. I'll focus on adding details there for now, but I can always add more to the rest of the draft later on!

[DRAFT]

[added vivid details]

Another problem you ^took care of was holding up the film's start
    thoughtfully

time until all the people in the theater was seated. Although you did

your best to make the lines move quickly, not everyone were seated

by 7:15. I was in this group, and I ~~saw what happened when~~
  witnessed, firsthand, the anxiety that began to spread as

people realized they might miss part of the movie. But by skipping

the coming attractions and starting the film at 7:30, you allowed

everyone to see the beginning.

Practice!

Now it's your turn. Make sure to include plenty of vivid details that will add energy and life to your writing.

Revising Clarify Writing

Word Choice/Clarity

The letter contains no irrelevant details.

Writing Strategy

Delete or revise details that don't support my main idea.

I always reread my draft to myself several times before I'm done. When I did it this time, I realized that my conclusion had some extra information that didn't really do much to support my purpose. Then, I realized the rubric says to avoid using irrelevant details, so I deleted them.

[DRAFT]

I'm happy to say that I count myself as one of those satisfied customers. You can be sure that I'll be back at your theater when one of the next blockbuster movies come to town. ~~I really hope it's another science fiction movie because those are my favorite movies of all. I also like action movies, but not as much as science fiction ones. Anyway.~~ Please keep up the excellent work. I'm sure it will pay off in the long run!

[deleted irrelevant details]

Practice!

Now it's your turn. Reread your draft and delete any details that don't relate to your purpose.

Reflect

Is my writing clearer and more vivid now?

Editing Check Sentences

Sentence Fluency

Concise sentences help the writing flow.

Writing Strategy Break up wordy sentences to keep my letter flowing.

Now I need to edit my writing. The rubric says it's important to use concise sentences, so I found a place where it helped to split one long sentence into two. It took some thought, but I was happy with the result.

[DRAFT]

[broke up a wordy sentence]

The last thing you did was give free tickets to the people who were still outside when the last show of the night sold out. I know that theater managers are not obligated to satisfy everyone who shows up on a particular night so considering this fact, I think your response was especially remarkable.

Practice!

Now it's your turn. Avoid confusing and boring writing by breaking up wordy sentences. This will really make your writing flow.

Editing Proofread Writing

Grammar/Mechanics

Spelling, punctuation, and capitalization are correct. All subjects and verbs agree.

Writing Strategy Make sure subjects and verbs agree.

Writer's Term

Subject-Verb Agreement

Every sentence has a **subject** and a **verb**. The subject is what the sentence is about. The verb tells what the subject does. The subject and verb must agree in number. If a subject is singular, the verb must be singular, too.

Now it's time to check my spelling, punctuation, and capitalization. The rubric also says to make sure that subjects and verbs agree. You can see some of my corrections below.

[corrected subject-verb agreement]

I am writing to thank you for the way you handled a really

tough situation on the night of August 5. As I'm sure you and your

        recall   night

staff ~~recalls~~, that was the opening ~~nite~~ of the summer's biggest

blockbuster, <u>Voyage to Mars</u>. The theater was filled with people,

but thanks to your quick thinking, we didn't have to wait long.

Practice!

Now it's your turn. Edit your draft for grammar and mechanics, making sure that all subjects and verbs agree.

For more practice with subject-verb agreement, use the exercises on the next two pages.

Reflect

Have my edits helped? Is my writing more fluid now?

Subject-Verb Agreement

The **subject** and **verb** in every sentence must agree in number, but figuring out whether a subject is singular or plural can be tricky.

- A **collective noun,** such as *crowd, group,* or *team,* names more than one person or object acting together as a group. Collective nouns are almost always singular.

  Example: The **crowd forms** different lines.

- Most **indefinite pronouns,** including *everyone, nobody, nothing, something,* and *anything,* are singular, except for *many* and *several,* which are considered plural.

  Example: Everyone has money for a ticket.

  Example: Many have tickets already.

- A **compound subject** that includes the conjunction *and* is plural, but if the compound subject includes *or* or *nor,* the verb agrees with the last item in the subject.

  Example: Sam and Jerry take people's tickets.

  Example: Either popcorn or **nachos are** fine.

- Every verb must agree with its subject and not with the object of the preposition that comes before the verb.

  Example: My **favorite** of all movies **is playing** at this theater.

Practice the Rule

Rewrite the paragraph below on a separate sheet of paper, using the verb in parentheses that agrees with the subject of the sentence.

When my mother and I (go/goes) to the grocery store, we always (looks/look) for your brand name on the shelves. Seeing one of your products (is/are) always reassuring to her. Everybody (know/knows) that your label means good quality and good taste. That's why my mother (know/knows) she can always count on you!

Apply the Rule

Read the following excerpt, looking for errors in subject-verb agreement. Then, rewrite the excerpt correctly on another sheet of paper.

17 West Washington Drive
Woodland Hills, CA 91364
March 13, 20—

Mr. Maxwell Jackson
Jackson Toy Company
1346 Industrial Drive
Hanover Park, IL 60103

Dear Mr. Jackson:

I am writing to tell you how much I enjoy your new game Do Tell. My family and I plays games every night, and we is always looking for good ones. One thing that are so great about Do Tell is that it have so many playing cards. My parents often buys a game, only to find that we use up all the cards in no time at all. But this is not the case with Do Tell. We'll definitely be playing it for a long time.

Another good thing about the game is its durability and its easy-to-read format. The vinyl-coated board help us keep it clean. Everyone like to eat while playing games in my house, and my little brother often spill things on the board. My mother tries to keep him from eating while he is playing, but it get pretty hard.

By far, my family's favorite thing about the game is that it is fun to play! My family laugh harder while playing Do Tell than during any other game we own. One thing that makes it so funny are the face in the middle of the game board. It almost looks as funny as some of the faces people makes while playing! My dad just scratches his head in amazement when he watch all of us laugh, and my mother and brother sometimes laughs so hard that they can't even breathe!

Writing a Business Letter

Publishing Share Writing

Send my letter to the appropriate recipient.

'___ve finally finished my business letter! Because it's a letter, the best way to publish it is to send it. But before I do, I'll read it to a classmate or a friend to get some final feedback. I'll also reread it to myself one more time to make sure it includes all of the items on my checklist.

My Checklist

✔ There is one main idea or purpose.

✔ I've included facts that support my main idea and deleted details that don't.

✔ My tone is polite and professional.

✔ Vivid details make my description lively and interesting.

✔ I used plenty of concise sentences to help the writing flow.

✔ Spelling, capitalization, and punctuation are all correct. All subjects and verbs agree.

Practice!

Now it's your turn. Make a checklist to check your business letter. Then, make a final draft to publish.

8301 Bell Avenue
Ivor, VA 23866
August 30, 20—

Mrs. Paula Locascio, Manager
Main Street Theater
2 Main Street
Ivor, VA 23866

Dear Mrs. Locascio:

I am writing to thank you for the way you handled a really tough situation on the night of August 5. As I'm sure you and your staff recall, that was opening night of the summer's biggest blockbuster, *Voyage to Mars*. The theater was filled with people, but thanks to your quick thinking, we didn't have to wait long.

The high heat and humidity also contributed to people's discomfort, but again you prevented what could have been an unbearable situation. Everyone standing—and wilting—outside thought your idea of passing out free ice water was fantastic! You made the wait as comfortable as possible, and the crowd really appreciated it.

Another problem you thoughtfully took care of was holding up the film's start time until all of the people in the theater were seated. Although you did your best to make the lines move quickly, not everyone was seated by 7:15. I was in this group, and I witnessed, firsthand, the anxiety that began to spread as people realized they might miss part of the movie. But by skipping the coming attractions and starting the film at 7:30, you allowed everyone to see the beginning.

The last thing you did was give free tickets to the people who were still outside when the last show of the night sold out. I know that theater managers are not obligated to satisfy everyone who shows up on a particular night. Considering this fact, I think your response was especially remarkable. By inviting those people back the next day and assuring them that they'd be the first ones allowed into the theater, you hung on to many customers.

I'm happy to say that I count myself as one of those satisfied customers. You can be sure that I'll be back at your theater when the next blockbuster movie comes to town. Please keep up the excellent work. I'm sure it will pay off in the long run!

Sincerely,

Josh Greene

Josh Greene

Josh Greene
8301 Bell Avenue
Ivor, VA 23866

Mrs. Paula Locascio
Main Street Theater
2 Main Street
Ivor, VA 23866

Reflect

What do you think? I hope I used all the traits of a good business letter. Check my work against the rubric, and don't forget to use the rubric to check your own business letter, too!

Ways to Publish a
Business Letter

As you decide how to publish your work, make sure you think about who will be reading it. Then, pick the best way to share it. Of course, publishing a letter usually means sending it to the recipient. But here are some other ways you can publish it.

 Submit it to the "Letter to the Editor" page of your local newspaper.

Post it on your blog or Web page, along with an explanation of why you wrote it.

Take your business letter home and share it with your family.

E-mail it to the intended recipient!

Writing Across the Content Areas
Business Letter

Your school subjects can be a source of writing ideas. So pick a subject and brainstorm as many topics that relate to it as you can. Here are some examples.

Language Arts
- Write a letter to your favorite author, describing what you liked best about one of his or her books.

- Want to publish a story or an article? First, write a letter to a newspaper or magazine, asking if they publish student work.

Social Studies
- Are you concerned about an issue in your community? Write your elected official about your thoughts.

- Write a company to give feedback on one of its products.

Art and/or Music
- Write to your favorite musician or band member, describing what you like best about his or her music.

- Do you want more community art, sculptures, murals, or other works in your city or town? Write your mayor and describe the situation.

What's a Scientific Observation?

It's writing that describes science experiments and summarizes what the observer has learned. When I write this kind of report, I like to make things as simple and clear as possible so that readers can follow my exact process.

What's in a Scientific Observation?

Voice
This is the style I use to present things to the reader. I'll narrate using the first-person *I*, but I'll remain objective and factual as I present my observation.

Organization
This is how I arrange my writing. I'll need to use clear labels to help readers follow my process and understand any conclusions.

Cause and Effect
A scientific observation describes test materials, experiments, and outcomes. After I explain the experiments, I'll note the causes and effects that were involved.

Conclusions
People perform experiments to test for certain results. My observation should end with the conclusions drawn from the experiments.

Why write a Scientific Observation?

There are many reasons to write a scientific observation. I write them all the time in science class, but here are some other purposes for this kind of writing.

Evidence

If I claim that one sneaker brand is better than another, I'll need evidence to explain why. If I run tests and write up what I observe, I can use this as proof of my claim.

Information

If I want to tell people about an experiment—like how my new backpack holds up under different kinds of weather—I can write an observation to inform readers of the results.

Organization

Science experiments involve a lot of elements: materials, procedures, results, tests, etc. I can write a scientific observation to organize and keep track of my information.

Scientific Observation Writing Traits

You can analyze a scientific observation in the same way that you look at other types of writing: by focusing on the six traits of good writing. I'll use these traits to help me write my observation.

Information/Organization	The writer describes several experiments. The observation includes causes and effects.
Voice/Audience	Scientific language is appropriate for the audience.
Content/Ideas	Diagrams enhance the description.
Word Choice/Clarity	Specific words show important connections throughout.
Sentence Fluency	Transitional phrases help the writing flow.
Grammar/Mechanics	Spelling, punctuation, and capitalization are correct. Colons and hyphens are used correctly.

I can use Hannah Prince's scientific observation on the next three pages as a model for my own writing. Later, we'll analyze how Hannah used the traits to help her write.

Observing Solar Collectors

By Hannah Prince

Did you know that solar energy doesn't cost a penny? Well, when I heard Voice that, I decided to conduct a series of experiments to find out how to improve the collection of solar energy. I predicted that the more insulation a collector was given the more heat it would collect.

MATERIALS

shoebox, larger box, masking tape, thermometer, clock or watch, black construction paper, clear plastic wrap, packing peanuts

PROCEDURES

Organization

Experiment 1

First, I taped a thermometer inside one of the long sides of a shoebox. (See Diagram 1.) Then, I placed the uncovered shoebox outside and turned it so that the bottom of the box was directly in the sun and the thermometer bulb was in the shade. I left the box in that position for 15 minutes.

I recorded the temperature inside the box at the start of the experiment and again 15 minutes later. Here are my observations. The temperature inside the box at the start of the experiment was 72°F (24°C). The temperature inside the box after 15 minutes was 98°F (36°C).

thermometer

shoebox

Diagram 1

Experiment 2

I did the experiment again, only this time I covered the inside of the shoebox with black construction paper. Then, I left the box for 15 minutes in the same position as before. (I did have to turn the box slightly to adjust for the movement of the sun.)

I again recorded the temperatures before and after the experiment. Here is what I observed. The temperature inside the box at the start of the experiment was 98°F (36°C). The temperature inside the box after 15 minutes was 98.5°F (36.25°C).

Experiment 3 ←——Organization

I did the experiment again. For this third time, however, I covered the top of the shoebox with clear plastic wrap. Then, I sealed the plastic wrap with masking tape so that no air could enter or leave the box. Next, I left the box for 15 minutes in the same position as before. (Again, I turned the box slightly to adjust for the movement of the sun.)

Once again, I recorded the temperatures and made these observations. The temperature inside the box at the start of the experiment was 98.5°F (36.25°C). The temperature inside the box after 15 minutes was 105°F (42°C).

Experiment 4

I did the experiment one last time. For this fourth time, I placed the shoebox inside another, larger box and then placed a layer of packing peanuts between the shoebox and the larger box. (See Diagram 2.) Next, I left the box for 15 minutes in the same position as before, again turning the box slightly to adjust for the movement of the sun.

Again, I recorded the temperatures and made these observations. The temperature inside the box at the start of the experiment was 105°F (42°C). The temperature inside the box after 15 minutes was 120+°F (50+°C).

thermometer

packing peanuts

big box

shoebox lined with black construction paper and sealed with clear plastic wrap

Diagram 2

OBSERVATIONS

Each change that I made to my solar collector caused the inside Cause and Effect of the shoebox to get hotter, resulting in a rise in temperature on the thermometer. When I placed the plain, uncovered shoebox in the sun, the Fahrenheit temperature increased 26°. When I covered the inside of the shoebox with black construction paper, the temperature increased another 0.5°. When I sealed the top of the box with plastic wrap, the temperature increased another 6.5°. When I placed the shoebox inside another box and put packing peanuts between them, the temperature increased another 15° before the thermometer topped out. Had my little thermometer gone beyond 120°F, I wonder how hot it would have gotten inside the shoebox! When I put my hand inside, the temperature change was pretty amazing. It felt almost twice as hot inside the shoebox as it felt outside that day.

CONCLUSIONS

I learned several things from my experiments: For one thing, I now Conclusions understand the basics of collecting solar energy. For another, I learned that solar energy really is a clean, efficient, and cost-effective way to heat a space. I also learned that the best way to gather the most heat with a solar collector is to place it inside a larger, well-insulated space. (I drew this conclusion because the insulation in Experiment 4 sent the temperature in the shoebox sky-high.) I was able to prove that my prediction was correct by doing these experiments. Since solar energy can be so powerful, I guess it's no wonder that people in regions where there is a lot of winter sun have been harnessing the sun's energy for centuries.

Scientific Observation

Rubric

The traits of a good scientific observation from page 128 have been used to make the rubric below. By using 1, 2, 3, or 4 check marks to judge each trait, you can decide how well any scientific observation was written.

	Excelling ✓✓✓✓	Achieving ✓✓✓	Developing ✓✓	Beginning ✓
Information/ Organization	The writer describes the causes and effects of several experiments.	The writer describes a few causes and effects of some experiments.	The writer describes a cause or effect of an experiment.	The writer should describe the causes and effects of several experiments.
Voice/ Audience	Scientific language is appropriate for the audience.	Scientific language is appropriate for the audience in many areas.	Scientific language is appropriate for the audience in some areas.	Scientific language should be appropriate for the audience.
Content/ Ideas	Several diagrams enhance the description.	A diagram enhances the description.	A diagram is included, but does not enhance the description.	Several diagrams should be included to enhance the description.
Word Choice/ Clarity	Specific words show important connections throughout.	Many specific words are used to show important connections.	Some specific words are used to show important connections.	More specific words are needed to show important connections.
Sentence Fluency	Transitional phrases help the writing flow throughout.	Many transitional phrases are used to help the writing flow.	Some transitional phrases are used to help the writing flow.	More transitional phrases are needed to help the writing flow.
Grammar/ Mechanics	Spelling, grammar, colons, and hyphens are used correctly.	There are one or two errors in spelling, grammar, colon, and hyphen usage.	There are several errors in spelling, grammar, colon, and hyphen usage.	There are many errors in spelling, grammar, colon, and hyphen usage.

Using the Rubric to Study the Model

Let's use the rubric to check Hannah's scientific observation, "Observing Solar Collectors." How many check marks would you give Hannah for each trait?

Information/Organization

- **The writer describes several experiments.**
- **The observation includes causes and effects.**

Hannah organizes her observation well. She lists everything she needs, and then she describes the four experiments, step-by-step. Next, she organizes her observations according to cause and effect, and then she wraps up with her conclusions.

[from the writing model]

CONCLUSIONS

I learned several things from my experiments: For one thing, I now understand the basics of collecting solar energy. For another, I learned that solar energy really is a clean, efficient, and cost-effective way to heat a space.

Voice/Audience

- **Scientific language is appropriate for the audience.**

Hannah uses scientific language throughout her report. You can tell she thought about her audience when she did this because the terms she uses are recognizable to almost anyone.

[from the writing model]

PROCEDURES

Experiment 1

First, I taped a thermometer inside one of the long sides of a shoebox.

Scientific Observation

• Diagrams enhance the description.

Hannah includes two labeled diagrams that illustrate what happened during the experiments. Diagram 1 shows exactly where in the shoebox Hannah placed the thermometer. Diagram 2 (shown below) shows how she placed the shoebox in the larger box.

[from the writing model]

thermometer

packing peanuts

big box

shoebox lined with black construction paper and sealed with clear plastic wrap

Diagram 2

• Specific words show important connections throughout.

I like how Hannah uses specific words to show important connections. This helps me understand the relationship between cause and effect. Take a look at the words I underlined below. See what I mean?

[from the writing model]

Each change that I made to my solar collector <u>caused</u> the inside of the shoebox to get hotter, <u>resulting</u> in a rise in temperature on the thermometer. <u>When</u> I placed the plain, uncovered shoebox in the sun, the Fahrenheit temperature increased 26°.

Sentence Fluency

• **Transitional phrases help the writing flow.**

I also like how Hannah uses transitional phrases such as *15 minutes later* and *after 15 minutes* to show the order of events. This puts everything in order and makes the observation easy to follow.

[from the writing model]

I recorded the temperature inside the box at the start of the experiment and again 15 minutes later. Here are my observations. The temperature inside the box at the start of the experiment was 72°F (24°C). The temperature inside the box after 15 minutes was 98°F (36°C).

Grammar/Mechanics

• **Spelling, punctuation, and capitalization are correct. Colons and hyphens are used correctly.**

In the passage below, Hannah uses a colon to separate the first two sentences, since the second one explains the first. She also uses a hyphen to connect *cost* and *effective*, which together, act as an adjective. I also think she must have edited for spelling and grammar because as far as I can tell, there are no mistakes.

[from the writing model]

I learned several things from my experiments: For one thing, I now understand the basics of collecting solar energy. For another, I learned that solar energy really is a clean, efficient, and cost-effective way to heat a space.

My Turn!

I'm going to write a scientific observation that describes something I'm curious about. I'll follow the rubric and use good writing strategies. Read on to see how I do it!

Writing a Scientific Observation

Information/Organization The writer describes several experiments.

Writing Strategy Observe and take notes.

Recently, my teacher asked us to record and write a scientific observation. I'm a total baseball freak, so I decided to do some baseball experiments. I recently read an article on how baseballs act under different conditions, so I decided to do a few of the experiments. I even got my brother Brian to help so that I could observe and take notes. I wrote down the question I wanted to answer, and then I continued from there.

My Notes

- **Question:** At what temperature (frozen, heated, or room temperature) will the rebound rate of a baseball be highest?

- **Prediction:** The warm baseball's rebound rate will be highest.

- **What I did:** Brian stood on a chair, held a tape measure 72 inches off the ground, and dropped a baseball straight down. I observed and recorded how high the ball bounced. I then divided that amount by 72 inches to get the rebound rate. We repeated the experiment three times with a cold baseball, a warm baseball, and a baseball at room temperature.

- **The Results:** The cold baseball had a rebound rate of 0.305. The warm baseball had a rebound rate of 0.236. The baseball at room temperature had a rebound rate of 0.292.

- **Conclusion:** My prediction was wrong. The cold baseball had the highest rebound rate, not the warm one.

Practice!

Now it's your turn. Choose a few experiments about something that interests you. Gather what you need. Then, run the experiments and describe what you observe.

Prewriting Organize Ideas

Information/Organization

The observation includes causes and effects.

Writing Strategy

Make Cause-and-Effect Links to organize my notes.

Writer's Term

Cause-and-Effect Links

Sometimes a single cause brings about a single effect. When this happens, you can use **Cause-and-Effect Links** to show each pair of events.

There are two kinds of organization in a scientific observation. Sequence is important because you need to follow the proper order of steps in an experiment so that your results will be accurate. Cause and effect are important because each cause can result in a different outcome. To track these causes and effects, I'll use Cause-and-Effect Links.

CAUSE-AND-EFFECT LINKS

 Cause: I refrigerated a baseball for eight hours. **Effect:** It rebounded 22 inches for a rebound rate of 0.305.

 Cause: I wrapped a baseball in a heating pad for eight hours. **Effect:** It rebounded 17 inches for a rebound rate of 0.236.

 Cause: I left a baseball on the counter overnight. **Effect:** It rebounded 21 inches for a rebound rate of 0.292.

Practice!

Now it's your turn. Use Cause-and-Effect Links to organize your notes.

Reflect

Do you think my Cause-and-Effect Links will help me?

Descriptive Writing ■ Scientific Observation   **137**

Drafting Write a Draft

Voice/Audience   Scientific language is appropriate for the audience.

Writing Strategy   Use scientific language that is appropriate for the audience.

Now I'm ready to start writing my scientific observation. I'll do my best with spelling and grammar, but right now I just want to focus on getting everything down on paper. Later, I'll reread the whole thing and make corrections.

According to the rubric, I need to use scientific language appropriate for my audience. I'll use the same four headings that Hannah used: MATERIALS, PROCEDURES, OBSERVATIONS, and CONCLUSIONS. I think these terms are pretty basic, so I don't think my readers will have any trouble understanding my report. Here's what I'll put in each section.

- MATERIALS: I'll list all the equipment that I'm going to need for my experiments.
- PROCEDURES: I'll describe how I set up my experiments, and I'll include the subheadings Experiment 1, Experiment 2, and Experiment 3.
- OBSERVATIONS: I'll describe the causes and effects of the experiments.
- CONCLUSIONS: I'll explain what I learned from the experiments.

Observing the Rebound Ratings of a Baseball
by Josh

[scientific language]

    I read in a book that in the 1950s, the Chicago White Sox used to keep their baseballs in a freezer before home games! That got me wondering: Does the temperature of a baseball noticably affect it's rebound rating? I decided to conduct some experiments to find out. (Note: The rebound rating is the ratio used to describe how well a ball bounces. To figure the rebound rating, take the length of the rebound and divide it by the length of the drop.) The book said that a baseball goes farther if the ball is warm. I predict that a ball that has been wrapped in a heating pad will bounce higher than the other balls tested.

MATERIALS

new baseball, heating pad, use of refrigerator, tape measure

PROCEDURES

Experiment 1

    I unwrapped a new baseball and placed it in the refrigerator. I took the ball out of the refrigerator and had my brother Brian help me test the ball's rebound rating. Brian stood on a chair in our kitchen and held a tape measure 72 inches (6 feet) off the ground. He dropped the baseball onto the hardwood floor. I watched the ball carefully.

    When it bounced back up, I looked at the tape measure and saw that it had rebounded 22 inches. Rebound rating: 22 in. ÷ 72 in. = 0.305

[scientific language]

[DRAFT]

Experiment 2

I let the ball return to room temperature. I wrapped a heating pad around it and set the temperature on "low." I took the ball out of the heating pad and had Brian help me test the ball's rebound rating. Brian had to stands on the same chair in the same spot in our kitchen. He held a tape measure 72 inches (6 feet) off the ground. Then he dropped the baseball onto the hardwood floor. I watched the ball carefully.

When it bounced back up, I looked at the tape measure and saw that it had rebounded 17 inches. Rebound rating: 17 in. ÷ 72 in. = 0.236

Experiment 3

I let the ball return to room temperature by letting it sit untouched on a counter. I had Brian help me test the ball's rebound rating. Brian stood on the same chair in the same spot in our kitchen. Again, he held a tape measure 72 inches (6 feet) off the ground. Then he dropped the baseball onto the hardwood floor. Again, I watched the ball carefully.

When it bounced back up, I looked at the tape measure and saw that it had rebounded 21 inches. Rebound rating: 21 in. ÷ 72 in. = 0.292

OBSERVATIONS

The baseball rebounded very differently under cold and hot conditions. When refrigerated, it rebounded to 22 inches (about a third of the height from which it was dropped). When heated, however, it only rebounded to 17 inches (about a fourth of the height from which it was dropped). That was a difference of 5 inches. When the ball returned to room temperature, its rebound rating was closer to the rating of the cold ball, but it wasn't quite as high.

CONCLUSIONS

I learned that the temperature of a baseball really does affect its variations in rebound rating, a colder ball has a grater rebound. In a baseball game, this would mean that when hit off a bat, a colder baseball would go farther than a warm one. So that must mean that a team that plays in a cool weather city would hit the ball farther than a team that plays in a warm weather city. I had predicted that the warmer ball would bounce higher. This is weird. How did I get these results? I'll repeat my experiments next week to see if I get the same results.

Practice!

Now it's your turn. Make sure to use scientific language that your readers will understand.

Reflect

Do you think my scientific language is appropriate for my audience?

Revising Extend Writing

Content/Ideas

Diagrams enhance the description.

Writing Strategy   Add diagrams to enhance the description.

Writer's Term

Diagrams

A **diagram** is a labeled drawing that shows how something works or how it is made. Diagrams are often used in reports to help explain complicated ideas.

You've probably tried to understand instructions that didn't have pictures. Well, that's when diagrams come in handy, and according to the rubric, I should include diagrams in my observation. So after I found a good spot, I drew a diagram and then inserted a reference for it in my report.

[DRAFT]

test the ball's rebound rating. Brian stood on a chair in our kitchen and held a tape measure 72 inches (6 feet) off the ground. He dropped the → (See Diagram 1.) baseball onto the hardwood floor. I watched the ball carefully.

[added a diagram]

baseball   72"

tape measure

Diagram 1

Practice!

Now it's your turn. Add a couple of diagrams to your draft to help readers understand your observation.

Revising Clarify Writing

Word Choice/Clarity

Specific words show important connections throughout.

Writing Strategy

Use specific words to show important connections.

The rubric says to use specific words to show important connections, so I reread my draft, looking for places where the connections I was making—linking cause and effect—were sort of unclear. Then, I changed words to make things clearer for the reader.

[DRAFT]

I learned that the temperature of a baseball really does ~~affect its~~ **cause** variations in rebound rating, a colder ball ~~has~~ **results in** a grater rebound. In a baseball game, this would mean that when hit off a bat, a colder baseball would go farther than a warm one. So that must mean that

[used specific words]

Practice!

Now it's your turn. Use specific words to show cause-and-effect connections.

Reflect

Have my revisions helped? Is my word choice clearer now?

Descriptive Writing ■ Scientific Observation **143**

Editing Check Sentences

 Sentence Fluency

Transitional phrases help the writing flow.

Writing Strategy   Use transitional phrases to help the writing flow.

Now I need to edit my writing. The rubric says to use transitional phrases to help my writing flow. This is important because I have to describe the experiments, step-by-step, and that can make the writing sound a little choppy. So I looked over my draft and found a few places where the writing seemed rough because each sentence started with the subject. I smoothed things out with some transitional phrases, and I even fixed an error in subject-verb agreement since I know that's important, too!

[DRAFT]

[used transitional phrases]

I let the ball return to room temperature. ~~The next day,~~ I wrapped a heating pad around it and set the temperature on "low." ~~Eight hours later,~~ I took the ball out of the heating pad and had Brian help me test the ball's rebound rating. Brian had to ~~stands~~ stand on the same chair in the same spot in our kitchen. He

[corrected subject-verb agreement]

Practice!

Now it's your turn. Use transitional phrases to make your writing flow.

Editing Proofread Writing

Grammar/Mechanics

Spelling, punctuation, and capitalization are correct. Colons and hyphens are used correctly.

Writing Strategy Make sure colons and hyphens are used correctly.

Writer's Term

Colons and Hyphens

A **colon (:)** is used to separate two independent clauses when the second one explains the first. It can also be used to introduce a list at the end of a sentence.
A **hyphen (-)** is used to separate words at the end of a line or to link two words that, when used together, act as an adjective.

The last thing to do is check my observation for incorrect spelling, punctuation, and capitalization. The rubric also says to make sure that colons and hyphens are used correctly. I checked my draft and fixed any errors that I saw.

[DRAFT]

[correctly used a colon]

cause

I learned that the temperature of a baseball really does affect its
                                                                  results in   greater
variations in rebound rating, a colder ball has a grater rebound. In

a baseball game, this would mean that when hit off a bat, a colder

baseball would go farther than a warm one. So that must mean that

a team that plays in a cool-weather city would hit the ball farther

than a team that plays in a warm-weather city. I had predicted that

[correctly used hyphens]

Practice!

Now it's your turn. Make sure that colons, hyphens, grammar, and mechanics are used correctly.

Grammar/Mechanics

For more practice with colons and hyphens, use the exercises on the next two pages.

Reflect

Did my edits make my writing clearer?

Colons and Hyphens

KNOW the RULE

A **colon** is used to separate two independent clauses when the second one explains the first.
    Example: I conducted an awesome experiment: I observed various items under a black light.
A **colon** can also be used to introduce a list at the end of a sentence.
    Example: Here is what I used: a white shirt, a pink shirt, nail polish, and fluorescent paint.

A **hyphen** is used to separate words at the end of a line or to link two words that, when used together, act as an adjective.
    Examples: black-light experiment; greenish-yellow tint

Practice the Rule

Copy the sentences below on a separate sheet of paper, inserting colons and hyphens where needed.

1. I will conduct an experiment I will observe the rebound ratings of three balls.
2. I predict that two balls will have similar rebound ratings the tennis ball and the basketball.
3. A golf ball is a lightning fast ball.
4. The golf ball's diameter is the smallest 1.68 inches.
5. British made golf balls are slightly smaller than American ones, so they probably have an even higher rebound rating.

Apply the Rule

Read the following passage, looking for colon and hyphen errors. Rewrite the corrected text on another sheet of paper.

Experiment

To begin my liquid density experiment, I filled three glasses with equal amounts of water. I also set out the following vegetable oil, soy sauce, and skim milk. Then, I measured out one teaspoonful of oil and poured it into a glass of water. I repeated this same process with the soy sauce and milk, making sure to rinse the liquid coated teaspoon after each different liquid.

OBSERVATIONS

The liquids behaved in the following ways Each one either floated on top of the water or sank to the bottom of the glass. When I poured in the oil, it floated on top of the water in little circles. But the soy sauce sank, and so did the milk.

CONCLUSIONS

I learned that oil was the least dense. Because it floated on top of the water, oil has a density of less than 1. Both the soy sauce and the skim milk sank, meaning they both have densities that are greater than 1. The experiment did leave me with one question What would happen if I tested the density of whole milk? Whole milk has fat in it, similar to that in oil. Will it float?

Publishing Share Writing

Include my observation in a display in my science classroom.

My scientific observation is done! Now I want to publish it. I could post it on the Web or read it to a friend. But a lot of kids like baseball, so I think my classmates will be interested in my results. That's why I want to include my final draft in a display in my science class. I'll read through it again right now to make sure it includes all of the items on my checklist.

My Checklist

✓ The observation describes several experiments.

✓ It includes causes and effects.

✓ Scientific language is appropriate for the audience.

✓ Diagrams clarify the description.

✓ Transitional phrases and specific words make the writing flow.

✓ Spelling, capitalization, and punctuation are all correct. Colons and hyphens are used correctly.

Practice!

Now it's your turn. Make a checklist to check your scientific observation. Then, make a final draft to publish.

Observing the Rebound Ratings of a Baseball

by Josh

I read in a book that in the 1950s, the Chicago White Sox used to keep their baseballs in a freezer before home games! That got me wondering: Does the temperature of a baseball noticeably affect its rebound rating? I decided to conduct some experiments to find out. (Note: The rebound rating is the ratio used to describe how well a ball bounces. To figure the rebound rating, take the length of the rebound and divide it by the length of the drop.) The book said that a baseball goes farther if the ball is warm. I predict that a ball that has been wrapped in a heating pad will bounce higher than the other balls tested.

MATERIALS

new baseball, heating pad, use of refrigerator, tape measure

PROCEDURES

Experiment 1

To begin my experiment, I unwrapped a new baseball and placed it in the refrigerator. After eight hours, I took the ball out of the refrigerator and had my brother Brian help me test the ball's rebound rating. Brian stood on a chair in our kitchen and held a tape measure 72 inches (6 feet) off the ground. (See Diagram 1.) Then, he dropped the baseball onto the hardwood floor. I watched the ball carefully.

When it bounced back up, I looked at the tape measure and saw that it had rebounded 22 inches. Rebound rating: 22 in. ÷ 72 in. = 0.305

baseball

72"

tape
measure

Diagram 1

Experiment 2

I let the ball return to room temperature. The next day, I wrapped a heating pad around it and set the temperature on "low." Eight hours later, I took the ball out of the heating pad and had Brian help me test the ball's rebound rating. Brian had to stand on the same chair in the same spot in our kitchen. Again, he held a tape measure 72 inches (6 feet) off the ground. Then, he dropped the baseball onto the hardwood floor. Again, I watched the ball carefully.

When it bounced back up, I looked at the tape measure and saw that it had rebounded 17 inches. Rebound rating: 17 in. $\div$ 72 in. $= 0.236$

Experiment 3

I let the ball return to room temperature by letting it sit untouched on a counter. After school the next day, I had Brian help me test the ball's rebound rating. Brian stood on the same chair in the same spot in our kitchen. Again, he held a tape measure 72 inches (6 feet) off the ground. Then, he dropped the baseball onto the hardwood floor. Again, I watched the ball carefully.

When it bounced back up, I looked at the tape measure and saw that it had rebounded 21 inches. Rebound rating: 21 in. ÷ 72 in. = 0.292

OBSERVATIONS

The baseball rebounded differently under cold and hot conditions. When refrigerated, it rebounded to 22 inches (about a third of the height from which it was dropped). When heated, however, it only rebounded to 17 inches (about a fourth of the height from which it was dropped). That was a difference of 5 inches. When the ball returned to room temperature, its rebound rating was closer to the rating of the cold ball, but it wasn't quite as high.

CONCLUSIONS

I learned that the temperature of a baseball really does cause variations in rebound rating: A colder ball results in a greater rebound. In a baseball game, this would mean that when hit off a bat, a colder baseball would go farther than a warm one. So that must mean that a team that plays in a cool-weather city would hit the ball farther than a team that plays in a warm-weather city. I had predicted that the warmer ball would bounce higher. This is weird. How did I get these results? I'll repeat my experiments next week to see if I get the same results.

Reflect

What do you think? Did I use all the traits of a good scientific observation in my writing? Check it against the rubric. Don't forget to use the rubric to check your own report, too.

Ways to Publish a
Scientific Observation

Before you publish your observation, think about your audience. This will help you pick the best way to share your work. Here are some publishing ideas.

 Read your observation to someone in your science class. Then, discuss his or her reaction.

 Submit your scientific observation to a school science club that would be interested in hearing about your work.

 Post your work on a Web site that publishes students' science experiments.

Include your scientific observation in a class book of lab reports.

 Take your work home and share it with your family.

Writing Across the Content Areas
Scientific Observation

Your school subjects can be a source of writing ideas. Pick a subject and brainstorm some topics. Here are some examples.

Science

- Observe the birds in your backyard and describe what you see. Then, put out a bird feeder. Now, describe your observations.

- Test the strength of different materials such as rubber bands and string by suspending the same weight from equal lengths of each. Then, write an observation.

Social Studies

- Test student food choices. Pick items to compare, and predict which will be more popular. Conduct a survey and describe the results.

- Find out the effect of television commercials on the average teenager. Watch three commercials and take notes on their contents, as well as your reaction. Then, write your observations.

Art and/or Music

- Which glass rings with a higher tone—one filled with more or less water? Write an observation.

- Make drawings using different art media such as chalk or charcoal. Write an observation about the benefits and drawbacks of each.

What's a Descriptive Vignette?

It's a short, descriptive sketch. The writer uses sensory details to describe a specific place, thing, or event. I think I'm going to like this kind of writing because I can challenge myself to bring description to life on the page!

What's in a Descriptive Vignette?

Organization
This is the structure of my description. I like to describe events from beginning to end, but sometimes I present things in order of importance or according to sensory details.

Narrator
The narrator is the person sharing the description. I do best when I describe something memorable, so I'll narrate an event that really stands out in my mind.

Sensory Details
Sensory details grab the reader's attention and bring the subject to life. Instead of *cold*, I'll write *nippy*, and I'll replace *nice scent* with *spicy aroma*. If I use details that appeal to all five senses, I'll create sharp, vivid images. Get the picture?

Figurative Language
This includes similes, metaphors, and personification. Similes and metaphors compare things, and personification brings an inanimate object to life. By including figurative language, you can help the reader see things in a new way.

Why write a Descriptive Vignette?

People write vignettes for many reasons. I'll list some here to help me decide what I want to write about.

Entertainment

I like to read descriptions of awesome places and amazing events. Entertaining the reader is one reason to write a descriptive vignette.

Personal Reflection

Personal reflection is a good reason to describe a subject that has a strong effect on me. When I describe something, I realize what it really means to me.

Information

A thing can make such an impression on me that I can't wait to tell people about it. If I include a lot of details, I can really inform my readers of the event.

Sharing

Have you ever felt the need to tell someone, "You've *got* to see this"? You might want to write so that you can share your description of a cool new gadget, a ball field, or your own science project.

Descriptive Vignette Writing Traits

I know that there are six traits of good writing. But what makes a good descriptive vignette? This list will help me write my description.

Information/Organization	A personal experience is described. Details are organized throughout.
Voice/Audience	Sensory details help the reader connect to the writing.
Content/Ideas	Figurative language enhances the description.
Word Choice/Clarity	Precise words make the description clear.
Sentence Fluency	Participial phrases create sentence variety.
Grammar/Mechanics	Spelling, punctuation, and capitalization are correct. Comparative and superlative forms are used correctly.

I can use Gina Bedow's descriptive vignette on the next page as a model for my own writing. Later, we'll check out how Gina used these traits to help her write.

The Concert

By Gina Bedow

Narrator

Last night I went to the most deafening concert I've ever attended. My ears are still ringing from the music, and my throat is still sore from screaming above the crowd. I guess you could say that I experienced the concert with all five of my senses!

Personification

The concert was outdoors, and there were food tents set up everywhere. The smoke from the barbecue ribs rose above the crowd. It curled a finger under Jackson's nose, beckoning him to eat. The pizza tent was next door, and Sharon couldn't resist the smell of fresh mozzarella. I chose corn on the cob. As I ate, butter dripped down my hand with each sweet, crunchy bite, and salt stung my lips like a thousand tiny bees.

Simile

Sensory Details

Personification Hunger satisfied, we found a place to sit about halfway up a hill. The grass felt cool and stiff as we spread out our blanket. Stretching drowsily, the sun soon sank behind the hill. I felt a little chilly, so I untied my sweater from around my waist and slipped it over my head. Its gentle caress felt soft and warm, and I secretly thanked my mom for making me take it along.

Organization After a while, the concert began. When the band hit the stage, the crowd sprang to its feet. I saw two girls, arms locked, in a jerky kind of square dance. To their right, a boy stood playing an imaginary drum set. To his right, a group of people clapped in time with the music.

And then it started raining—hard. Within minutes, we were all drenched, and so was the ground. It was now a toboggan run of mud. I couldn't stand it anymore. I took off my shoes and socks, rolled up my jeans, and went flailing down the hill. There's nothing quite like the feel of cold, wet mud against the skin. By the time I finished, I looked like someone had turned me upside down and dipped me in a vat of chocolate.

Metaphor

Simile

The band tried to get everyone's attention by playing louder than the roar of the crowd. The bass was so loud that it rattled my bones. I plugged my ears with cotton, and it's a good thing I did! A few hours later, my ears were still ringing, and I practically had to shout to hear myself.

When I got home, my parents asked how the night had gone. I just laughed and shouted, "I'll tell you tomorrow, when I get my hearing back!"

Descriptive Vignette

Rubric

The traits of a good descriptive vignette from page 156 have been used to make the rubric below. By using 1, 2, 3, or 4 check marks to judge each trait, you can decide how well any descriptive vignette was written.

	Excelling ✓✓✓✓	Achieving ✓✓✓	Developing ✓✓	Beginning ✓
Information/ Organization	One experience is described. Details are organized throughout.	Most of an experience is described. Details are mostly organized.	Some of an experience is described. Details are loosely organized.	More description is needed. Details should be organized.
Voice/ Audience	Sensory details help the reader connect to the writing.	Some sensory details are included for the reader.	A few sensory details are included for the reader.	More sensory details are needed to help the reader connect to the writing.
Content/ Ideas	Figurative language enhances the description.	Much figurative language is used.	Some figurative language is used.	More figurative language is needed to enhance the description.
Word Choice/ Clarity	Precise words make the description clear.	Many precise words are used.	Some precise words are used.	More precise words are needed to make the description clear.
Sentence Fluency	Participial phrases create sentence variety throughout.	Some participial phrases are used.	A few participial phrases are used.	More participial phrases are needed to create sentence variety.
Grammar/ Mechanics	Spelling, grammar, and comparative/ superlative forms are used correctly.	There are a few errors in spelling, grammar, and comparative/ superlative usage.	There are some errors in spelling, grammar, and comparative/ superlative usage.	There are many errors in spelling, grammar, and comparative/ superlative usage.

Descriptive Vignette

Using the Rubric to Study the Model

Now, let's use the rubric to check Gina's vignette, "The Concert." How many check marks would you give Gina for each trait?

Information/ Organization

- A personal experience is described.
- Details are organized throughout.

Gina organizes her vignette into paragraphs that focus on specific sensory details. She focuses on smell and taste in the first body paragraph, and she describes how things feel in the second. In the third body paragraph, Gina focuses on what she saw.

[from the writing model]

I saw two girls, arms locked, in a jerky kind of square dance. To their right, a boy stood playing an imaginary drum set. To his right, a group of people clapped in time with the music.

Voice/ Audience

- Sensory details help the reader connect to the writing.

Gina is really good at painting mental pictures. She uses details that appeal to the reader's senses of sight, smell, taste, sound, and touch. This passage contains one of my favorite descriptions. I could really visualize the different foods. I could almost smell them and taste them myself.

[from the writing model]

The smoke from the barbecue ribs rose above the crowd. It curled a finger under Jackson's nose, beckoning him to eat. The pizza tent was next door, and Sharon couldn't resist the smell of fresh mozzarella. I chose corn on the cob. As I ate, butter dripped down my hand with each sweet, crunchy bite, and salt stung my lips like a thousand tiny bees.

Descriptive Vignette

Content/Ideas

• **Figurative language enhances the description.**

Gina makes her description even more vivid by using similes, metaphors, and other figurative language. In the passage below, Gina uses personification to describe both the sun and her sweater as if they were living beings. I realize these are just objects that don't have the ability to act, but Gina finds a creative way to bring them to life.

> [from the writing model]
>
> Stretching drowsily, the sun soon sank behind the hill. I felt a little chilly, so I untied my sweater from around my waist and slipped it over my head. Its gentle caress felt soft and warm, and I secretly thanked my mom for making me take it along.

Word Choice/Clarity

• **Precise words make the description clear.**

I really appreciate the way Gina keeps her writing interesting. Instead of using vague, generic words that readers see all the time, she picks the exact words for what she wants to say. Check out the precise details in this passage. Instead of *wet*, Gina uses *drenched*. She could have written *went down the hill*, but *flailing down the hill* says it so much better.

> [from the writing model]
>
> Within minutes, we were all drenched, and so was the ground. It was now a toboggan run of mud. I couldn't stand it anymore. I took off my shoes and socks, rolled up my jeans, and went flailing down the hill.

Sentence Fluency

• Participial phrases create sentence variety.

I remember what a participle is! It's a verb form that ends in *–ing* or *–ed*, and when it's included in a group of words or a phrase that acts as an adjective, it's called a participial phrase. In the passage below, Gina uses the participial phrase *Hunger satisfied* to describe the group of concert-goers.

[from the writing model]

Hunger satisfied, we found a place to sit about halfway up a hill.

Grammar/Mechanics

• Spelling, punctuation, and capitalization are correct. Comparative and superlative forms are used correctly.

Gina knows how to use the correct comparative and superlative forms of adjectives and adverbs. She uses the comparative form to compare two objects or people and the superlative form to compare three or more. Notice her use of the superlative adjective form *most deafening* to explain that this was the loudest concert she has ever attended.

[from the writing model]

Last night I went to the most deafening concert I've ever attended.

Gina also uses the comparative adverb form *louder* to explain how loud the band played.

[from the writing model]

The band tried to get everyone's attention by playing louder than the roar of the crowd.

My Turn!

I'm going to write a descriptive vignette about something that's meaningful to me. I'll follow the rubric and use good writing strategies. Read on to see how I do it!

Prewriting Gather Information

Information/Organization

A personal experience is described.

Writing Strategy

Choose a personal experience. Jot down notes about what I heard, smelled, tasted, and touched.

I live near the Atlantic Ocean, and I like to hang out at the beach. When I daydream about it, I can imagine what things sound, smell, and taste like. So when my teacher said we were going to write descriptive vignettes, choosing my topic was a no-brainer. I just visualized a bunch of details about the beach. Then, I jotted them down.

My Notes About the Beach

✔ sun feels warm on my skin
✔ sunscreen smells like coconuts
✔ seagulls are calling overhead
✔ smell of salt is in the air
✔ ocean waves are crashing
✔ little kids are playing, talking, laughing, calling
✔ warm sand feels soft when my feet sink in
✔ water tastes salty on my lips
✔ salt dries my lips, hair, skin
✔ peanut butter and jelly sandwich tastes great (a tradition!)

Practice!

Now it's your turn. Choose a memorable experience to describe. Gather information by noting sensory details.

Information/Organization   Details are organized throughout.

Writing Strategy   Make a Web to organize my notes.

Writer's Term___

Web
A **Web** organizes ideas around one topic. The topic goes in the center. Categories related to the topic are attached to it, and details are attached to each category.

The rubric says I should organize my details. I think a Web will help me categorize my notes. Then, I can use the Web categories as starting points for each of the paragraphs in my vignette. Since I can see almost everything I sense, I won't include sight as a category.

Web

kids laughing & shouting

seagulls calling

coconut sunscreen

salty air

waves crashing

SOUND

at the beach

SMELL

pb & j

warm, smooth sand

TOUCH

TASTE

hot sun

skin dry from salt

salty water

Practice!

Now it's your turn. Organize details by using your notes to create a Web.

Reflect

How did I do? Do you think my Web will help me structure my vignette?

Writing a Descriptive Vignette

Drafting Write a Draft

Voice/Audience

Sensory details help the reader connect to the writing.

Writing Strategy

Help the reader visualize by including plenty of sensory details.

OK, now I'm ready to write. I'm just going to focus on getting my ideas down. I'll do my best with spelling and grammar, but I know that when I finish, I can go back and correct any mistakes. For now, though, I'm going to make sure that my subjects and verbs agree.

According to the rubric, my descriptive vignette should contain sensory details to help the reader picture what I put on the page. Here's what I plan to do in my lead paragraph: After introducing my topic, I'll add a few sensory details that explore it in some way. Then, I'll use my Web to help me organize groups of sensory details into paragraphs.

[DRAFT]

[correct use of subject-verb agreement] **A Day at the Beach**

There is nothing I like better than a day at the beach, with all its sights, sounds, and sensations. Everything about it is so familiar. My most favorite thing about the beach is the sound. If I close my eyes and consintrate, I can hear the water right now. I also enjoy the sound of the seagulls circling overhead. I take pleasure in the children's voices, too. Some children talk quietly as they build sandcastles. Others giggle and squeal as they horse around in the water and are overcome by the waves. Some even call to their parents as they find "treasures" in the sand. Every new shell is a glistening piece of gold; every fossil is the more rare gem of all.

[sensory details]

and then there are the feelings. The water is coolest and most refreshing than I remember as I immerse myself under its surface. When I emerge, I can feel its stinging saltiness as it dries on my lips. When I've had enough, I trudge slowly back to my blanket. Every time I step, my foot is swallowed by the sand and disappears into its softness.

Practice!

Now it's your turn. Write a draft using sensory details from your Web to paint vivid pictures for the reader.

Reflect

What do you think? Are my details colorful enough? Will they help the reader visualize the scene?

Revising Extend Writing

Figurative language enhances the description.

Writing Strategy   Add figurative language.

Writer's Term

Figurative Language

Figurative language includes **simile, metaphor,** and **personification**. A simile is a comparison of two things, using *like* or *as*: *The girl sang like a bird.* A metaphor is also a comparison, but it says that one thing is another: *The sun is a fiery lion.* Personification is the technique of giving human qualities to an animal, object, or idea: *The dog smiled.*

After I finished writing my draft, I realized that the rubric said I needed to include figurative language. I then found a few spots where I could add some figures of speech to liven things up.

[DRAFT]

[added a simile]   [added personification]

all its sights, sounds, and sensations. Everything about it is so
→ that it feels like my second home
familiar. My most favorite thing about the beach is the sound. If
                          It sings an endless song that swells and roars.
I close my eyes and consintrate, I can hear the water right now.
                    Their squawking is a rhythmic lullaby.
I also enjoy the sound of the seagulls circling overhead. I take

[added a metaphor]

Practice!

Now it's your turn. Add some figurative language to freshen up your writing.

Revising Clarify Writing

Word Choice/ Clarity

Precise words make the description clear.

Writing Strategy

Replace clichés, vague words, and overused words with precise words.

✏ Writer's Term

Clichés, Vague Words, and Overused Words

A **cliché** is an expression such as *white as snow* that is used so often that it becomes stale. **Vague words** don't present a precise picture. For example, *James looked* is not as specific as *James stared intently*. **Overused words** have been used so often that they become repetitive and boring. Instead of constantly writing *Rob said,* try using *Rob replied* or *Rob stated.*

I read my draft to a classmate. She liked it, but she noticed that I used some vague words. She also spotted two clichés near the end. The rubric says to replace this kind of language with precise words, so that's what I did. I also remembered to make sure I used colons and hyphens correctly.

[DRAFT]

[replaced cliché with precise words]

cramped with hunger

I'm ~~so hungry I can eat a horse~~, so I pull out my traditional

peanut butter and jelly

beach snack: a sandwich.

[correct use of colon]

[added precise words]

Practice!

Now it's your turn. Replace vague and overused language with precise words.

Reflect

Have my revisions made my word choice clearer?

Editing Check Sentences

 Sentence Fluency

Participial phrases create sentence variety.

Writing Strategy   Use participial phrases to create sentence variety.

✎ Writer's Term

Participial Phrases

A **participial phrase** is a group of words that includes a participle, or a verb form that ends in –*ed* or –*ing*. A participle acts as an adjective in a participial phrase by modifying the subject of a sentence.

Now it's time to edit my writing. The rubric says to use participial phrases so that my sentences don't all sound the same. I looked over my draft to see if there were any repetitive sentence patterns, and sure enough, there were. To vary my writing, I changed the beginning of each of those sentences.

[DRAFT]

[formed participial phrases]

I'm startled from my daydream, I realize that I'm not at the beach at all. I am holding my pen, I am writing and dreaming about the beach.

 Practice!

Now it's your turn. Use participial phrases to add variety to your writing.

Editing Proofread Writing

Grammar/Mechanics Spelling, punctuation, and capitalization are correct. Comparative and superlative forms are used correctly.

Writing Strategy Make sure comparative and superlative forms are used correctly.

Writer's Term

Comparative and Superlative Forms
The **comparative form** of an adjective or adverb compares two people, places, things, or actions. The **superlative form** compares three or more people, places, things, or actions.

Now it's time to check for errors in spelling, punctuation, and capitalization. The rubric also says to make sure that comparative and superlative forms are used correctly.

[DRAFT]

call to their parents as they find "treasures" in the sand. Every

new shell is a glistening piece of gold; every fossil is the ~~more rare~~ rarest

gem of all.

[correct superlative form]

Practice!

Now it's your turn. Edit for errors in grammar and mechanics, and make sure that comparative and superlative forms are used correctly.

Grammar/Mechanics

For more practice with comparative and superlative forms, use the exercises on the next two pages.

Reflect

Do my edits work well? Did participial phrases freshen up my writing?

Comparative and Superlative Forms

KNOW the RULE

The **comparative form** of an adjective or adverb compares two people, places, things, or actions.
- Add an *–er* ending to short adjectives and adverbs to create the comparative form.
  Examples: loud, loud**er**; small, small**er**
- Use the word *more* or *less* before long adjectives and adverbs (of three or more syllables) to create the comparative form.
  Examples: wonderful, **more** wonderful, **less** wonderful

The **superlative form** compares three or more people, places, things, or actions.
- Add an *–est* ending to short adjectives and adverbs to create the superlative form.
  Examples: loud, loud**est**; small, small**est**
- Use the word *most* or *least* before long adjectives and adverbs (of three or more syllables) to create the superlative form.
  Examples: wonderful, **most** wonderful, **least** wonderful

Practice the Rule

On a separate sheet of paper, write the word or phrase in parentheses that correctly completes each sentence. Then, write whether that form is comparative or superlative.

1. The (more memorable/most memorable) teacher I've ever known was my swim instructor.
2. I swim (more skillfully/most skillfully) than my brother.
3. When I swam (slower/slowest) than he did, he used to tease me.
4. I've heard that Mediterranean beaches have the (more beautiful/most beautiful) sand.
5. Though the butterfly is (harder/more hard) than the breaststroke, I still want to learn it.

Apply the Rule

Read the following vignette, watching for errors in comparative and superlative usage. On a separate sheet of paper, rewrite the corrected text.

I went to the more wonderful restaurant in the whole world last night! Their menu had more items than I've ever seen before. There were seven kinds of pasta dishes, and each one sounded deliciouser than the next. Just when I thought I had chosen the one that sounded more delectable, the waiter told me about the evening's special, which sounded even most luscious.

The special was something called surf and turf. The "surf" was a whole lobster. I would have to crack it open and dip each piece in my own cup of melted butter. The "turf" was a small steak, called a filet mignon, that was wrapped in bacon. My mom told me that filet mignon is tenderer than any other steak she has eaten. The surf and turf sounded so good that I decided to order it.

When the food came, it smelled wonderful. My lobster was the most sweet seafood I've ever eaten! Sometimes I had trouble cracking open the hard shell, but my dad helped me out. His hands are more strong than mine. Oh, and my mom was right about the filet mignon. It seemed to melt in my mouth.

Boy, was I full! I didn't think I could eat another thing . . . until I saw that there was chocolate cake for dessert!

Publishing Share Writing

Read my vignette to a friend.

My descriptive vignette is finished! Now it's time to publish it. I could publish my work in one of several ways. I could submit it to a magazine or newspaper for publication, post it on the Web, or even add it to our class journal. But I'd like to read this one to a friend. Before sharing my vignette, I want to read through it one last time to make sure it includes all of the items on my checklist.

My Checklist

- ✔ My vignette describes a personal experience.
- ✔ The details are organized.
- ✔ Sensory details and figurative language paint vivid pictures.
- ✔ Clichés and vague language have been replaced with precise words.
- ✔ Participial phrases add variety.
- ✔ Spelling, capitalization, and punctuation are all correct. Comparative and superlative forms are used correctly.

Practice!

Now it's your turn. Make a checklist to check your descriptive vignette. Then, make a final draft to publish.

A Day at the Beach

By Josh

There is nothing I like better than a day at the beach, with all its sights, sounds, and sensations. Everything about it is so familiar that it feels like my second home. My favorite thing about the beach is the sound. If I close my eyes and concentrate, I can hear the water right now. It sings an endless song that swells and roars. I also enjoy the sound of the seagulls circling overhead. Their squawking is a rhythmic lullaby. I take pleasure in the children's voices, too. Some children talk quietly as they build sandcastles. Others giggle and squeal as they frolic in the water and are overcome by the waves. Some even call to their parents as they find "treasures" in the sand. Every new shell is a glistening piece of gold; every fossil is the rarest gem of all.

And then there are the feelings. The water is cooler and more refreshing than I remember as I immerse myself under its surface. When I emerge, I can feel its stinging saltiness as it dries on my lips. When I've had enough, I trudge slowly back to my blanket. Every time I step, my foot is swallowed by the sand and disappears into its softness.

The sun beams down at me like a loving friend. Its hot breath warms my skin and hair and dries me again. As I dry, the saltwater parches my skin. It feels as tight on my body as shrink-wrap.

I'm cramped with hunger, so I pull out my traditional beach snack: a peanut butter and jelly sandwich. It is a savory blend of sweet, nutty, and salty flavors. Sticking to the roof of my mouth, the peanut butter prompts me to wash it down with some water.

Startled from my daydream, I realize that I'm not at the beach at all. I am holding my pen, writing and dreaming about the beach.

Reflect

Did I use all the traits of a good vignette in my writing? Check it against the rubric. Don't forget to use the rubric to check your own work, too.

Ways to Publish a
Descriptive Vignette

While trying to decide how to publish your work, you should also think about who will be reading it. Then, you can pick the best way to share it. Here are some publishing ideas.

 Read your work to your writing partner. Then, discuss his or her reaction.

 Submit your vignette to a local newspaper or magazine that publishes student work.

 If you have a Web page or a blog, post your description there. Then, wait for feedback.

 Include your vignette in a class anthology or journal.

 Add your work to a personal scrapbook or your writing journal.

Writing Across the Content Areas
Descriptive Vignette

You can get all kinds of writing ideas at school. Pick your favorite subject, and brainstorm some related topics. Check out these examples.

Math
- Write about a sporting event during which your favorite team won by making the final tie-breaking score.

- Describe what you would do with your paycheck. Would you save the money or spend it?

Social Studies
- Describe an important local statue, monument, or memorial.

- Watch a debate between political candidates, or follow a political campaign. Then, describe the highlights.

Art and/or Music
- Review a local concert or a new CD. Describe the band or singer and the type of music played.

- Visit an art museum and describe your favorite exhibit, painting, or sculpture.

DESCRIPTIVE test writing

Read the Writing Prompt

You will be given a writing prompt when you take a test. Most writing prompts have three parts:

Setup This is the introduction to the writing prompt. It gives you some background information so that you can begin to think about your topic.

Task This part of the writing prompt tells you what you're supposed to write: a descriptive vignette.

Scoring Guide This section tells how your writing will be scored. To do well on the test, you should include everything on the list.

Remember the rubrics you've been using? When you take a writing test, you won't always have all of the information that's on a rubric. But don't worry. The scoring guide is just like a rubric. It tells you everything you need to think about in order to do well on a written test. Like the rubrics you're used to seeing, most scoring guides are based upon the six traits of writing:

Think about a memorable personal experience. What is it about this event that stands out in your mind?

Write a descriptive vignette that describes a memorable personal experience.

Be sure your writing

- is well organized.

- has an appropriate tone that keeps the reader interested.

- contains sensory details throughout.

- has precise words throughout.

- contains clauses that strengthen weak sentences.

- contains correct grammar, punctuation, capitalization, and spelling.

Writing Traits
in the Scoring Guide

Not every writing prompt will include each of the six writing traits, but the one on page 177 does. Study the chart below to help you understand how this scoring guide relates to the writing traits in the rubrics you're used to using.

 Information/Organization
- Be sure your writing is well organized.

 Voice/Audience
- Be sure your writing has an appropriate tone that keeps the reader interested.

 Content/Ideas
- Be sure your writing contains sensory details throughout.

 Word Choice/Clarity
- Be sure your writing has precise words throughout.

 Sentence Fluency
- Be sure your writing contains clauses that strengthen weak sentences.

 Grammar/Mechanics
- Be sure your writing contains correct grammar, punctuation, capitalization, and spelling.

Amy Lee's vignette is on the next page. Did she follow the scoring guide?

Summer at the Park

by Amy Lee

It was the second week of summer vacation, but the weather had been chilly and wet. Today, however, the clouds were nowhere to be seen. The sun's rays shone through my bedroom window and woke me from my slumber. It finally felt as though summer had arrived.

My sister, my mom, and I decided to start the season with a picnic at the park. When we arrived, we discovered we were not the only ones lured by the warm weather. Kids were riding their bikes along the winding paths while mothers pushed babies and toddlers along in strollers. The picnic tables were taken, so we laid out our big, comfy blanket on the grass.

I sat for a few minutes and watched the young children running through the fountains, splashing and laughing. Then, I kicked off my flip-flops and moved them from the blanket to the grass. Although the sun was warm, the grass was still cool and damp.

I got out my book of poems, which I had checked out from the library. As soon as school had ended, I went straight to the library to load up on reading material. Amber, on the other hand, put on her headphones so she could listen to the new CD she had just purchased. It was time to settle in, so I rolled over on my stomach and started to read.

"Amy," my mother said, "wake up. It's lunchtime."

Without realizing it, I had fallen asleep, lulled by the warmth of the sun and the sounds of children playing. I stretched my body from head to toe and sat back up. Mom had packed sweet, juicy honey chicken and a thermos of tangy, homemade lemonade. For dessert, she brought fresh, sweet purple plums. "The first of the season," she told us.

After lunch, Amber and I ran down to the fountains. Water squirted up and drenched us, and we laughed and screamed, just like the other kids.

It didn't take long for us to dry off in the sun. By now, even the grass was dry. Eventually, we packed up our bags and headed back to the car. Even though I was sad the day was over, I was happy that summer had finally come!

Using the Scoring Guide to Study the Model

Now let's use the scoring guide to check Amy's writing test, "Summer at the Park." How well does her vignette meet each of the six writing traits?

• **The vignette is well organized.**

Amy's story is well organized. Because she describes events in chronological order, her vignette is easy to follow.

My sister, my mom, and I decided to start the season with a picnic at the park. When we arrived, we discovered we were not the only ones lured by the warm weather. Kids were riding their bikes along the winding paths while mothers pushed babies and toddlers along in strollers. The picnic tables were taken, so we laid out our big, comfy blanket on the grass.

• **The vignette has an appropriate tone that keeps the reader interested.**

Since this is a vignette about an upbeat, informal event, Amy uses a friendly tone to capture her reader's interest. She uses words and images that make me feel like I'm part of the story. I mean, who can't relate to a summertime nap in the sun?

Without realizing it, I had fallen asleep, lulled by the warmth of the sun and the sounds of children playing. I stretched my body from head to toe and sat back up.

Content/Ideas

• **The vignette contains sensory details throughout.**

Amy uses plenty of sensory details to help the reader visualize her day at the park. Her description of the picnic lunch really makes my mouth water!

Mom had packed sweet, juicy honey chicken and a thermos of tangy, homemade lemonade. For dessert, she brought fresh, sweet purple plums. "The first of the season," she told us.

Word Choice/Clarity

• **The vignette has precise words throughout.**

Amy is not vague with her description. She uses precise words to describe her day. In the passage below, she doesn't just say the kids were playing; she says they were "splashing and laughing." She could've said she took off her shoes, but instead, she says, "I kicked off my flip-flops."

I sat for a few minutes and watched the young children running through the fountains, splashing and laughing. Then, I kicked off my flip-flops and moved them from the blanket to the grass. Although the sun was warm, the grass was still cool and damp.

Using the Scoring Guide to Study the Model

- **The vignette contains clauses that strengthen weak sentences.**

Amy uses clauses to add detail to her sentences and strengthen her writing. I think the clauses also add good sentence variety. What do you think?

I got out my book of poems, which I had checked out from the library. As soon as school had ended, I went straight to the library to load up on reading material. Amber, on the other hand, put on her headphones so she could listen to the new CD she had just purchased. It was time to settle in, so I rolled over on my stomach and started to read.

- **The vignette contains correct grammar, punctuation, capitalization, and spelling.**

It looks like Amy used correct grammar, spelling, capitalization, and punctuation. I know it's important to check for these kinds of mistakes, and I'll be sure to keep that in mind as I write. But you should check for proper grammar and mechanics in your writing, too. Don't forget that this can be done at every step of the writing process!

Planning My Time

Before handing out a writing prompt, our teacher always tells us how much time we'll have to finish a test. Since I already know the steps of the writing process, I like to think about how much total time I'll need for each step. If the test takes an hour, here's one way that I can plan my time. When taking a writing test, you should plan your time, too. Believe me, it helps!

Step 4:
Editing
10 minutes

Step 1:
Prewriting
25 minutes

Step 3:
Revising
10 minutes

Step 2:
Drafting
15 minutes

Prewriting Study the Writing Prompt

Writing Strategy Study the writing prompt to be sure I know what to do.

After my teacher gives me a writing prompt, I study it to make sure I know exactly what I should do. A writing prompt usually has three parts, even though they aren't always labeled. When you study the writing prompt, you should first find the setup, the task, and the scoring guide. Then, you can label them like I did below. Circle key words in the setup and the task that tell what kind of writing you need to do and who your audience will be. I circled my topic in blue, and I circled what kind of writing I'll be doing (a descriptive vignette) in orange. Since the writing prompt doesn't say who the audience is, I'll write for my teacher.

My Writing Test Prompt

Setup —— Think about the (seasons of the year.)

Task —— Write (a descriptive vignette) about a specific activity that you like to do during one of the four seasons.

Be sure your writing

Scoring Guide
- is well organized.
- has an appropriate tone that keeps the reader interested.
- contains sensory details throughout.
- has precise words throughout.
- contains clauses that strengthen weak sentences.
- contains correct grammar, punctuation, capitalization, and spelling.

ow it's time to think about how the scoring guide relates to the six writing traits in the rubrics you've studied. Not all of the traits will be included in every scoring guide, but you'll still want to remember them all in order to write a good vignette.

- **Be sure your writing is well organized.**

I'll work hard at every step along the way to make sure my writing is well organized.

- **Be sure your writing has an appropriate tone that keeps the reader interested.**

Since this is a descriptive vignette, I'll be sure to use a tone that's less formal and more upbeat.

- **Be sure your writing contains sensory details throughout.**

I know how important description is, so I'll remember to use plenty of sensory details in my story.

- **Be sure your writing has precise words throughout.**

As I write, I'll try to avoid using vague, dull words. Precise words are more exact.

- **Be sure your writing contains clauses that strengthen weak sentences.**

I think that using a clause here and there will help add detail and variety to my sentences.

- **Be sure your writing contains correct grammar, punctuation, capitalization, and spelling.**

I'll be sure to think about using proper grammar and mechanics as I write!

Prewriting Gather Information

Writing Strategy Respond to the task.

I know that good writers gather information before they start to write. I'll begin by rereading the task, since that's the part of the writing prompt that tells what I'm supposed to do. But I have to remember that time is limited! That's why it's a good idea to think about how I'm going to respond before I start writing.

My task is to write a descriptive vignette about one of the seasons. Since I wrote about summer once before, I think I'll write about winter this time. Last year, my friends and I made our own outdoor hockey rink, so I think I'll write about that. I'll jot down some notes right now.

Task —

Write a descriptive vignette about a specific activity that you like to do during one of the four seasons.

Notes

- ✔ Built a hockey rink; had to wait for it to freeze
- ✔ Found out it froze
- ✔ Wore warm clothes; different than inside hockey
- ✔ Had to skate around to warm up
- ✔ Played a game of hockey
- ✔ Can't wait to play again

Remember! Before you write, think about how you'll respond to the task in the writing prompt. Then, write some notes to help you gather information.

Prewriting **Organize Ideas**

Writing Strategy **Choose a graphic organizer.**

The clock is ticking, so I have to begin organizing my ideas right away. First, I'll choose a graphic organizer. I remember plenty of sensory details about the time we built our rink. But I think I'll use a Story Map to help me remember the order of events.

Title of My Story: "Winter On Ice"
Setting
Where: Outdoor hockey rink, behind Austin's barn   **When:** Last winter

---

Major Character: Me (Josh)
Minor Character(s): Austin, Colin

Theme: Wintertime is fun.

Plot

Event 1	Event 2	Event 3	Event 4
My friends and I built an outdoor hockey rink.	I found out the rink was frozen, and I "suited up."	We warmed up by skating around the rink.	We played a game of hockey.

Outcome: We hoped the weather would stay cold, and we couldn't wait to play again.

Remember! Choose a graphic organizer that will help you sequence ideas before you write.

Reflect
Do you think my Story Map will help me as I write?

Prewriting Check the Scoring Guide

Information/Organization

Writing Strategy Check my graphic organizer against the scoring guide.

There's not much time to revise when you write for a test. That's why prewriting is really important! Before I start to write my draft, I'm going to check my Story Map against the scoring guide in the writing prompt.

Title of My Story: "Winter On Ice"
Setting
Where: Outdoor hockey rink, behind Austin's barn   **When:** Last winter

Major Character: Me (Josh)
Minor Character(s): Austin, Colin

Theme: Wintertime is fun.

Plot

Event 1	Event 2	Event 3	Event 4
My friends and I built an outdoor hockey rink.	I found out the rink was frozen, and I "suited up."	We warmed up by skating around the rink.	We played a game of hockey.

Outcome: We hoped the weather would stay cold, and we couldn't wait to play again.

Information/ Organization

- Be sure your writing is well organized.

I'll use the events from my Story Map to form paragraphs that flow from one main idea to the next.

Voice/ Audience

- Be sure your writing has an appropriate tone that keeps the reader interested.

The theme from my Story Map will remind me to use a fun, upbeat tone.

Content/ Ideas

- Be sure your writing contains sensory details throughout.

Like I said, I remember that day really well. As I write, I'll include all the sensory details I can remember.

Word Choice/ Clarity

- Be sure your writing has precise words throughout.

My Story Map only shows the main events, but I don't think it will be hard to avoid dull words when I write. This is an exciting memory!

Sentence Fluency

- Be sure your writing contains clauses that strengthen weak sentences.

As I write, I'll be sure to use clauses to add detail to weak sentences.

Grammar/ Mechanics

- Be sure your writing contains correct grammar, punctuation, capitalization, and spelling.

When I edit my draft, I'll check for proper grammar and mechanics.

Reflect

My Story Map doesn't cover every point in the scoring guide, but there is a lot of good information there. Is there anything I forgot to include?

Remember! Before you write, you'll want to reread the writing prompt to be sure you're on track with what needs to be done.

Write a Draft

Writing Strategy Use an appropriate tone to keep the reader interested.

I have to remember that I'm writing a descriptive vignette. That means the reader should be able to visualize my story. Playing outdoor hockey in the winter is something I really enjoy doing, so I'll be sure to use a fun, upbeat tone.

Now, how should I begin my story? The first event listed on my Story Map is the building of our outdoor hockey rink. I think I'll begin there.

Winter on Ice

by Josh

I remember it like it was yesterday. My friends and I actually built our own outdoor hockey rink!

We set up our rink in a field behind Austin's barn. We laid four 2x4s in a big rectangle on the ground, and we flooded it with water. Since it was already wintertime, all we had to do was weight for the water to freeze. About a week later, Austin called to say it was time—the rink had frozen.

I immediately went to my closet to pull out my warmest clothes. I stopped when I saw my hockey shorts and jersey. You see, I always wear my team uniform. But today, we would be playing

Proofreading Marks

⌐	Indent	ℓ	Take out something
≡	Make a capital	⊙	Add a period
/	Make a small letter	⑤Ⓟ	Spelling error
∧	Add something	¶	New paragraph

outside! And we wear the most mismatched clothing ever! We wear long pants and sweats, sweatshirts and turtlenecks, knit hats and helmets, and plenty of pads. So I "suited up" in my warmest gear, and I rubbed my toes to warm them before putting on my skates.

Soon, we were all on the rink. Although there was snow on the ground, it wasn't snowing at the moment. Other than the action on the ice, everything around us seemed so still. We all skated back and forth across the rink, just to keep warm.

Then, Colin dropped the puck. Game on! He shouted. Soon, we were shouting to each other and passing the puck back and forth across the rink. We were sweating through our clothes, and steam was rising from our bodies. The game didn't even matter anymore: We were playing hockey on our very own rink!

After nearly two hours, we were wet and tired. We sat down in the snow banks and realized it was long past time to get a drink. We grabbed our thermoses and started to sip on hot coco, cider, and tea. As we sat there, I realized we weren't only drinking in the frothy liquid, we were also drinking in the sights and sounds of a frozen winter day.

Remember! Write with an appropriate tone to keep your reader's interest.

Reflect

Is my tone upbeat? Does it hold your interest?

Revising Extend Writing

Content/Ideas

Writing Strategy Add sensory details.

Since my draft is complete, I can go back and read it to see if I missed anything. The scoring guide says to add sensory details, and I think this is a good idea because it will help the reader visualize the story. So I went back and added some details to an area in my draft that I thought could use more description.

[DRAFT]

[added sensory details]

, shushing along and scraping through the ice

Soon, we were all on the rink. Although there was snow on the ground, it wasn't snowing at the moment. Other than the action on the ice, everything around us seemed so still. We all skated back and forth across the rink, just to keep warm.

Remember! Add sensory details to make your writing more descriptive. Think about expressing in words how something looked, smelled, felt, sounded, and tasted.

Revising Clarify Writing

Word Choice/ Clarity

Writing Strategy Replace vague words with precise words.

I reread my paper once again to see if there was anywhere that I needed to be clearer. The scoring guide says I should replace vague words with precise words. I think some of my explanations in the final paragraph are a little dull, so I'll replace them with precise words.

[DRAFT]

[used precise words]

soaked and worn out   plopped

After nearly two hours, we were ~~wet and tired~~. We ~~sat~~ down in

quench our thirst
the snow banks and realized it was long past time to ~~get a drink~~.

Remember! The words that you choose to use in your story make a big difference. Replace dull words with precise words to make your writing lively and original.

Reflect

How do you think my vignette is shaping up? Have my revisions helped to make it a better story?

Editing Check Sentences

Sentence Fluency

Writing Strategy Use clauses to strengthen weak sentences.

OK, I'm almost done. I'm ready to edit my writing, so I'll turn to the scoring guide for another helpful hint. It says that I should use clauses to strengthen weak sentences, and when I reread my draft, I found a few places where the sentences seemed a little dull. I went ahead and added some clauses to spice things up.

[DRAFT]

[added clauses]

I immediately went to my closet to pull out my warmest clothes.
when I play indoors,
I stopped when I saw my hockey shorts and jersey. You see, I

always wear my team uniform. But today, we would be playing
when Colin and Austin and I play hockey outside,
outside! And we wear the most mismatched clothing ever! We wear

Remember! Add clauses to weak sentences to make them more interesting.

Editing Proofread Writing

Writing Strategy   Check my grammar, punctuation, capitalization, and spelling.

Now there's just one last step. The scoring guide says to check my grammar and mechanics, so I'll read my draft one last time to make sure there aren't any mistakes. If there are, I'll just correct them on the page, so that my teacher can see that I tried my best. I've got five minutes left, so I better get started.

Winter on Ice

by Josh

I remember it like it was yesterday. My friends and I actually built our own outdoor hockey rink!

We set up our rink in a field behind Austin's barn. We laid four 2x4s in a big rectangle on the ground, and we flooded it with water. Since it was already wintertime, all we had to do was ~~weight~~ wait for the water to freeze. About a week later, Austin called to say it was time—the rink had frozen.

I immediately went to my closet to pull out my warmest clothes. I stopped when I saw my hockey shorts and jersey. You see, I when I play indoors, always wear my team uniform. But today, we would be playing

Remember! Check your grammar, punctuation, capitalization, and spelling every time you write for a test.

when Colin and Austin and I play hockey outside,
outside! And we wear the most mismatched clothing ever! We wear

long pants and sweats, sweatshirts and turtlenecks, knit hats and

helmets, and plenty of pads. So I "suited up" in my warmest gear,

and I rubbed my toes to warm them before putting on my skates.

, shushing along and scraping through the ice

Soon, we were all on the rink. Although there was snow on the

ground, it wasn't snowing at the moment. Other than the action on

the ice, everything around us seemed so still. We all skated back

and forth across the rink, just to keep warm.

Then, Colin dropped the puck. "Game on!" He shouted. Soon, we

were shouting to each other and passing the puck back and forth

across the rink. We were sweating through our clothes, and steam

was rising from our bodies. The game didn't even matter anymore:

We were playing hockey on our very own rink!

soaked and worn out   plopped

After nearly two hours, we were wet and tired. We sat down in

quench our thirst

the snow banks and realized it was long past time to get a drink.

cocoa

We grabbed our thermoses and started to sip on hot coco, cider,

and tea. As we sat there, I realized we weren't only drinking in the

frothy liquid, we were also drinking in the sights and sounds of a

frozen winter day.

Reflect

Did I miss anything? I'll check my writing against
the scoring guide one last time before turning it
in. Remember to use your writing prompt's scoring
guide to check your writing when you take a test.

I'm done! I never knew taking a test could be so easy! I guess when you use the scoring guide, it really helps out. But also remember to keep in mind these important tips when you write for a test.

TEST TIPS

1. **Study the writing prompt before you start to write.** Most writing prompts have three parts: the setup, the task, and the scoring guide. The parts probably won't be labeled. You'll have to figure them out for yourself!

2. **Make sure you understand the task before you start to write.**

   - Read all three parts of the writing prompt carefully.

   - Circle key words in the task part of the writing prompt that tell what kind of writing you need to do. The task might also identify your audience.

   - Make sure you know how you'll be graded.

   - Say the assignment in your own words to yourself.

3. **Keep an eye on the clock.** Decide how much time you will spend on each part of the writing process and try to stick to your schedule. Don't spend so much time on prewriting that you don't have enough time left to write.

4. **Reread your writing. Compare it to the scoring guide at least twice.** Remember the rubrics you've used? A scoring guide on a writing test is like a rubric. It can help you keep what's important in mind.

5. **Plan, plan, plan!** You don't get much time to revise during a test, so planning is more important than ever.

6. **Write neatly.** Remember, if the people who score your test can't read your writing, it doesn't matter how good your essay is!

EXPOSITORY
writing explains something to the reader.

Hi, I'm Briana. In school, I'm studying expository writing. I think this will really help me because sometimes when I try to explain something, the information just doesn't come out right. I often skip over important details because I'm so excited about what I have to say. But I think studying expository writing will teach me to organize my ideas.

IN THIS UNIT

1 **Book Report: Response to Literature**

2 **Research Report**

3 **How-To Guide: Instructional Text**

4 **Writing for a Test**

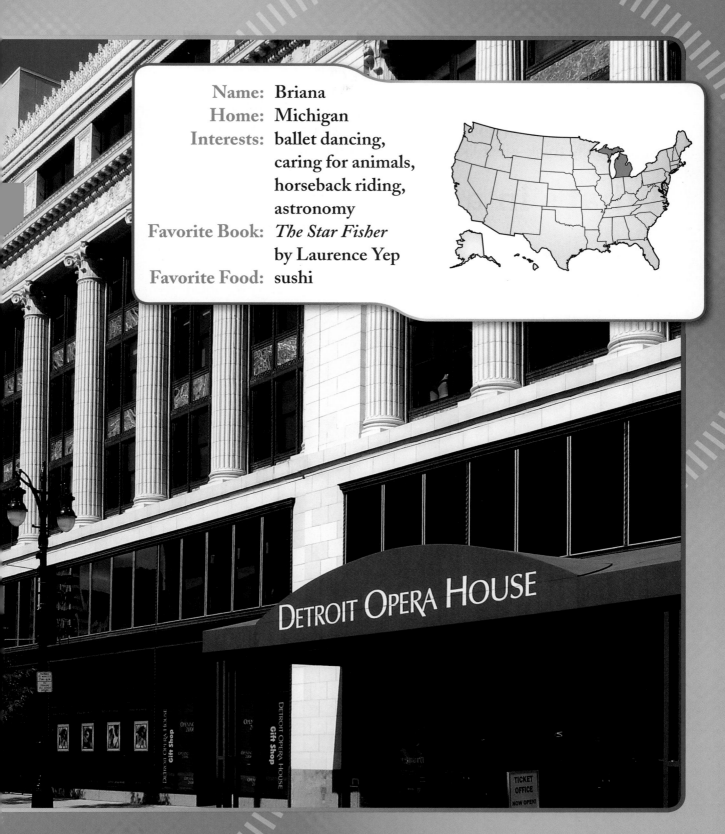

Name: Briana
Home: Michigan
Interests: ballet dancing, caring for animals, horseback riding, astronomy
Favorite Book: *The Star Fisher* by Laurence Yep
Favorite Food: sushi

DETROIT OPERA HOUSE

What's a Book Report?

It's a report that summarizes a book and explains what the reader liked and disliked about it. I'm going to enjoy writing a book report because I can say what I really think—just like a real book reviewer.

What's in a Book Report?

Summary
To understand my report, readers will need to know something about the book. I'll include a short summary that contains just the right amount of background information.

Pros and Cons
My report will include my responses to the book's strengths (pros) and weaknesses (cons). To help keep me focused, I'll organize pros and cons according to order of importance.

Viewpoint
The viewpoint is my honest opinion. It is my overall response to the book. I'll make sure that my report contains a strong, clear viewpoint.

Examples
I'll use examples to back up my opinions. I'll include direct quotations or paraphrases from the book to explain what I mean.

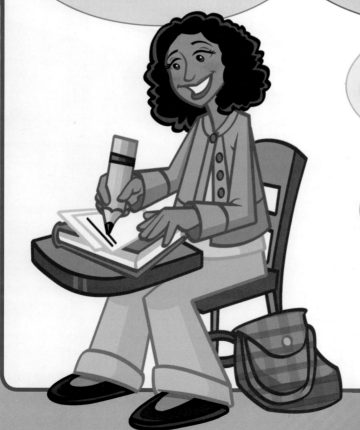

Why write a Book Report?

There are many different reasons for writing a book report. I wrote several of them here. Take a look!

Entertainment

A book report can be entertaining. The writer's style and presentation of information can make the response fun to read.

Information

People often read reviews to find out what a book is about and whether it's worth reading. Providing this kind of information is one good reason for writing a book report.

Influence

A writer might feel strongly about a particular book. If so, he or she can influence people to either read the book or avoid it.

Compare and Contrast

A particular book might be similar to other books in style, plot, characters, and/or theme. Or one book might be totally different from others that are written by the same author. Comparing and contrasting books is one purpose for writing a book report.

Book Report: Response to Literature Writing Traits

I know that there are six traits of good writing. Here's a list of what makes a good book report. I'll use it to help me write.

Information/ Organization	The writing contains many responses. Responses are organized by order of importance.
Voice/ Audience	The purpose is understandable to the reader.
Content/ Ideas	Examples support responses throughout.
Word Choice/ Clarity	Active voice clarifies the writing throughout.
Sentence Fluency	Many declarative sentences present facts.
Grammar/ Mechanics	Spelling, punctuation, and capitalization are correct. Introductory verbal phrases are used correctly.

I can use Lizzie Webber's book report on the next page as a model for my own writing. Later, we'll check out how Lizzie used the traits to help her write.

King of Shadows

A book report by Lizzie Webber

Summary

I would like to tell you about a really interesting book. *King of Shadows* was written by Newbery winner Susan Cooper. The book is about a group of young American actors called the Company of Boys. They travel to London's new Globe Theatre to put on Shakespeare's play *A Midsummer Night's Dream*. One of the actors, Nathan Field, gets seriously ill. He falls asleep one night and awakens the next morning to find that he's still in London, only now the year is 1599. No longer acting in the Company of Boys, Nat is now in the Lord Chamberlain's Men, performing alongside William Shakespeare.

Pros Several things appeal to me about this book. I like the way that Cooper seamlessly weaves fact and fiction together. Using the same play as the backdrop for both time periods, she moves Nat, as well as her readers, back and forth between the present and the past. For example, Nat is rehearsing to play Puck in the present, so he fits Puck's role in the past.   Examples

Cooper also changes the characters' speech from modern American English (in the present) to Elizabethan English (in the past). This clarifies when and where the action takes place.

Cons But I have to admit that there were also times when I was frustrated by *King of Shadows*. For example, I didn't know until the very end why Nat had to go back to 1599. Once I knew, the whole story made perfect sense. I also didn't know why the author spent so much time on details that, at the time, seemed unimportant. For example, near the beginning of the book, Cooper takes a whole paragraph to describe a muscle twitch under Richard Burbage's left eye. When I got to the end of the book, however, I realized why that twitch was so important. That's when I realized that all of Cooper's details are intentional, right down to the names of the directors: Richard Burbage in the past, and Arby (RB), which stands for Richard Babbage, in the present.

Viewpoint

Overall, I highly recommend *King of Shadows*, as I'm sure everyone will be delighted when the secret of the book is revealed.

Book Report
Rubric

The traits of a good book report from page 202 have been used to make the rubric below. By using 1, 2, 3, or 4 check marks to judge each trait, you can decide how well any book report was written.

	Excelling ✓✓✓✓	Achieving ✓✓✓	Developing ✓✓	Beginning ✓
Information/ Organization	The writing contains many responses; they are ordered by importance.	The writing contains some responses; most are ordered by importance.	The writing contains a few responses; some are ordered by importance.	The writing needs responses, organized by order of importance.
Voice/ Audience	The purpose is understandable to the reader.	The purpose is mostly understandable.	The purpose is understandable in some places.	The purpose needs to be understandable.
Content/ Ideas	Examples support responses throughout.	Examples are used in many places.	Examples are used in some places.	More examples are needed for support.
Word Choice/ Clarity	Active voice clarifies the writing throughout.	Active voice is used in many places.	Active voice is used in some places.	Active voice should clarify the writing throughout.
Sentence Fluency	Many declarative sentences present facts.	Some declarative sentences are used.	A few declarative sentences are used.	Many declarative sentences should be used to present facts.
Grammar/ Mechanics	Spelling, grammar, and introductory verbal phrases are used correctly.	There are a few errors in spelling, grammar, and introductory verbal phrase usage.	There are several errors in spelling, grammar, and introductory verbal phrase usage.	There are many errors in spelling, grammar, and introductory verbal phrase usage.

Using the Rubric to Study the Model

Book Report

Now, let's use the rubric to check Lizzie Webber's book report, "King of Shadows." How many check marks would you give Lizzie for each trait?

Information/Organization

- **The writing contains many responses.**
- **Responses are organized by order of importance.**

After Lizzie summarizes the book, she describes some of its pros, or strengths. Then, she describes some of its cons, or weaknesses. She begins with the more important points and works down to the less important points. Here's how she begins the body of her response.

> [from the writing model]
>
> Several things appeal to me about this book. I like the way that Cooper seamlessly weaves fact and fiction together. Using the same play as the backdrop for both time periods, she moves Nat, as well as her readers, back and forth between the present and the past.

Voice/Audience

- **The purpose is understandable to the reader.**

Lizzie states her purpose in the first sentence of the lead paragraph. This way, her audience knows that what follows is the author's opinion about a specific book, which is named in the second sentence.

> [from the writing model]
>
> I would like to tell you about a really interesting book. *King of Shadows* was written by Newbery winner Susan Cooper.

Content/Ideas

- **Examples support responses throughout.**

Whether she is writing about the book's pros or cons, Lizzie uses examples to support her responses. Here's a passage where she begins with a response and then supports it with a specific example from the book.

[from the writing model]

I also didn't know why the author spent so much time on details that, at the time, seemed unimportant. For example, near the beginning of the book, Cooper takes a whole paragraph to describe a muscle twitch under Richard Burbage's left eye. When I got to the end of the book, however, I realized why that twitch was so important.

Word Choice/Clarity

- **Active voice clarifies the writing throughout.**

Lizzie uses the active voice to present her report. This makes her writing clear and easy to read. For instance, she could've used this wordy, passive construction in her report: The characters' speech was changed by Cooper from modern American English (in the present) to Elizabethan English (in the past). But she used the following active sentence instead.

[from the writing model]

Cooper also changes the characters' speech from modern American English (in the present) to Elizabethan English (in the past).

Sentence Fluency

- Many declarative sentences present facts.

Lizzie uses declarative sentences to present facts. She makes clear statements and keeps the writing simple. These declarative sentences from her opening paragraph show what I mean.

[from the writing model]

The book is about a group of young American actors called the Company of Boys. They travel to London's new Globe Theatre to put on Shakespeare's play *A Midsummer Night's Dream*.

Grammar/Mechanics

- Spelling, punctuation, and capitalization are correct. Introductory verbal phrases are used correctly.

I know that a verbal is a verb form that acts like a noun, adjective, or adverb, and I appreciate how Lizzie uses verbal phrases to begin some of her sentences. This pattern adds variety to her writing. Look at the following example, in which the introductory verbal phrase *Using the same play as the backdrop for both time periods* clearly describes the subject *she*.

[from the writing model]

Using the same play as the backdrop for both time periods, she moves Nat, as well as her readers, back and forth between the present and the past.

My Turn!

I'm going to write a book report about a book I recently read. I'll follow the rubric and use good writing strategies. Read along to find out how I do it!

Prewriting Gather Information

Information/Organization

The writing contains many responses.

Writing Strategy

Read a book on a topic that interests me. Then, list my responses about the book.

When my teacher said to write a book report, the first thing I did was choose a book. I take ballet, and I absolutely love to dance. So I chose *Another Way to Dance* by Martha Southgate. After I finished reading, I looked back through the book and jotted down some things that I liked and disliked about it. I put smiley faces next to the pros and frowns next to the cons.

Another Way to Dance

- ☺ interesting and well-developed main characters
- ☹ the same things said too many times
- ☹ too much obsessing on Vicki's part
- ☺ very good/accurate descriptions of Vicki's ballet classes
- ☺ realistic feelings and actions toward Vicki's family members
- ☹ corny and overused ending

Practice!

Now it's your turn. Choose a book to read. Then, jot down notes about the things you liked and disliked.

Prewriting Organize Ideas

Information/Organization
Responses are organized by order of importance.

Writing Strategy
Make a Pro-and-Con Chart to organize my responses by order of importance.

Writer's Term

Pro-and-Con Chart

A **Pro-and-Con Chart** can help you organize your opinions about a book. By presenting a book's **pros** (good points) and **cons** (bad points) in order of their importance, you can tell your reader what the book is about, as well as why you liked and/or disliked it.

The rubric says my responses should be organized by order of importance, so I took my list of likes and dislikes and made it into a Pro-and-Con Chart. You can see how I put the most important ideas at the top of each column and worked down from there.

PRO-AND-CON CHART

PROS	CONS
very good/accurate descriptions of Vicki's ballet classes	the same things said too many times
realistic feelings and actions toward Vicki's family members	too much obsessing on Vicki's part
interesting and well-developed main characters	corny and overused ending

Practice!

Now it's your turn. Organize your book report by making a Pro-and-Con Chart that lists your responses in order of importance.

Reflect

Is my Pro-and-Con Chart clearly organized? Do you think it will help me stay focused as I write?

Drafting Write a Draft

Voice/Audience   The purpose is understandable to the reader.

Writing Strategy   State my purpose so the reader will understand why I'm writing.

✏️ Writer's Term_____

Purpose

Sometimes an author has more than one **purpose**. An author's purpose can include any one or more of the following:

- to inform or explain
- to entertain or amuse
- to persuade or convince
- to express a feeling, an idea, or an opinion

I'll use my Pro-and-Con Chart to help me write my draft. According to the rubric, my purpose needs to be clear. I could write in favor of the book I read, or I could write against it. But in this case, my purpose is more neutral: I'd like to summarize the book and then share my opinions about the way the author presented her information. Of course, the reader will want to know which book I'm reporting on, so I'll begin by naming it.

I'll do my best with grammar and spelling errors. But mainly, I just want to concentrate on getting my ideas down. I can always go back later to proofread.

[DRAFT]

<u>Another Way to Dance</u>

A book report by Briana

[purpose for writing]

After reading <u>Another Way to Dance</u> by Martha Southgate, I had mixed opinions. I'd like to share some of them with you now. Having studied ballet myself, I found the premise of the book particularly interesting. A fourteen-year-old African American girl named Vicki is accepted into the summer dance program at the School of American Ballet in New York City. The book chronicles everything that happens to her Vicki that summer. She experiences several things that help her mature, including an exciting first date and a devastating encounter with a racist schoolmate.

In many ways, I think the author does a good job of describing Vicki and her experiences. As I read them, I could almost smell the dance studio, hear the music and activity, and feel my muscles straining to move along with Vicki's.

Practice!

Now it's your turn. When you write your draft, make sure to state your purpose so that it's clear to the reader.

Reflect

What do you think? Is my purpose appropriate for a book report?

Revising Extend Writing

Content/Ideas   Examples support responses throughout.

Writing Strategy   Add examples to support my responses.

Writer's Term

Examples

Examples are pieces of information that support a topic, a statement, an idea, or an opinion. An example can be a fact, a description, a quotation, or a paraphrase of an author's exact words.

In my introduction, I gave my purpose for writing and a brief description of what the book is about. In the body, I presented my opinions of the book, based on my list of pros and cons. The rubric says that I need examples to support my responses, so I added some description from the book to make my opinions even stronger.

[DRAFT]

In many ways, I think the author does a good job of describing

Vicki and her experiences. For example, the passages describing Vicki's ballet classes are very accurate and detailed. As I read them, I could almost smell the

dance studio, hear the music and activity, and feel my muscles straining

to move along with Vicki's.   [added an example]

Practice!

Now it's your turn. Add examples that support your opinions.

Revising Clarify Writing

Word Choice/ Clarity

Active voice clarifies the writing throughout.

Writing Strategy

Change passive voice to active voice to make the report clearer.

✏️ Writer's Term____

Active Voice/Passive Voice

If the subject of a sentence performs the action, the verb is in the **active voice**. If the subject is acted upon by something else, the verb is in the **passive voice**. The active voice makes sentences stronger.
Active voice: Janice sang a lively song.
Passive voice: A lively song was sung by Janice.

The rubric says that active voice will clarify my writing. So I reread part of my draft where I had used passive voice. Then, I changed it to active voice.

[DRAFT]

[changed passive voice to active]

I especially liked Vicki's "Aunt" Hanna, her girlfriend Stacey, her

boyfriend Michael, and Michael's mother. ~~Vicki is shown by~~ Michael and

show Vicki ⟵

Stacey, that there's another way to view the world around her. ~~And she~~

show Vicki ⟵

~~is shown by~~ Stacey and Michael's mother, that there's another way to

dance.

Practice!

Now it's your turn. Read through your draft to see where you can change passive voice to active voice to clarify your writing.

Reflect

Did my changes make my writing clearer? Did I use the active voice correctly?

Editing Check Sentences

Sentence Fluency

Many declarative sentences present facts.

Writing Strategy   Use declarative sentences to present facts.

✏️ **Writer's Term**

Declarative Sentences
Different types of sentences have different uses.
A **declarative sentence** is a statement that
ends with a period.

Now, it's time to edit. The rubric says to use declarative sentences to present facts. When I reread my draft, I ran across a question that would be better stated as a declarative sentence. I didn't change any of my exclamatory sentences, since they express feelings rather than state facts.

[DRAFT]

[used a declarative sentence]

~~Doesn't it bug you when an author keeps~~ The author kept talking about the same things

over and over. Vicki's constant fantasizing about Baryshnikov is one

example. I mean, every ballet dancer loves Misha. But please, give me

a break!

Practice!

Now it's your turn. Make stronger statements by using declarative sentences to present facts.

Editing Proofread Writing

Grammar/Mechanics Spelling, punctuation, and capitalization are correct. Introductory verbal phrases are used correctly.

Writing Strategy Make sure introductory verbal phrases are used correctly.

Writer's Term

Introductory Verbal Phrases
A **verbal** is a verb form that acts like a noun, an adjective, or an adverb. An **introductory verbal phrase** comes at the beginning of a sentence and describes the subject.

According to the rubric, I should pay special attention to introductory verbal phrases. These phrases can make my writing more interesting, but I need to make sure that I use them correctly. Here's how I edited one sentence.

[DRAFT]

[corrected subject of introductory verbal phrase]

I also got tired of the fact that Vicki was such a high-maintenance character. Constantly crying over one thing or another, ~~I wished~~ she made me wish she would just stop!

Practice!

Now it's your turn. Edit your draft for spelling, punctuation, and capitalization. Also, make sure each introductory verbal phrase correctly describes its subject.

Grammar/Mechanics

For more practice with introductory verbal phrases, use the exercises on the next two pages.

Reflect

I worked hard to use declarative sentences to present facts and to make sure I used verbal phrases correctly. Did it help my writing?

Introductory Verbal Phrases

A **verbal** is a verb that ends in either *–ed* or *–ing* and acts as a noun, an adjective, or an adverb. An **introductory verbal phrase** comes at the beginning of a sentence and describes the subject.

Correct:

Laughing loudly, Andrew enjoyed the show. (The introductory verbal phrase is *Laughing loudly*, and the verbal is *Laughing*. The verbal phrase describes the subject *Andrew*.)

When the introductory verbal phrase doesn't describe the subject, it causes confusion for the reader. Here is an example of a verbal phrase that does not describe the subject.

Incorrect:

Laughing loudly, the show was enjoyable for Andrew. (Here again, the phrase is *Laughing loudly*, but it incorrectly describes *the show*.)

Practice the Rule

Number a separate sheet of paper 1–5. Then, write the introductory verbal phrase from each sentence, underlining the verbal in each. If the verbal correctly describes the subject of the sentence, write the subject after the phrase. If the verbal does not describe the subject, rewrite the rest of the sentence correctly.

1. Sitting on the couch like a friend, my favorite book awaits me.
2. Filled with humorous stories, I can hear its pages call to me.
3. Salvaged by several tapings, I see its cover wink at me.
4. Smiling in anticipation, I pick up the book.
5. Slowly spinning on my heel, I turn and sit down.

Apply the Rule

Read the following passage, noting any mistakes in the use of introductory verbal phrases. Then, rewrite the passage correctly on a separate sheet of paper.

To Kill a Mockingbird
a book report

It's not often that a book surprises me, but <u>To Kill a Mockingbird</u> by Harper Lee sure did. As soon as I finished the last page, I wanted to tell people about it. Suggesting I read it independently, my teacher gave me this book. Knowing it was famous, the book had to be boring and irrelevant, I figured. Boy, was I wrong! <u>To Kill a Mockingbird</u> has got to be the best book I've ever read.

<u>To Kill a Mockingbird</u> is set during the Great Depression in the South. The main character is a girl named Scout Finch, who lives with her brother, Jem, and her father, Atticus. The two children befriend Dill and Boo Radley, and the story gets interesting when Atticus Finch defends a black man who has been unjustly accused of a serious crime.

Discovering that the book was first published back in 1960, the story would contain nothing I could relate to. But I got hooked on the first page because the author gives Scout, who narrates in the first person, such a strong voice. Piquing my interest on the first page, I included interesting questions that made me want to read further.

Publishing Share Writing

Display my book report on a bulletin board in the school library.

Now that I've finished my book report, how should I publish it? I could read it to a friend or post it in the classroom, but I'd reach a larger audience if I posted it in the school library. First, I'll get permission from the school librarian. Then, I'll make a clean copy that's easy to read. I should remember to print each page on one side only, in case I have to pin my report to the bulletin board. Before I post it, though, I'll read through it one last time to make sure it includes all of the items on my checklist.

My Checklist

✔ My responses are organized by order of importance.

✔ My purpose is easy to understand.

✔ Examples from the book support my opinions.

✔ Active voice makes the writing clear.

✔ Declarative sentences present facts.

✔ Spelling, capitalization, and punctuation are all correct. Introductory verbal phrases are used correctly.

Practice!

Now it's your turn. Make a checklist to check your book report. Then, make a final draft to publish.

Another Way to Dance

A book report by Briana

After reading *Another Way to Dance* by Martha Southgate, I had mixed opinions. I'd like to share some of them with you now. Having studied ballet myself, I found the premise of the book particularly interesting. A fourteen-year-old African American girl named Vicki is accepted into the summer dance program at the School of American Ballet in New York City. The book chronicles everything that happens to Vicki that summer. She experiences several things that help her mature, including an exciting first date and a devastating encounter with a racist schoolmate.

In many ways, I think the author does a good job of describing Vicki and her experiences. For example, the passages describing Vicki's ballet classes are very accurate and detailed. As I read them, I could almost smell the dance studio, hear the music and activity, and feel my muscles straining to move along with Vicki's.

I also think that the author does a good job of capturing Vicki's complicated feelings toward her family. Since her parents are newly divorced, Vicki feels a mixture of sympathy and resentment toward them. She also feels that she can't be entirely honest with her mother, so she bottles up her emotions. I think all of this is quite realistic.

One more thing I think the author does well is reveal the personalities of some of the characters. I especially liked Vicki's "Aunt" Hannah, her girlfriend Stacey, her boyfriend Michael, and Michael's mother. Michael and Stacey show Vicki that there's another way to view the world around her. Stacey and Michael's mother show Vicki that there's another way to dance.

There were, however, some things that I didn't like about the book. The author kept talking about the same things over and over. Vicki's constant fantasizing about Baryshnikov is one example. I mean, every ballet dancer loves Misha. But please, give me a break! After a while, I was bored with all that fantasizing. I was much more interested in Vicki's real relationship with Michael than the one that goes on in her head.

I also got tired of the fact that Vicki was such a high-maintenance character. Constantly crying over one thing or another, she made me wish she would just stop! It's not that some of her problems weren't completely valid. It's just that after a while, they got really old. Many times, I just wanted to tell her, "Calm down, girl! Just get over yourself and relax! And join the real world while you're at it."

After all that reading, the thing that disappointed me the most was the ending. It sounded like such a cliché. I was really hoping that the author would include a juicy morsel to chew on for a while after I finished the book—some theme or life lesson that Vicki learned after all that obsessing. Instead, I got a corny and overused ending.

Well, if you love ballet—and you really love Baryshnikov—*Another Way to Dance* is worth the read. But if you tend to get impatient with reading about the struggles of a confused and insecure adolescent, you might want to pass on this one.

Reflect

What do you think? Did I use all the traits of a good book report in my writing? Check it against the rubric. Don't forget to use the rubric to check your own book report, too.

Ways to Publish a Book Report

As you decide how to publish your work, it's a good idea to think about who might want to read it. That way, you can figure out the best way to share it. Here are some ideas for publishing your book report.

 Read your paper aloud to the class. Then, discuss whether other students have read the same book.

 Find a Web site where others have posted reviews of your book. Then, upload your work.

 Mail your work to a newspaper or book review publication that accepts student work.

 Include your report as part of a multimedia presentation.

 Include your report as part of a class publication called "Should You Read This Book?"

Writing Across the Content Areas
Book Report

Your school subjects can be a great source of writing ideas. Choose a subject and see how many related topics you can brainstorm. Check out these examples.

Science
- Read a biography about a famous scientist. Then, write a book report.

- Write about a science-fiction book.

Social Studies
- Read a nonfiction book on an era you'd like to know more about. Then, respond by writing a book report.

- Write about a historical fiction book.

Art and/or Music
- Read a biography about an artist or musician. Then, respond by writing a book report.

- Read a book about your favorite form of art. Then, write a book report.

What's a Research Report?

It's a report containing information that a writer discovers about a topic after asking questions and researching the answers. I'd like to learn more about research assignments so that they won't seem so overwhelming.

What's in a Research Report?

Narrow Topic
I need to make sure my topic is specific enough to cover it in my report. For example, "Ancient Egypt" is too broad; "Becoming a Scribe" is more specific.

Attention-Grabbing Introduction
I want to make sure that I grab the reader's attention in my introduction. I can do this by starting with an interesting fact or quote about my topic.

Quotes and Paraphrases
When I need information that supports a main point in my report, I'll use an exact quote from an expert, or I'll use my own words to paraphrase someone else's ideas.

Works Consulted
It's important to list all the sources that I used while writing. I'll do this in my list of Works Consulted. This way, readers will know where I got my information.

Why write a Research Report?

I'm not yet sure why I want to write a research report, but here are some different reasons I'm thinking about.

Information

Whether it's background on a general topic or in-depth knowledge about something more specific, discovering information and sharing it with the reader is one good reason for writing a research report.

Compare and Contrast

Sometimes people best understand a topic when they compare it to something else. For instance, you might understand soccer better if you compare it to rugby. Examining similarities and differences is one purpose for writing a research report.

Understand Issues

Writing a research report can help a person understand important issues. If a writer decides to research a current event, he or she will probably find out what caused the event.

Make Decisions

People often read about a topic before they make an important decision such as getting a dog, becoming a vegetarian, or studying abroad. Researching a topic in order to make an informed decision is a good reason to write a research report.

Research Report Writing Traits

I know that there are six traits of good writing. Here's a list of what makes a good research report. I'll use this list to help me write.

Information/ Organization	The report focuses on one topic. The report is well organized.
Voice/ Audience	The introduction is attention grabbing.
Content/ Ideas	Quotes and paraphrased information are included throughout.
Word Choice/ Clarity	Citations and the Works Consulted are correct.
Sentence Fluency	The report contains introductory verbal phrases, which provide sentence variety.
Grammar/ Mechanics	Spelling, punctuation, and capitalization are correct. Compound and complex sentences are formed correctly.

I can use Julie Fleming's research report on the next three pages as a model for my own writing. Later, we'll check out how Julie used the traits to help her write.

UNDERSTANDING PHOBIAS

by Julie Fleming

Attention-Grabbing Introduction

Narrow Topic

Fears—we all have them. Walking alone at night, crossing dangerous intersections, and speaking in front of a crowd are all common fears. However, fears become abnormal when they become so irrational or exaggerated that a person never leaves the house. That's when fears turn into phobias.

Fear is a normal response to a scary situation. A phobia is an unreasonable response and is not normal. A phobia keeps people from doing the things that they want or need to do, such as going to work, school, or attending social functions. Judy Monroe, author of *Phobias: Everything You Wanted to Know, But Were Afraid to Ask,* quotes Anne Marie Albana at the Center of Stress and Anxiety Disorders at the State University of New York at Albany: "A phobia is an unrealistic fear that is all out of proportion to the actual threat. The fear of spiders, for instance, would be present even when there were no spiders around" (15–16). There are more than 500 phobias currently listed on the Internet. They fall into three common types: specific phobia, social phobia, and agoraphobia. Let's look at them one at a time.

Quote

The most common type is a specific phobia, or a simple phobia. As the name suggests, a specific phobia is an unreasonable fear of a specific thing, animal, or situation. Most specific phobias are related to the fear of animals, environments, or bodily harm or injury. Fear of animals is the most common. Which animal is feared most? The results of a 2001 Gallup poll put snakes at the top of the list.

Specific environmental phobias include fear of storms, lightning, thunder, and earthquakes. Others include the fear of school, elevators, cars, airplanes, open spaces, closed spaces, and heights. Specific body phobias include the fear of pain, germs, blood, and terminal illnesses.

The second type of phobia is related to social fear. People with social phobias have intense fear of social situations. An example of an especially difficult social phobia is a situation in which a person thinks that he or she will be watched and judged by others. People with social phobias spend great amounts of time trying to avoid public situations. For some, drinking a cup of coffee or writing a check in public is enough to cause immense fear.

⌐ **Paraphrase**

According to the American Psychological Association (APA), the most common social phobia is giving a speech in public. However, others include eating in restaurants, attending parties, dating, playing sports, and dancing.

The third kind of phobia, and the most disabling one, is agoraphobia. Of the people with agoraphobia, women outnumber men two to one. The most common fears suffered by these people are the fear of leaving home and the fear of being in a public place that would be difficult to leave quickly.

Agoraphobia sounds quite similar to social phobia, but they differ in one major way. Although people with social phobias fear looking foolish in public, people with agoraphobia fear having anxiety attacks and losing control. Symptoms of an anxiety attack could include chest pains and a racing heart, shortness of breath, hot or cold flashes, nausea, sweating, and fainting. These symptoms can last from several minutes to several hours. Fearing these symptoms, many people with this phobia do not ever leave home.

What are the causes of all of these phobias? Several theories exist. Among them is the belief that phobias are psychological. Judy Monroe states: **Quote** ↵

> Some researchers say that phobias arise when people ignore unresolved problems and conflicts. If someone has a stressful home life, for example, and never gets any help, then that person's anxiety will grow. Over time, that anxiety can change into a phobia. The phobia is the way that person manages the fearful situation. It symbolizes the real fear and allows the person to focus all fear onto one situation or thing. (70–71)

Other researchers believe that people's body chemistry makes them more prone to phobias. Still other researchers say that phobias are hereditary. A person with agoraphobia, for example, often has a parent or other relative who also has the condition.

Another theory states that phobias can be learned, either by watching a family member or by having an unpleasant personal experience. If a person were to become frightened while trapped in an elevator, he or she might develop claustrophobia, an irrational fear of closed spaces.

Yet another theory, offered by Dr. Harold Levinson, states that 90 percent of all phobias are caused by physical problems with the inner ear. Levinson reports that he has helped many patients with a combination of therapy and medicines for inner-ear disorders.

The good news about phobias is that there are many effective ways to treat and to cure them. One of the newest is virtual-reality therapy. The virtual-reality simulator, which works like an arcade game, gradually and safely exposes a person to the situation they most fear. In this way, patients can be exposed to airplanes, elevators, balconies, footbridges, different kinds of audiences, and even a jungle in Vietnam, all without leaving the room.

Well before virtual-reality therapy was invented, therapists were taking their patients on trips to real places. Through the USAir (currently US Airways) Fearful Flyer Program, people with aerophobia actually worked on their fear of flying by taking a short flight with their instructor and classmates.

Doctors prescribe antidepressants and anti-anxiety drugs to some people with phobias. Other treatments include individual therapy, group therapy, and self-help books. Also effective are programs that combine breathing and meditation exercises with vitamins, herbs, and foods that fight stress.

Many researchers feel that the most important way for people to overcome their phobias is to seek help in confronting them. According to an article in *Time International,* "The harder phobics work to avoid the things they fear, the more the brain grows convinced that the threat is real" (60).

Confronting fears helps people with phobias get rid of them. This works in much the same way that turning on the light helps children see that the "monster" in the corner is really a chair piled with clothes. Of course, facing fears isn't easy for patients with phobias. But if done gradually and gently, many can greatly decrease their fears, if not overcome them completely.

Works Consulted

Dolliver, Mark. "These Are a Few of Our Least-Favorite Things." *AdWeek* 26 Mar. 2001, eastern ed.: 15.

"Fear Not! PHOBIAS: For Millions of Sufferers, Science Is Offering New Treatments—and New Hope." *Time International* 14 May 2001: 60.

Heller, Sharon, Ph.D. *The Complete Idiot's Guide to Conquering Fear and Anxiety.* New York: Alpha Books, 1999.

Monroe, Judy. *Phobias: Everything You Wanted to Know, But Were Afraid to Ask.* Springfield: Enslow, 1996.

Stern, Richard. *Mastering Phobias: Cases, Causes, and Cures.* New York: Penguin, 1996.

Works Consulted

Research Report

Rubric

The traits of a good research report from page 226 have been used to make the rubric below. By using 1, 2, 3, or 4 check marks to judge each trait, you can decide how well any research report was written.

	Excelling ✓✓✓	Achieving ✓✓✓	Developing ✓✓	Beginning ✓
Information/ Organization	The report focuses on one topic; it is well organized.	Most of the report focuses on one topic; it is mostly organized.	Some of the report focuses on one topic; it is organized in some places.	The report should focus on one topic; it should be well organized.
Voice/ Audience	The introduction is attention grabbing.	The introduction is interesting.	The introduction is mildly interesting.	The introduction should be attention grabbing.
Content/ Ideas	Quotes and paraphrased information are included throughout.	Quotes and paraphrased information are included in some places.	Quotes and paraphrased information are included in a few places.	Quotes and paraphrased information should be included throughout.
Word Choice/ Clarity	Citations and the Works Consulted are correct.	Citations and the Works Consulted are mostly correct.	There are some errors in citations and in the Works Consulted.	Citations and the Works Consulted need to be correct.
Sentence Fluency	Introductory verbal phrases provide sentence variety throughout.	Introductory verbal phrases provide some sentence variety.	Introductory verbal phrases provide little sentence variety.	More introductory verbal phrases are needed for sentence variety.
Grammar/ Mechanics	Spelling, grammar, and compound/ complex sentences are correct.	There are a few errors in spelling, grammar, and compound/ complex sentences.	There are several errors in spelling, grammar, and compound/ complex sentences.	There are many errors in spelling, grammar, and compound/ complex sentences.

Research Report
Using the Rubric to Study the Model

Now, let's use the rubric to check Julie Fleming's research report, "Understanding Phobias." How many check marks would you give Julie for each trait?

 Information/ Organization

- **The report focuses on one topic.**
- **The report is well organized.**

Julie focuses her report on the topic of phobias. Her paper has a clear introduction, body, and conclusion, and she puts information in a logical order, including subpoints for all of her main points. In this excerpt, Julie breaks the main topic into three subpoints: specific phobias, social phobias, and agoraphobia.

[from the writing model]

There are more than 500 phobias currently listed on the Internet. They fall into three common types: specific phobia, social phobia, and agoraphobia. Let's look at them one at a time.

 Voice/ Audience

- **The introduction is attention grabbing.**

Julie captures the audience's interest in her introduction. She describes something everyone can relate to—fears. Then, she hooks readers with specific details.

[from the writing model]

Fears—we all have them. Walking alone at night, crossing dangerous intersections, and speaking in front of a crowd are all common fears. However, fears become abnormal when they become so irrational or exaggerated that a person never leaves the house. That's when fears turn into phobias.

Content/Ideas

- **Quotes and paraphrased information are included throughout.**

Julie quotes experts as she discusses different definitions and theories about phobias. She also paraphrases ideas by putting them in her own words. By including ideas from several specialists in the field of mental health, Julie makes her report more credible.

[from the writing model]

According to the American Psychological Association (APA), the most common social phobia is giving a speech in public. However, others include eating in restaurants, attending parties, dating, playing sports, and dancing.

Word Choice/Clarity

- **Citations and the Works Consulted are correct.**

When Julie uses an exact quotation in the body of her report, she always makes sure to first provide a brief introduction to the quote. Then, she uses parentheses to indicate the page number(s) on which the information can be found in its original source. Julie also includes a list of Works Consulted at the end of her report, so that readers can view full source information.

[from the writing model]

Judy Monroe, author of *Phobias: Everything You Wanted to Know, But Were Afraid to Ask,* quotes Anne Marie Albana at the Center of Stress and Anxiety Disorders at the State University of New York at Albany: "A phobia is an unrealistic fear that is all out of proportion to the actual threat. The fear of spiders, for instance, would be present even when there were no spiders around" (15–16).

Sentence Fluency

• The report contains introductory verbal phrases, which provide sentence variety.

I appreciate the way Julie uses different types of sentences to make her writing more interesting. This example shows how she uses an introductory verbal phrase to avoid an otherwise wordy sentence.

[from the writing model]

Fearing these symptoms, many people with this phobia do not ever leave home.

Grammar/Mechanics

• Spelling, punctuation, and capitalization are correct. Compound and complex sentences are formed correctly.

Julie uses the proper conjunctions and punctuation to join compound and complex sentences. Notice how she uses a comma and the conjunction *but* to join these two independent clauses into one compound sentence.

[from the writing model]

Agoraphobia sounds quite similar to social phobia, but they differ in one major way.

This next sentence is a complex sentence with both a dependent and an independent clause, and again, Julie uses a comma to separate the two.

[from the writing model]

According to the American Psychological Association (APA), the most common social phobia is giving a speech in public.

I'm going to write a research report about an interesting topic. I'll follow the rubric and use good writing strategies. Read along to see how I do it.

Prewriting Gather Information

Information/Organization	The report focuses on one topic.
Writing Strategy	Choose a topic, survey some sources, and make a 3 W's Chart. Then, make note cards.

My teacher told us that we'd be writing research reports. I really like watching the night sky with my telescope, so I decided to choose a topic related to astronomy. I just read an article about deadly asteroid threats, so I chose asteroids as my topic. My first step was to look at books and magazine articles, so I went to the library and searched for information about asteroids. Here's a list of some of the information I read for my report.

Source	Why I Chose It
"Deadly Space Threats Get More Attention." The Columbus Dispatch	Newspaper article about asteroids and comets that could hit Earth
"Danger from the Sky." Cricket	Magazine article about asteroids and meteors
The Search for the Killer Asteroid	Book about the times that asteroids have hit Earth

Practice!

Now it's your turn. Choose a topic and gather information from sources.

3 W's Chart

A **3 W's Chart** organizes your ideas about a topic. It lists **what** your questions are, **what** information you already know, and **where** you might find answers to your questions.

After I chose my topic and began my research, I decided to make a 3 W's Chart to organize the information that I found. Notice on my chart how some of the information can be found in more than one place. This is good because if I find the same information in different sources, it's probably correct.

3 W'S CHART

What are some of my questions?	What do I already know?	Where can I find answers/explanations?
What are asteroids, and where are they found?	They're pieces of rock that move through space.	The Search for the Killer Asteroid
What are the differences among asteroids, meteoroids, meteors, and meteorites?	I'm not sure—will need to find out.	article in Cricket magazine, The Search for the Killer Asteroid
What important meteorites have hit Earth? What were their effects?	One hit Arizona around 50,000 years ago. It left a huge crater.	Web site on Barringer Meteorite Crater, Cricket article
Why are scientists so concerned about asteroids, and why do they study them so closely?	They're afraid one could slam into Earth and cause mass destruction—and possible extinction.	Internet article from Space.com, newspaper article on space threats, MIT Web site, Cricket article
Is there any way to stop asteroids from slamming into Earth?	I don't know—will need to find out.	The Search for the Killer Asteroid, newspaper article on space threats, Cricket article

Practice!

Now it's your turn. Make a 3 W's Chart to decide what you want to know, what you already know, and where you can find the answers.

Writer's Term

Note Cards

A **note card** is a place, usually an index card, to put information about a topic. It should contain the following:

- a label identifying the topic
- a "page number" so the cards don't get mixed up
- the question(s) from your 3 W's Chart that you would like to get answered
- information relating to the topic (either paraphrased or directly quoted), followed by an *F* for *Fact* or an *O* for *Opinion*
- the source of the information

Use one note card for each source.

After I made my 3 W's Chart, I made note cards. Near the top of each card, I wrote one or more questions from my 3 W's Chart. Then, I used each card to focus on information that would answer the question(s) at the top.

Asteroids   **1**

3 W's Question: What are asteroids, and where are they located?
- They're lumps of rock and/or metal; also called minor planets. **F**
- Most are found between Mars and Jupiter, in the asteroid belt. **F**
- Some come dangerously close to Earth. **O**
- Some scientists believe that an asteroid may someday cause mass destruction and the extinction of our species. **O**

From: "Danger from the Sky." <u>Cricket</u> Oct. 1998: 22–26.

Practice!

Now it's your turn. Use your 3 W's Chart to make note cards.

Reflect

My 3 W's Chart helped me decide what kind of information I needed to gather. Do you think my note cards will help me focus on subtopics?

Prewriting Organize Ideas

Information/Organization   The report is well organized.

Writing Strategy   Make an Outline to organize my information.

Writer's Term

Outline

An **Outline** shows the main points and the supporting details of the paragraphs in an essay. A **Topic Outline** contains words and phrases to help a writer organize information. A **Sentence Outline** contains complete sentences. Use the same form for both outlines:

- Use Roman numerals (I, II, III) for major sections or topics.
- Use capital letters (A, B, C) for major paragraphs.
- Use Arabic numerals (1, 2, 3) for the supporting details within each paragraph.
- Use lowercase letters (a, b, c) for less important details within each paragraph.
- Use a period after each symbol.

I created a Topic Outline to organize the body of my report. I gave the Outline the same title as my report. Then, I listed the main ideas and supporting details in the order that I plan to discuss them.

Outline

Asteroid Alert!

I. Asteroids ←——— **first main idea**
   A. What they are ←— **paragraph topic**
      1. space rock and/or metal
      2. leftover debris from formation of universe ⎦ ←— **supporting details**
   B. Where they are
      1. between Mars and Jupiter, in asteroid belt
      2. kept there by Jupiter's gravity

II. Differences among asteroids, meteoroids, meteors, meteorites

    A. Meteoroids: pieces of asteroids that have collided

    B. Meteors: meteoroids that fall into Earth's atmosphere

        1. meteors that pass near/over Earth: near-Earth objects (NEOs)

        2. meteors that make bright streaks across sky: shooting, or falling, stars

    C. Meteorites: meteors that fall to Earth

III. Important meteorites that have damaged Earth

    A. Barringer Meteorite Crater, Arizona (a.k.a. Meteor Crater)

        1. hit Earth 50,000 years ago

        2. was traveling 28,600 mph

        3. made a crater 4,150 feet wide and 570 feet deep

        4. meteorite estimated at 100 feet in diameter and 300,000 tons

    B. Tunguska Valley, Siberia

        1. exploded above Earth in 1908

        2. could be seen 466 miles away in daylight

        3. could be felt 50 miles away

        4. started a 30-mile area on fire

    C. Yucatán Peninsula, Mexico

        1. hit Earth 65 million years ago

        2. was 5 miles wide

        3. was traveling 150,000 mph

        4. changed Earth's climate

        5. believed to have caused extinction of dinosaurs

    D. The moon

        1. hit Earth 4.5 billion years ago

        2. was the size of Mars

        3. was traveling 25,000 mph

        4. sent rubble into orbit

        5. orbiting rubble formed the moon

IV. Why scientists are concerned about asteroid activity

    A. Two NEOs passed less than 500,000 miles (6 hours) away

        1. March 1989

        2. October 2001

B. One NEO passed within 280,000 miles
   1. June 1996
   2. would have been as destructive as all nuclear weapons at once
C. Earth will be threatened by asteroids again
   1. asteroids 1 kilometer (0.62 miles) across
      a. hit every 100,000 to 300,000 years
      b. would disrupt global climate
      c. could cause extinction of some species
   2. asteroids 100 meters (328 feet) across or larger
      a. hit every 1,000 to 3,000 years
      b. could eliminate a city
      c. could create a tsunami
V. Actions scientists are taking to avoid disaster
   A. Researchers are locating, recording, and rating new asteroids
   B. Scientists are proposing ways of destroying or averting asteroids
      1. attach rocket engine to asteroid and alter its orbit
      2. destroy asteroid with an atomic bomb

Practice!

Now it's your turn.
Organize ideas by using your note cards to make an Outline.

Reflect

Am I on the right track? Does my Outline make sense?

Drafting Write a Draft

Voice/Audience

The introduction is attention grabbing.

Writing Strategy

Use my Outline to draft my report. Remember to include an introduction that grabs the reader's attention.

Now, I'm ready to write my research report. It's going to be pretty long, so for now, I'll just focus on getting my ideas down. I'll do my best with spelling and grammar, but I can fine-tune everything later on.

I checked the rubric, and it says that my introduction should grab the reader's attention. But how should I do that? I could start with a surprising quote or fact, but since I plan on including a lot of facts in the body of my writing, I don't really want to begin that way. I mean, I know this is a fact-based research paper, but that doesn't mean my opening paragraph can't be fun.

I've got an idea! I've always thought it would be fun to be a TV news announcer, so I think I'll open with a news scene.

[DRAFT]

Asteroid Alert!

by Briana

[attention-grabbing introduction]

"We interupt this program to bring you a special report. Scientists at the University of Arizona's Spacewatch center have downgraded their previous Torino Scale rating of Asteroid 2003CB from 1 to 0. This means that the likelihood of the asteroid's collision with Earth is less likely than something the same size hitting Earth within the next few decades. Citizens all over the globe can now breathe easier as they look into friendlier skies. . . . And now we return you to your regularly scheduled program."

Is the paragraph fact or fiction? It's hard to tell. That's because it's filled with facts. For one, there really is a Spacewatch center in Arizona where scientists study the skies for asteroid "attacks" and near misses. For another, the torino scale exists, too. Adopted in 1999 the scale is used to measure and categorize the risk that asteroids and other near Earth objects (NEOs) pose to Earth.

Practice!

Now it's your turn. Draft an introduction using interesting details to capture your reader's attention.

[DRAFT]

Just what are asteroids, and why are they important? Simply put, asteroids are pieces of space rock, or metal, or both. Also called planetoids or minor planets, they range in size from just a few yards across to several hundred miles across.

Many scientists believe that asteroids are leftover "space debris" from some heavenly bodies that collided when the universe formed. Most asteroids are located between the orbits of Mars and Jupiter in an area known as the asteroid belt. They are located there because Jupiter's gravitational pull on the asteroids is stronger than any other planet's. When Jupiter's orbit changes, an asteroid's orbit also will change, and it will be pulled into another planet's orbit. When an asteroid gets pulled into Earth's orbit, it will begin to travel toward Earth. This is why an asteroid sometimes gets close to, or even crashes into, Earth.

What are meteoroids, meteors, and meteorites? When asteroids collide with each other they shatter into smaller pieces called meteoroids. These meteoroids sometimes fall into Earth's atmosphere. When they do they are called meteors. Meteors that pass near Earth are called near Earth objects, or NEOs. The ones that burn up as they streak brightly across the sky are called shooting stars. The ones that hit Earth before they burn up are called meteorites.

[DRAFT]

Some meteorites have been large enough to form craters when they hit Earth. The best example of a crater is the Barringer Meteorite Crater in Arizona. (It is also known as the Meteor Crater.) About 50,000 years ago, a meteorite traveling almost 28,600 miles per hour struck Arizona in the area between what are now the towns of Winslow and Flagstaff. It created a crater about 4,150 feet wide and 570 feet deep. Scientists estimate that the meteorite was 100 feet in diameter and 300,000 tons in weight.

Another meteorite exploded several miles above the Tunguska Valley in Siberia in 1908. This explosion was so bright that it could be seen 466 miles away in broad daylight. The explosion was so powerful that it could be felt as far as 50 miles away. It also started a forest fire 30 miles wide.

Practice!

Now it's your turn. Use the information in your Outline to draft your research report.

Reflect

What do you think? Will my introduction grab the reader's attention?

Revising Extend Writing

Content/Ideas   Quotes and paraphrased information are included throughout.

Writing Strategy   Add quotes and paraphrased information from experts.

Writer's Term

Paraphrase/Plagiarize

To **paraphrase** is to restate the meaning of a particular passage in your own words.
Don't **plagiarize**! To plagiarize means to present another person's writing as your own work.

The rubric says that a good research report includes quotes and paraphrased information. When I finished my draft, I reread it and realized that I hadn't included any quotes at all. I'm no expert, so quoting specialists should make my report more credible. But I didn't want to add just any old quotes. I knew they should add to the information I already had, so I went back through my note cards and found some good information.

I know I have to be careful not to use an author's words without giving proper credit, so I'll make sure to introduce quotes properly. After all, I don't want to get into trouble for stealing another person's work!

[DRAFT]

Although scientists often disagree on how much money and time should be spent tracking NEOs, most agree that Earth could someday be threatened by a devastating asteroid.

What actions are being taken to avoid NEO crashes? Researchers all over the world are continuing to locate new asteroids. Once located, each asteroid's size and orbit is measured and recorded.

[added quotes]

According to an article written by Robert Roy Britt, a collision with a large asteroid "would rock the planet, disrupt the global climate for years, and could render some species extinct." Britt also says, "Such an event could eliminate a city or create a tsunami that might inundate shore communities and even large cities along multiple coastlines."

Practice!

Now it's your turn. Add quotes and paraphrased information to support your main points.

Reflect

What do you think? Did the added quotes help strengthen the point I was trying to make?

Revising Clarify Writing

Word Choice/ Clarity

Citations and the Works Consulted are correct.

Writing Strategy

Make sure I have cited all quotes correctly. Then, make my list of Works Consulted.

After I added quotes and paraphrased information, I checked the rubric one more time. It says to make sure all quotes are cited correctly. Anytime I use a quote without introducing it with the author's name, article, or book title, I know I should add that information in parentheses at the end of the quote. I should also include a list of Works Consulted at the end of my report so that readers will know the full source information for each source I used in my report.

✏️ Writer's Term

Citing Sources: Works Consulted

When **citing sources,** list where you found borrowed information. The examples below show how to present this information in a list of **Works Consulted**. Place the list at the end of your paper and include each source used, regardless of whether direct quotes were pulled from that source. Pay special attention to the order of the information and the use of punctuation. Listings in a Works Consulted are arranged alphabetically according to authors' last names. When there is no author, use the first word in the title. In addition, use the styles shown here.

To cite a book:

Author's last name, author's first name. *Book title*. City of publication: Publisher, date of publication.

To cite a magazine or a newspaper article:

Author's last name, author's first name. "Article title." *Magazine/newspaper title* Date of publication: page number(s).

To cite an article in an on-line periodical:

Author's last name, author's first name. "Article title." *On-line periodical title* Date of publication. Date of access <Web address>.

To cite a Web site:

Author's last name, author's first name. *Web site title*. Date of last update. Sponsor of Web site. Date of access <Web address>.

[DRAFT]

[added Works Consulted]

Works Consulted

Bridges, Andrew. "Deadly Space Threats Get More Attention." The Columbus Dispatch 13 May 2001: C4.

Britt, Robert Roy. "Asteroid Discoveries May Outpace Ability to Assess Threat to Earth." Space.com 19 Oct. 2001. 20 Oct. 2006 <http://www.space.com/scienceastronomy/solarsystem/asteroid.html>.

"Danger from the Sky." Cricket Oct. 1998: 22–26.

"MIT Researcher Creates Scale to Assess Earth-Asteroid Close Encounters." MIT News 22 July 1999. 20 Oct. 2006 <http://web.mit.edu/newsoffice/nr/1999/asteroid.html>.

Vogt, Gregory L. The Search for the Killer Asteroid. Brookfield: Millbrook, 1994.

What is the Barringer Meteorite Crater? 1998. The Cyrus Company. 20 Oct. 2006 <http://www.barringercrater.com/science/main/htm>.

Practice!

Now it's your turn. Make sure that you correctly cite quotes and include a Works Consulted at the end of your report.

Reflect

Did I format my Works Consulted correctly?

Editing Check Sentences

Sentence Fluency

The report contains introductory verbal phrases, which provide sentence variety.

Writing Strategy Use introductory verbal phrases to vary my sentences.

Now I'm going to edit my draft. The rubric says I should use introductory verbal phrases to vary my sentences, so I looked over my draft to see where I could do this. I had trouble with verbal phrases when we learned about them in class. So while I work to add them, I'll also make sure that I use them correctly!

[DRAFT]

About 50,000 years ago, a meteorite traveling almost 45,000 miles per hour struck Arizona in the area between what are now the towns of Winslow and Flagstaff. ~~It created~~ Creating a crater about 4,150 feet wide and 570 feet deep. ~~Scientists estimate that~~ the meteorite was 100 feet in diameter and 60,000 tons in weight. estimated by scientists to be

[correctly used an introductory verbal phrase]

Practice!

Now it's your turn. Add variety to your writing with the use of introductory verbal phrases.

Editing Proofread Writing

Grammar/Mechanics

Spelling, punctuation, and capitalization are correct. Compound and complex sentences are formed correctly.

Writing Strategy

Make sure I've formed compound and complex sentences correctly.

Writer's Term

Compound Sentences/Complex Sentences

A **compound sentence** consists of two closely related independent clauses joined by a comma and a coordinating conjunction (*and, but, or*) or by a semicolon. A **complex sentence** consists of an independent clause and a dependent clause that begins with a subordinating conjunction (*although, because, if, as,* or *when*).

Now I need to check for errors in spelling and punctuation. The rubric also says that I should pay special attention to compound and complex sentences. Here's how I edited two complex sentences.

[DRAFT]

[correctly formed complex sentences]

What are meteoroids, meteors, and meteorites? When asteroids collide with each other, they shatter into smaller pieces called meteoroids. These meteoroids sometimes fall into Earth's atmosphere. When they do, they are called meteors. Meteors that

Practice!

Now it's your turn. Edit your draft for spelling, punctuation, and capitalization. Also, make sure you've formed compound and complex sentences correctly.

Grammar/Mechanics

For more practice forming compound and complex sentences, use the exercises on the next two pages.

Reflect

I used verbal phrases for sentence variety, and I edited two complex sentences. Did I miss anything?

Compound and Complex Sentences

A **compound sentence** consists of two closely related independent clauses. An independent clause can stand alone as a sentence, but two independent clauses should be joined by a comma and a coordinating conjunction (*and, but, or*) or by a semicolon.

Example: An NEO passes Earth, **but** a meteorite hits it.
Example: An NEO passes Earth; a meteorite hits it.

A **complex sentence** consists of an independent clause and a dependent clause joined by a comma. A dependent clause cannot stand alone as a sentence because it begins with a subordinating conjunction such as *although, because,* or *when*.

Example: Because some asteroids are potentially harmful, scientists keep watching the skies.
Example: When an asteroid poses no threat to Earth, it gets a Torino rating of 0.

Practice the Rule

Number a separate sheet of paper 1–5. Read the sentences below. Write *CX* if the sentence is complex. Write *CD* if the sentence is compound. Then, copy each dependent clause onto the paper.

1. The Torino Impact Hazard Scale is relatively new; it was adopted in 1999.
2. It was developed by Richard Binzel; he worked on it for several years.
3. Because so many new asteroids were being discovered, Binzel felt the need to help the public understand them.
4. When a new asteroid is discovered, scientists gather information about it.
5. They calculate where the asteroid will be in the future, and they assign a rating to it.

Apply the Rule

Read the research report, looking for errors in the use of compound/ complex sentences. Then, rewrite the passage correctly on a separate sheet of paper.

A meteor is the streak of light that appears when a meteorite, an actual piece of falling rock, enters Earth's atmosphere. Meteorites are genuine bits of our solar system. Most of them have broken off of asteroids, which are space rocks that are too small to be classified as planets. Some meteorites come from comets, which are balls of ice and frozen gas.

When a meteor shower occurs the sky lights up with thousands of meteor trails. Scientists use the path of Earth's rotation to predict these spectacular light shows, which repeat each year as the planet crosses the path of a comet.

Regular meteor showers have names that come from the constellations that produce them. Because it originates in the constellation Leo one shower is called the Leonids. You can find out when the Leonids and other regular meteor showers are scheduled to appear by checking one of several sources. Weather forecasters keep track of these displays and you can also check for schedules on Web sites such as www.nasa.com.

Publishing Share Writing

Include my report as part of a multimedia presentation.

I finished my research report, and now I want to publish it. I could show it to some classmates or read it aloud. But I think my report begs for multimedia! I can sit at a desk in the front of the classroom like a TV reporter and deliver the special announcement in the beginning of my report. Then, I can move away from the desk and present the rest of my report as a slide show. Before I do this, though, I'll read through my paper one last time to make sure it includes all of the items on my checklist.

My Checklist

✔ The report includes one well-organized topic.

✔ The introduction grabs the reader's attention.

✔ Quotes and paraphrased information support main points.

✔ All quotes are cited correctly, and the Works Consulted is well formatted.

✔ Introductory verbal phrases add sentence variety.

✔ Spelling, capitalization, and punctuation are all correct. Compound and complex sentences are also used correctly.

Practice!

Now it's your turn. Make a checklist to check your research report. Then, make a final draft to publish.

Asteroid Alert!

by Briana

"We interrupt this program to bring you a special report. Scientists at the University of Arizona's Spacewatch center have downgraded their previous Torino Scale rating of Asteroid 2003CB from 1 to 0. This means that the likelihood of the asteroid's collision with Earth is less likely than something the same size hitting Earth within the next few decades. Citizens all over the globe can now breathe easier as they look into friendlier skies. . . . And now we return you to your regularly scheduled program."

Is the paragraph fact or fiction? It's hard to tell. That's because it's filled with facts. For one, there really is a Spacewatch center in Arizona where scientists study the skies for asteroid "attacks" and near-misses. For another, the Torino Scale exists, too. Adopted in 1999, the scale is used to measure and categorize the risk that asteroids and other near-Earth objects (NEOs) pose to Earth.

Just what are asteroids, and why are they important? Simply put, asteroids are pieces of space rock, or metal, or both. Also called planetoids or minor planets, they range in size from just a few yards across to several hundred miles across.

Many scientists believe that asteroids are leftover "space debris" from some heavenly bodies that collided when the universe formed. Most asteroids are located between the orbits of Mars and Jupiter in an area known as the asteroid belt. They are located there because Jupiter's gravitational pull on the asteroids is stronger than any other planet's. When Jupiter's orbit changes, an asteroid's orbit will also change, and it will be pulled into another planet's orbit. When an asteroid gets pulled into Earth's orbit, it will begin to travel toward Earth. This is why an asteroid sometimes gets close to, or even crashes into, Earth.

What are meteoroids, meteors, and meteorites? When asteroids collide with each other, they shatter into smaller pieces called meteoroids. These meteoroids sometimes fall into Earth's atmosphere. When they do, they are called meteors. Meteors that pass near Earth are called near-Earth objects, or NEOs. The ones that burn up as they streak brightly across the sky are called shooting stars. The ones that hit Earth before they burn up are called meteorites.

Some meteorites have been large enough to form craters when they hit Earth. The best example of a crater is the Barringer Meteorite Crater in Arizona. (It is also known as the Meteor Crater.) About 50,000 years ago, a meteorite traveling almost 28,600 miles per hour struck Arizona in the area between what are now the towns of Winslow and Flagstaff. Creating a crater about 4,150 feet wide and 570 feet deep, the meteorite was estimated by scientists to be 100 feet in diameter and 300,000 tons in weight.

Another meteorite exploded several miles above the Tunguska Valley in Siberia in 1908. This explosion was so bright that it could be seen 466 miles away in broad daylight. The explosion was so powerful that it could be felt as far as 50 miles away. It also started a forest fire 30 miles wide.

An even more important impact happened 65 million years ago. Scientists believe that an asteroid at least five miles wide crashed into Mexico's Yucatán Peninsula at about 150,000 miles per hour. This crash sent dust and other debris high into Earth's atmosphere. The debris blocked so much of the sunlight for so long that Earth's climate changed entirely. Much of the plant life died. This caused the plant-eating dinosaurs to die off. This, in turn, caused the meat-eating dinosaurs to die off because their food supply had disappeared.

Many astronomers believe that the most violent asteroid impact of all might have occurred 4.5 billion years ago. At that time, an asteroid the size of Mars traveled more than 25,000 miles per hour before smashing into Earth. This sent a huge amount of rubble into orbit. For a while, the rubble just continued to orbit Earth. Over time, however, due in part to Earth's gravitational pull, the rubble came together and formed the moon.

Because of many NEOs' potential for destruction, scientists all over the world have become concerned about asteroids. Two particularly frightening NEOs, sighted in March 1989 and October 2001, sped past Earth at a distance of less than 500,000 miles—twice the distance to the moon—and missed a collision with Earth by a mere six hours.

In June 1996, an even scarier near-miss occurred when Asteroid 1996 JA1 passed within only 280,000 miles of Earth. Scientists estimate that if that asteroid had crashed into Earth, it would have had as much destructive power as all the nuclear weapons on Earth exploding at the same time.

Although scientists often disagree on how much money and time should be spent tracking NEOs, most agree that Earth could someday be threatened by a devastating asteroid. According to an article written by Robert Roy Britt, a collision with a large asteroid "would rock the planet, disrupt the global climate for years, and could render some species extinct." Britt also says, "Such an event could eliminate a city or create a tsunami that might inundate shore communities and even large cities along multiple coastlines."

What actions are being taken to avoid NEO crashes? Researchers all over the world are continuing to locate new asteroids. Once located, each asteroid's size and orbit is measured and recorded. Then, the asteroid is assigned a rating on the Torino Scale, which, according to Carl Pilcher, Science Director for solar system exploration in the NASA Office of Space Science in Washington, D.C., "is a major advance in our ability to explain the hazard posed by a particular NEO." Carl further explains, "If we ever find an object with a greater value than one, the scale will be an effective way to communicate the resulting risk" ("MIT").

Scientists are also proposing ways to destroy or avert devastating NEOs that might be on their way to Earth. One proposal is to attach rocket engines to the asteroids to alter their orbit and move them out of Earth's path. Another proposal is to destroy the asteroids with spacecraft loaded with atomic bombs.

Scientists remain alert, but fortunately, Earth has not had to take on an NEO yet. Thankfully, "the attack of the killer asteroid" is still only fiction.

Works Consulted

Bridges, Andrew. "Deadly Space Threats Get More Attention." *The Columbus Dispatch* 13 May 2001: C4.

Britt, Robert Roy. "Asteroid Discoveries May Outpace Ability to Assess Threat to Earth." *Space.com* 19 Oct. 2001. 20 Oct. 2006 <http://www.space.com/scienceastronomy/solarsystem/asteroid.html>.

"Danger from the Sky." *Cricket* Oct. 1998: 22–26.

"MIT Researcher Creates Scale to Assess Earth-Asteroid Close Encounters." *MIT News* 22 July 1999. 20 Oct. 2006 <http://web.mit.edu/newsoffice/nr/1999/asteroid.html>.

Vogt, Gregory L. *The Search for the Killer Asteroid.* Brookfield: Millbrook, 1994.

What is the Barringer Meteorite Crater? 1998. The Cyrus Company. 20 Oct. 2006 <http://www.barringercrater.com/science/main/htm>.

Reflect

What do you think? Did I use all of the traits of a good research report in my writing? Check it against the rubric. Don't forget to use the rubric to check your own report, too.

Ways to Publish a Research Report

When it's time to publish your work, you should stop and think about who will be reading it. That way, you can figure out the best way to share it. Here are some ideas for publishing your research report.

 Include your report as part of a broader collection of writings on a similar topic.

 Post your report on a Web site that relates to your topic.

 Include your work as part of a class bulletin board or display.

 Display your paper in your science or social studies classroom.

 Take your work home and share it with your family.

Writing Across the Content Areas
Research Report

You can brainstorm ideas for a research report by thinking about your school subjects. Choose a subject and see how many related topics you can write about. Check out these examples.

Science
- Report on an exciting technological development in a field such as computers, robotics, or medicine.

- Write about ecology, focusing your research on habitats, climate changes, pollution, or alternative fuels.

Language Arts
- Should the text of whole books be available for free on the Internet? Research and write about this issue.

- Explore how many alphabet systems are currently in use in the world today.

Art and/or Music
- Compare the old technology of records with today's digital compact discs.

- Before modern chemicals gave us artificial colors, what did people use for dyes and paints? Write about the world of natural coloring agents.

What's a How-To Guide?

It explains how to do something or how to put something together. I'm looking forward to this kind of writing because I often get instructions when I buy certain products—and some of them aren't helpful at all. Hopefully I will learn to do a better job when I write my own how-to guide!

What's in a How-To Guide?

Explanation
This is the point of a how-to guide: to explain clearly, and in great detail, how to do something or put something together.

Sequence
A how-to guide should be structured so that it presents the sequential steps of a process. I'll keep this in mind when I organize my ideas.

Friendly Tone
This is how I want my guide to sound. The best instructions "speak" to readers in a friendly way, taking them by the hand and guiding them through the steps of a process. I'll try to use a friendly tone when I write my guide.

Visual Aids
Sometimes words alone can't explain a particular part or step in a process. That's why it's important to include pictures, drawings, or diagrams in a how-to guide.

Why write a How-To Guide?

There are many reasons for writing a how-to guide. I'll list some here.

Information

A how-to guide can explain how something—a computer, an engine, a radio—works. Educating readers about what goes on behind the scenes is one good reason for writing a guide.

Construction

Writing a how-to guide is probably the best way to tell others how to put something together—whether it's a bicycle, a bookcase, or a barn.

Process

You don't have to build something to need instructions. Writing a how-to guide is also a good way to explain a process such as drawing scenery or conducting a successful Internet search.

Action

Sometimes, a writer needs to give orders. In this case, writing a how-to guide can be a good way to tell the reader what actions to take. For instance, parents might need to leave a list of instructions for a babysitter or leave a note on the refrigerator telling their kids which chores to do.

How-To Guide: Instructional Text Writing Traits

I know that there are six traits of good writing. Here's a list of what makes a good how-to guide. I'll use it to help me write.

Information/Organization	Every step of a process is explained. All of the steps are in sequential order.
Voice/Audience	The tone is friendly throughout.
Content/Ideas	Pictures and explanative details are used throughout.
Word Choice/Clarity	All jargon is explained.
Sentence Fluency	Compound and complex sentences add variety to the writing.
Grammar/Mechanics	Spelling, punctuation, and capitalization are correct. All appositives have been set off with commas.

I can use Adrian Desmond's how-to guide on the next three pages as a model for my own writing. Later, we'll see how Adrian used the traits to help him write.

"Building" a Sailboat Cake

by Adrian Desmond

For years, my brother has dreamed of owning a sailboat. For his birthday this year, I decided to build him one—well, sort of. I made him a sailboat cake. It was pretty easy once I got started. And if I could do it, so could you! Here are the steps to follow to make a sailboat cake.

<u>First,</u> decide on the kind of cake you want to make. <u>Next,</u> buy a boxed cake mix that will work in a pan that is 13 × 9 × 2 inches, and buy one package, 7.2 ounces, of white frosting mix. Bake the cake according to the directions on the package. <u>When it's done,</u> set the cake pan on a rack until the cake is cool enough to cut. <u>Then,</u> cut the cake diagonally into three pieces, as shown in Diagram 1. (You may want to leave the cake in the pan, which makes the pieces easier to handle.) <u>Finally,</u> place the uncovered pan of cut cake pieces in the freezer, and set a timer for one hour. Freezing the pieces will make them easier to frost.

Sequence

Visual Aid

Diagram 1

Friendly Tone

While the cake is in the freezer, you'll need to do two things. First, prepare the frosting according to the directions on the package. When it is nice and fluffy, put one cup of it into a medium-sized bowl. Take a few tablespoons of frosting from there, and put it into a small-sized bowl. Then, set all three bowls aside. Next, make an ocean on which to set your sailboat. You can do this by covering a 20 × 18-inch tray or piece of heavy cardboard with aluminum foil.

When the timer sounds, take the pieces of cake out of the freezer and arrange them into a sailboat, as shown in Diagram 2. As you arrange the sails, leave plenty of space between them for the mast, the pole from which the sails are hung.

main sail

jib
Note: this piece
must be flipped
over

hull

Visual Aid

Diagram 2

Before you add the mast, frost the sails. Use the frosting from the largest bowl to carefully frost the sails. You may want to make a few waves in the frosting to suggest an ocean breeze. If you want, you can put some of the frosting from this bowl into a square plastic bag with one corner cut off. Then, you can squeeze the frosting out to make a cloud and sea gulls. (See Diagram 3.) Next, take the medium-sized bowl of frosting and gently fold one tablespoon of cocoa into it. When the frosting is well blended, spread it over the hull, the long body of the sailboat. Finish off the hull by adding some portholes, or windows: Take five white, ring-shaped candies, and place them as you see them in Diagram 3. Finally, make water by mixing blue food coloring into the small bowl of frosting. Use another square plastic bag with a corner cut off to draw some waves.

Now it's time for the mast. Roll up a 14 × 4-inch sheet of aluminum foil and place it between the sails. If you wish to add a bit of color, attach a red paper flag at the top.

Now your cake is ready to set sail. Wish your "passengers" *bon voyage,* as well as *bon appétit*!

Visual Aid

Diagram 3

How-To Guide

Rubric

The traits of a good how-to guide from page 260 have been used to make the rubric below. By using 1, 2, 3, or 4 check marks to judge each trait, you can decide how well any how-to guide was written.

	Excelling ✓✓✓✓	Achieving ✓✓✓	Developing ✓✓	Beginning ✓
Information/Organization	Every step of a process is explained in sequential order.	Most steps are explained; many are sequentially ordered.	Many steps are explained; some are sequentially ordered.	Every step of a process should be explained in sequential order.
Voice/Audience	The tone is friendly throughout.	The tone is friendly in many places.	The tone is friendly in some places.	The tone needs to be friendlier throughout.
Content/Ideas	Pictures and explanative details are used throughout.	Pictures and explanative details are used in some places.	Pictures and explanative details are used in a few places.	More pictures and explanative details are needed.
Word Choice/Clarity	All jargon is explained.	Most jargon is explained.	Some jargon is explained.	All jargon should be explained.
Sentence Fluency	Compound and complex sentences add variety to the writing.	Some compound and complex sentences are used.	A few compound and complex sentences are used.	More compound and complex sentences are needed for variety.
Grammar/Mechanics	Spelling, grammar, and appositive punctuation are correct.	There are a few errors in spelling, grammar, and appositive punctuation.	There are several errors in spelling, grammar, and appositive punctuation.	There are many errors in spelling, grammar, and appositive punctuation.

How-To Guide
Using the Rubric to Study the Model

Now, let's use the rubric to check Adrian Desmond's how-to guide, "'Building' a Sailboat Cake." How many check marks would you give Adrian for each trait?

 Information/Organization

- **Every step of a process is explained.**
- **All of the steps are in sequential order.**

Adrian does a good job of organizing his guide into sequential steps. The following passage is a good example. Notice how each main step flows smoothly to the next.

[from the writing model]

First, decide on the kind of cake you want to make. Next, buy a boxed cake mix that will work in a pan that is 13 × 9 × 2 inches, and buy one package, 7.2 ounces, of white frosting mix. Bake the cake according to the directions on the package. When it's done, set the cake pan on a rack until the cake is cool enough to cut.

 Voice/Audience

- **The tone is friendly throughout.**

I like the way Adrian's writing sounds sort of chatty, as if he's right there talking the reader through the process of making the cake. This friendly tone helps make the instructions easier to follow.

[from the writing model]

While the cake is in the freezer, you'll need to do two things. First, prepare the frosting according to the directions on the package. When it is nice and fluffy, put one cup of it into a medium-sized bowl. Take a few tablespoons of frosting from there, and put it into a small-sized bowl. Then, set all three bowls aside.

Content/Ideas

- Pictures and explanative details are used throughout.

Adrian uses a lot of details so that the reader can understand each step. It's also good that he includes diagrams because the pictures help make everything clear. In this passage, Adrian uses both details and a reference to the diagram on the page to explain what he means.

[from the writing model]

When the timer sounds, take the pieces of cake out of the freezer and arrange them into a sailboat, as shown in Diagram 2. As you arrange the sails, leave plenty of space between them for the mast, the pole from which the sails are hung.

Word Choice/Clarity

- All jargon is explained.

Adrian's instructions are clear and easy to follow because he defines technical words, or jargon. In this example, I underlined the two words that might be unfamiliar terms to the reader. You can see how Adrian defines each one, right after using it.

[from the writing model]

When the frosting is well blended, spread it over the <u>hull</u>, the long body of the sailboat. Finish off the hull by adding some <u>portholes</u>, or windows.

• **Compound and complex sentences add variety to the writing.**

Adrian doesn't stick with just one sentence pattern; instead, he uses different kinds of sentences to add variety. Take a look at the passage below. Notice how Adrian uses a complex sentence followed by a compound statement. This makes his writing flow from one point to the next.

[from the writing model]

When it is nice and fluffy, put one cup of it into a medium-sized bowl. Take a few tablespoons of frosting from there, and put it into a small-sized bowl.

• **Spelling, punctuation, and capitalization are correct. All appositives have been set off with commas.**

I can tell that Adrian proofread his writing because I didn't find any mistakes. He also uses appositives correctly. I know that an appositive is a phrase that defines a noun and that it needs to be set off from the rest of the sentence by a comma. In this passage, notice how Adrian correctly inserts a comma to separate the definition of a mast from the rest of the sentence.

[from the writing model]

As you arrange the sails, leave plenty of space between them for the mast, the pole from which the sails are hung.

My Turn!

I'm going to write a how-to guide about something I can do well. I'll follow the rubric and use good writing strategies. Read on to see how I do it!

Prewriting Gather Information

Information/Organization   Every step of a process is explained.

Writing Strategy   Choose a process to explain. List the main steps in the process.

I'm really crazy about horses, and I love to go riding every chance I get. A lot goes into preparing for a safe and enjoyable ride—for both the rider and the horse. Since my assignment was to write a how-to guide, it seemed only natural to write about tacking up. Tacking up involves getting a horse ready to ride by putting on its bridle and saddle. Before I started writing my explanation, I thought it would be useful to make a checklist of the main steps involved in the process. Here's what I came up with.

Tacking Up—Main Steps

- ✔ Position the bridle, and put the bit in the horse's mouth.
- ✔ Pull the bridle over the horse's ears.
- ✔ Buckle the noseband and the throatlatch, making sure they are not too tight.
- ✔ Position the blanket or saddle pad over the horse's withers.
- ✔ Place the saddle on top of the blanket.
- ✔ Fasten and adjust the girth, making sure it is not too tight.
- ✔ Check the fit one last time to make sure the horse is comfortable.

Practice!

Now it's your turn. Choose a process to explain. Then, jot down the major steps involved in completing the task.

Prewriting Organize Ideas

All of the steps are in sequential order.

Writing Strategy

Make a Sequence Chain to arrange steps in a sequential order.

Writer's Term

Sequence Chain

A **Sequence Chain** shows the chronological steps of a complex process. Some of the steps might have substeps. These should be placed, in order, below each step.

Nearly every step I included on my checklist has at least one substep. To keep things organized, I used a Sequence Chain.

SEQUENCE CHAIN

Topic: Tacking Up

Step 1: Position bridle; put bit in mouth.
  a. Use thumb to guide bit in.
  b. Make sure it clears horse's teeth.

Step 2: Pull bridle over ears.
  a. Pull ears through headstall and browband.
  b. Pull forelock out from under browband.

Step 3: Buckle noseband and throatlatch comfortably.
  a. Fit two fingers under noseband.
  b. Fit width of hand between throatlatch and cheek.

Step 4: Position blanket or pad over withers.
  a. Slide blanket or pad back so hair lies flat.

Step 5: Place saddle on top of blanket.
  a. Unfold girth and let it hang down.
  b. Reach carefully under belly and grab girth strap.

Step 6: Fasten and adjust girth by slipping fingers between girth and horse's body.

Step 7: Make one last check for fit by checking for pinched skin.

Result: The horse is tacked up and ready to ride.

Practice!

Now it's your turn. Use a Sequence Chain to organize the steps of your process.

Reflect

Do you think my Sequence Chain will help me keep my writing organized?

Drafting Write a Draft

Voice/Audience The tone is friendly throughout.

Writing Strategy Use a friendly tone to explain each step to the reader.

Now I'll use my Sequence Chain to help me write my draft. According to the rubric, I should use a friendly tone. I know I won't be able to talk to my audience face-to-face, but I can pretend. I can use casual phrases and expressions that I normally use while speaking.

I also know how impersonal directions can be, especially when it sounds like they were written with no particular person in mind. So I'll also use the second person pronoun *you* to address my readers.

Right now, I won't worry too much about grammar and spelling errors. I just want to concentrate on presenting the steps in a way that will keep readers interested. However, I know that I've had trouble with introductory verbal phrases in the past, so I'll make sure to use them correctly.

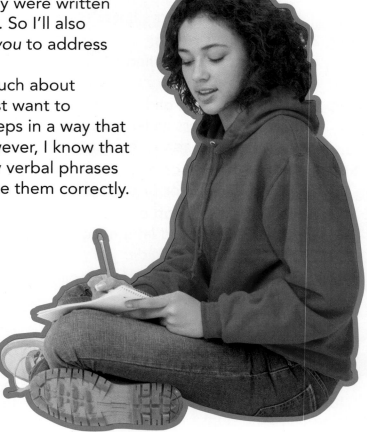

[DRAFT]

Tacking Up a Horse

by Briana [used a friendly tone]

Have you ever watched someone fit a horse with a bridle and a saddle? If you have, you've seen the process of "tacking up." Tacking up properly is very important. Below are the steps involved in the process of tacking up. If you follow these steps carefully, you're sure to make the ride enjoyable, for both horse and rider alike.

First, you will need to put on the horse's bridle. Begin by unfastening all of the buckles. When finished, you should put the bit into the horse's mouth. To insert the bit without hurting the horse, first slide your thumb into its mouth. Then, gently guide the bit into place, making sure it clears the teeth and rests comfterbly on the tongue.

Once the bit is positioned, slide the bridle over the horse's head. Then, pull the forelock out from under the browband. [correct use of an introductory verbal phrase]

Practice!

Now it's your turn. Use a friendly tone to address your readers.

Reflect

Is my tone friendly enough? Are there any places where I could be friendlier?

Revising Extend Writing

Content/Ideas   Pictures and explanative details are used throughout.

Writing Strategy   Add pictures and explanative details.

I just reread my draft, and it feels like something is missing. The rubric says to use pictures and explanative details, so I'll reread my draft, looking for places to further my explanation with helpful diagrams and specific details.

[DRAFT]

Have you ever watched someone fit a horse with a bridle and a saddle? If you have, you've seen the process of "tacking up." Tacking up properly is very important. Below are the steps involved in the process of tacking up. If you follow these steps carefully, you're sure to make the ride enjoyable, for both horse and rider alike.

If the process is not followed correctly, a person could cause a horse discomfort or injury.

[added explanative details]

[DRAFT]

[added explanative details]

(Remember to always stand to the left of the horse.)

First, you will need to put on the horse's bridle. Begin by unfastening

all of the buckles. When finished, you should put the bit into the horse's

mouth. To insert the bit without hurting the horse, first slide your thumb

, behind its teeth
into its mouth. Then, gently guide the bit into place, making sure it

clears the teeth and rests comfterbly on the tongue.
Be careful not to hurt its ears as you pull them through the headstall
    Once the bit is positioned, slide the bridle over the horse's head.
                                            and browband.
Then, pull the forelock out from under the browband.

Next, position the noseband and throatlatch and buckle them
            by slipping two fingers between it and the horse's nose
securely. Check that the noseband is not too tight. Check the

throatlatch by putting a hand's width between it and the horse's
(See Diagram 1.)
cheek.

[added a picture]

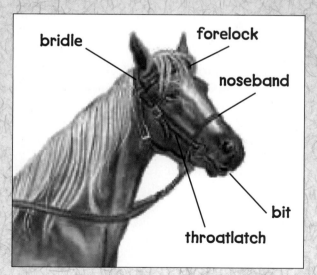

Diagram 1

bridle   forelock

noseband

bit

throatlatch

Now it's your turn. Add explanative details and pictures to
make your guide easier to understand.

Revising Clarify Writing

Word Choice/ Clarity

All jargon is explained.

Writing Strategy

Make sure all jargon has been explained.

I read my how-to guide to a classmate who told me that he'd never tacked up a horse before. He was confused by some of the terms I used. The rubric says that I should explain all jargon used in my writing, so I defined any terms that I thought were specific to horseback riding.

Writer's Term

Jargon

Jargon is the language used by a group of people to describe their profession, trade, or hobby. One group (such as nurses or horseback riders) might not understand the jargon used by another group (such as athletes or skydivers). For this reason, whenever jargon is used, it should always be carefully explained.

[DRAFT]

(Remember to always stand to the left of the horse.)

First, you will need to put on the horse's bridle. Begin by unfastening
[explained jargon] ⟶ , or headgear
all of the buckles. When finished, you should put the bit into the horse's
(The bit helps the rider control the horse.)
mouth. To insert the bit without hurting the horse, first slide your thumb
, behind its teeth
into its mouth. Then, gently guide the bit into place, making sure it

clears the teeth and rests comfterbly on the tongue.

[DRAFT]

Be careful not to hurt its ears as you pull them through the headstall
Once the bit is positioned, slide the bridle over the horse's head.
, the long hair between the horse's ears, ← and browband.
Then, pull the forelock out from under the browband.
, the straps across the horse's nose and face,
Next, position the noseband and throatlatch and buckle them
by slipping two fingers between it and the horse's nose
securely. Check that the noseband is not too tight. Check the

throatlatch by putting a hand's width between it and the horse's
(See Diagram 1.)
cheek.

[explained jargon]

bridle
forelock
noseband

Diagram 1

bit
throatlatch

Practice!

Now it's your turn. Review your draft to see if you've included jargon. If so, add an explanation for each term.

Reflect

I added a diagram and some explanative details to clarify jargon and important steps. Do my additions help? Do they make things clearer?

Editing Check Sentences

Sentence Fluency

Compound and complex sentences add variety to the writing.

Writing Strategy

Use compound and complex sentences for variety.

Now I'm going to edit my draft. The rubric says to include compound and complex sentences for variety. I remember learning about these kinds of sentences not too long ago. Since I already know how to use them correctly, I'll focus on using them to add variety to my writing, just like the rubric says. Take a look at the passage below to see how I created variety by forming a complex sentence out of two closely related statements that both started with the same subject: *You.*

[DRAFT]

[added variety by forming a complex sentence]

Before
~~You are almost~~ finished tacking up, You should check one last time to make sure everything fits the horse comfterbly.

Practice!

Now it's your turn. Use compound and complex sentences to add variety to your writing.

Editing Proofread Writing

Grammar/Mechanics Spelling, punctuation, and capitalization are correct. All appositives have been set off with commas.

Writing Strategy Check to see that appositives have been set off with commas.

Writer's Term

Appositives
An **appositive** is a word or a phrase that identifies a noun. An appositive usually follows the noun it identifies, and it is usually separated from the rest of the sentence by one or more commas.

Now I need to check for errors. I always check spelling, punctuation, and capitalization, but the rubric says I should also check to see if appositives have been set off with commas. I used appositives to explain jargon, and lucky for me, I remembered to use the correct punctuation.

[DRAFT]

Be careful not to hurt its ears as you pull them through the headstall
Once the bit is positioned, slide the bridle over the horse's head. and browband.
, the long hair between the horse's ears,
Then, pull the forelock out from under the browband.

———— [correct use of appositive] ————

Practice!

Now it's your turn. Edit your draft for spelling, punctuation, and capitalization. Make sure that appositives have been set off with commas.

For more practice with appositives, use the exercises on the next two pages.

Reflect

What do you think of my edits? I tried hard to vary my writing, and I think I used all appositives correctly. Does my writing flow better now?

Appositives

An **appositive** is a word or a phrase that identifies a noun. An appositive usually follows the noun it identifies, and it is usually separated from the rest of the sentence by one or more commas.

If the appositive appears at the end of a sentence, put a comma right after the noun being identified.

Example: I usually ride Daisy, **my favorite horse**.

If the appositive appears mid-sentence, put one comma before it and one comma after it.

Example: Daisy, **my favorite horse,** has brown and white spots.

Practice the Rule

Number a separate sheet of paper 1–5. Then, copy each of these sentences. After each one, write the appositive and the noun it identifies.

1. My family, the Mirabelli family, loves to have lots of parties.

2. Whenever there's a party at my house, I like to make my favorite appetizer, "The Ball."

3. The Ball, a cheese ball made with cream cheese, was named by my cousin Patty.

4. Patty, the daughter of Uncle Wes and Aunt Mary, says that The Ball is her favorite food.

5. The recipe, a six-step process, is really quite easy to follow.

Apply the Rule

Read the passage below, looking for errors in appositive punctuation. Then, rewrite the text correctly on a separate sheet of paper.

How To Make a Paperweight

Do you want to liven up your desk or study area? This guide will show you how to turn an ordinary rock, some paints, and a little imagination into a colorful paperweight.

The first step in this process finding a good rock is easy. The best one for the job is about the size of a baseball. However, your rock does not have to be perfectly round. After you've found a rock you like, the next step is to clean it. Hold it under running water or soak it for 5–10 minutes until its surface is free of all visible dirt. Rub it with a towel, and then let it sit in the open until it feels dry to the touch.

While your rock dries, prepare your work area a table or the floor, by covering it with newspapers or an old sheet. Gather paints and brushes. You may also want to gather ideas from books that show appealing designs or patterns. Plan out your design by sketching a few ideas on paper. You can turn your rock into something animate a pet or a funny face. You can paint pictures of leaves or ladybugs, or you can drip on random doodles—anything goes!

Publishing Share Writing

Present my guide as a speech for a small group of classmates.

Now that I've finished my how-to guide, I need to decide how to publish it. I could post it on-line or on a class bulletin board. But my classmates know I love to horseback ride, so I think it would be fun to read my paper as a speech. I can enlarge the diagrams and make them into posters, and I can use a model of a tacked up horse while I talk. To prepare, I'm going to practice in front of a mirror until I feel comfortable. But before I present, I'll read through my guide one last time to make sure it includes all of the items on my checklist.

My Checklist

✔ Every step of a process is explained.

✔ The tone is friendly and inviting.

✔ Pictures and details help explain complicated steps.

✔ All jargon is explained.

✔ Compound and complex sentences add variety to the writing.

✔ Spelling, punctuation, and capitalization are correct. Appositives are set off with commas.

Practice!

Now it's your turn. Make a checklist to check your how-to guide. Then, make a final draft to publish.

Tacking Up a Horse
by Briana

Have you ever watched someone fit a horse with a bridle and a saddle? If you have, you've seen the process of "tacking up." Tacking up properly is very important. If the process is not followed correctly, a person could cause a horse discomfort or injury. Below are the steps involved in the process of tacking up. If you follow these steps carefully, you're sure to make the ride enjoyable, for both horse and rider alike.

First, you will need to put on the horse's bridle, or headgear. (Remember to always stand to the left of the horse.) Begin by unfastening all of the buckles. When finished, you should put the bit into the horse's mouth. (The bit helps the rider control the horse.) To insert the bit without hurting the horse, first slide your thumb into its mouth, behind its teeth. Then, gently guide the bit into place, making sure it clears the teeth and rests comfortably on the tongue.

Once the bit is positioned, slide the bridle over the horse's head. Be careful not to hurt its ears as you pull them through the headstall and browband. Then, pull the forelock, the long hair between the horse's ears, out from under the browband.

Next, position the noseband and throatlatch, the straps across the horse's nose and face, and buckle them securely. Check that the noseband is not too tight by slipping two fingers between it and the horse's nose. Check the throatlatch by putting a hand's width between it and the horse's cheek. (See Diagram 1.)

Diagram 1

Now, it is time to put on the saddle. To begin, position a blanket or saddle pad over the horse's withers, or shoulders. Slide the blanket or pad back so that the horse's hair lies flat and doesn't get pulled the wrong way. Place the saddle on top of it. Unfold the girth, the strap that goes underneath the horse, and let it hang down. Then, reach under the horse's belly and grab the girth strap. Fasten the girth and then adjust it. Again, make sure it's not too tight by running your hand between it and the horse's body.

Before you finish tacking up, you should check one last time to make sure everything fits the horse comfortably. Then, gently pull the horse's forelegs forward to release any skin that might be pinched or wrinkled. And there you have it—your horse is tacked up! Now, you're ready for a wonderful ride.

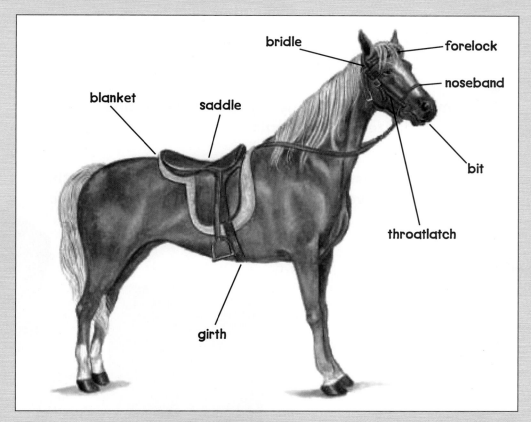

Diagram 2

Reflect

What do you think? Did I use all of the traits of a good how-to guide in my writing? Check it against the rubric. Don't forget to use the rubric to check your own guide, too.

Ways to Publish a How-To Guide

As you decide how to publish your work, you should think about who might want to read it. That way, you can figure out the best way to share it. Here are some ideas for publishing your how-to guide.

 Turn your how-to guide into a multimedia demonstration and present it to a group of classmates.

 Submit your work to a newspaper or magazine that specializes in your topic.

 Post your guide on a Web site where others have posted writing related to your topic.

 Include your work as part of a class collection of how-to guides called "You Can Do It!"

 Post your paper on a school or class bulletin board.

 Take your guide home and share it with your family.

Writing Across the Content Areas
How-To Guide

Your school subjects can be a surprising source of writing ideas. Choose a subject and see how many related topics you can brainstorm. Check out these examples.

Science
- Have you ever made a homemade volcano or other science project? Explain the steps in a how-to guide.

- Explain how to make your favorite recipe.

Social Studies
- Have you ever conducted a survey? Write about your survey process.

- Do you have a test-preparation strategy that results in success? Explain it in a guide called "How to Study For a Test."

Art and/or Music
- Describe a special skill such as how to work with digital photographs or how to make beaded jewelry.

- Explain the basics of learning to play a musical instrument.

EXPOSITORY test writing

Read the Writing Prompt

When you take a writing test, you will be given a writing prompt. Most writing prompts have three parts:

Setup This part of the writing prompt gives you the background information you need to get ready to write.

Task This part of the writing prompt tells you exactly what you are supposed to write: a how-to guide.

Scoring Guide This section tells how your writing will be scored. To do well on the test, you should include everything on the list.

Remember the rubrics you've used? When you take a writing test, you don't always have all of the information that's on a rubric, but the scoring guide is a lot like a rubric. It lists everything you should think about as you write. Like the rubrics you've previously used, most scoring guides are based on the six traits of writing:

Writing MODEL Prompt

Think of a chore that you enjoy. This should be something that others normally find dull or routine. For example, do you like to tinker around, cleaning, washing, and/or organizing things? Do you enjoy cooking, baking, or washing the family car?

Write a how-to guide explaining how to accomplish a chore that you actually enjoy.

Be sure your writing

- is sequentially ordered.

- contains a lot of explanative details that help the reader understand the process.

- is supported with factual information.

- has been checked for proper use of homophones.

- flows smoothly.

- contains correct grammar, punctuation, capitalization, and spelling.

Writing Traits
in the Scoring Guide

Reread the scoring guide in the writing prompt on page 287. Not every test prompt will include each of the six writing traits, but this one does. You can use the following chart to help you better understand the connection between the scoring guide and the writing traits in the rubrics you've used.

 Information/Organization
- Be sure your writing is sequentially ordered.

 Voice/Audience
- Be sure your writing contains a lot of explanative details that help the reader understand the process.

 Content/Ideas
- Be sure your writing is supported with factual information.

 Word Choice/Clarity
- Be sure your writing has been checked for proper use of homophones.

 Sentence Fluency
- Be sure your writing flows smoothly.

 Grammar/Mechanics
- Be sure your writing contains correct grammar, punctuation, capitalization, and spelling.

Look at Kyle Greer's how-to guide on the next page. Did he follow the scoring guide?

HOW TO MOW A LAWN

by Kyle Greer

Are you looking for a great way to earn extra money? If so, I have the perfect job for you: mowing other people's lawns. Here are the steps to take to mow a great lawn.

First, you'll need to get your equipment ready. You can use a gas mower, an electric mower, or a push mower. I think the gas and electric mowers are better because they are easier to handle. If you use a gas mower, be sure that it has enough gas and oil. An electric mower, like the one that I use, needs to be charged, so be sure to charge yours. Also, most mowers have settings for grass length, so make sure your mower is set properly.

Then, you'll need to walk through the yard that you're going to mow, picking up items that will get in your way, such as rocks and sticks or toys. It's important to do this because otherwise it can wreak havoc on your mower's blades, ruin the items that you mow over, and/or cause things to fly up toward you as you mow.

Before you start your mower, you'll want to put on safety glasses or goggles, as well as sneakers or work boots to protect your feet. Now, you're ready to start the power. You do this by either pushing a button or using the pull cord. Once the mower is started, mow along the outside of the lawn. Go in one direction across the lawn and then back in the other direction right beside where you first mowed. Repeat this again and again until you reach the edge of the lawn opposite to where you first began.

I use a mulching mower that cuts up the grass clippings and puts them back into the grass as I mow. But if you use a mower that has a grass collector, you will periodically need to check the bag on the mower to see how full it is getting. When it gets full, you will need to empty the clippings into a bag that you can leave for the homeowner to either use as compost or properly dispose of. Be sure to turn the mower off or make sure that the blade is stopped before emptying the bag.

Now the lawn is mowed. Turn off the mower and check your work one last time to be sure you didn't miss anything. Good job!

Using the Scoring Guide to Study the Model

Now we'll use the scoring guide to check Kyle's writing test, "How to Mow a Lawn." Let's see how well his essay meets each of the six writing traits.

Information/Organization

- **The guide is sequentially ordered.**

Kyle wrote the steps in his guide in the order that they are to be followed. He begins with a short explanation of equipment preparation. Then, he explains the importance of removing items from the grass and putting on safety gear before mowing the lawn. I like the way Kyle ordered his guide, and the way he stresses safety, too.

Before you start your mower, you'll want to put on safety glasses or goggles, as well as sneakers or work boots to protect your feet. Now, you're ready to start the power.

Voice/Audience

- **The writing contains a lot of explanative details that help the reader understand the process.**

Kyle tells his readers what to do and why they should do it. To help his readers better understand the process, he also talks about how he does these things.

Now, you're ready to start the power. You do this by either pushing a button or using the pull cord. Once the mower is started, mow along the outside of the lawn. Go in one direction across the lawn and then back in the other direction right beside where you first mowed. Repeat this again and again until you reach the edge of the lawn opposite to where you first began.

Content/Ideas

• **The guide is supported with factual information.**

Kyle doesn't just give his opinion or point of view when he explains how to mow a lawn; he also points out the facts, such as what is needed to prepare equipment.

If you use a gas mower, be sure that it has enough gas and oil. An electric mower, like the one that I use, needs to be charged, so be sure to charge yours. Also, most mowers have settings for grass length, so make sure your mower is set properly.

Word Choice/Clarity

• **The writing has been checked for proper use of homophones.**

Kyle uses homophones correctly. He uses *It's* instead of *Its*, and he uses the word *wreak* instead of *reek*, which has a totally different meaning!

It's important to do this because otherwise it can wreak havoc on your mower's blades, ruin the items that you mow over, and/or cause things to fly up toward you as you mow.

Using the Scoring Guide to Study the Model

• **The writing flows smoothly.**

Kyle's story flows smoothly. Even though it's step-by-step, the writing still contains enough sentence variety to make it interesting and easy to read.

I use a mulching mower that cuts up the grass clippings and puts them back into the grass as I mow. But if you use a mower that has a grass collector, you will periodically need to check the bag on the mower to see how full it is getting. When it gets full, you will need to empty the clippings into a bag that you can leave for the homeowner to either use as compost or properly dispose of.

• **The writer correctly uses grammar, punctuation, capitalization, and spelling.**

I think Kyle's how-to guide is error-free. But I know it's important to check for mistakes in my own work, so I'll be sure to do this as I write. And remember, you should check for proper grammar and mechanics at every step of the writing process so that you can avoid having errors on your final test, too!

Planning My Time

When our teacher gives us a writing prompt, she always tells us how much time we'll have to complete the test. I'm already familiar with the writing process, so I'll think about how much time I need for each step. Then, I'll add it all up to see if it meets the amount of time my teacher has given us. She has allowed us an hour for this test, so here's how I plan to organize my time. Remember, planning your time will help you, too!

Step 4:
Editing
10 minutes

Step 1:
Prewriting
25 minutes

Step 3:
Revising
10 minutes

Step 2:
Drafting
15 minutes

Prewriting Study the Writing Prompt

Writing Strategy Study the writing prompt to be sure I know what to do.

I always study my writing prompt so that I know exactly what I'm supposed to do. I know that it usually has three parts, and that it will help to first find and then label the setup, task, and scoring guide. You should also circle key words in the setup and the task that show what kind of writing you need to do and who your audience will be. I used orange to circle my topic and red to circle my task. The writing prompt doesn't say who the audience is, but my purpose is to teach someone to do something, so I'll keep that in mind as I write.

My Writing Test Prompt

Setup — Think about something you know how to do really well. Is there anything about this activity that others would find useful?

Task — Write a how-to guide that "teaches" others how to do something beneficial.

Scoring Guide — Be sure your writing

- is sequentially ordered.
- contains a lot of explanatory details that help the reader understand the process.
- is supported with factual information.
- has been checked for proper use of homophones.
- flows smoothly.
- contains correct grammar, punctuation, capitalization, and spelling.

Think about how the scoring guide meets the writing traits in the rubrics you've used. All of the traits might not be included in every scoring guide, but you'll want to think about each of them in order to write a good essay.

- Be sure your writing is sequentially ordered.

I want to be sure I write all the steps in the correct order.

- Be sure your writing contains a lot of explanative details that help the reader understand the process.

I need to include details that explain each step of the process. This way, my readers will really understand what I'm talking about.

- Be sure your writing is supported with factual information.

I'd better include facts for credibility.

- Be sure your writing has been checked for proper use of homophones.

Sometimes it's easy to mix up words while writing, so I'll make sure that I've used homophones correctly.

- Be sure your writing flows smoothly.

I can make my writing flow smoothly by using different kinds of sentence patterns.

- Be sure your writing contains correct grammar, punctuation, capitalization, and spelling.

I'll remember to check grammar and mechanics throughout the writing process.

Prewriting Gather Information

Writing Strategy Respond to the task.

It's important to gather information before writing, so I'll take another look at the writing prompt. Since there's not a lot of time when taking a test, it's important to think about how you'll respond to the task before you start to write.

My task says that I have to write a guide that teaches others how to do something. I've already written a how-to guide on tacking up a horse, but since I love animals so much, I know there has to be something else involving animals that I can teach others how to do. I always watch my aunt's dog when she is out of town, and I even take care of our neighbor's cats when she's away. I'll bet I can write a good how-to guide on being a pet sitter! I'll quickly write down some notes about it.

Task ⎯⎯ Write a how-to guide that "teaches" others how to do something beneficial.

Notes

 Take good care of animals when you pet-sit.

 Get instructions from the owners.

 Make sure pets have food and water.

Remember! Before you begin writing, think about how you are going to respond to the task. Then, jot down a few notes.

Prewriting Organize Ideas

Writing Strategy Choose a graphic organizer.

Since I don't have much time, I'll start organizing my ideas. The scoring guide says my writing should be in sequential order, so I'll use a Sequence Chain to organize the steps in my how-to guide.

Topic: How to be a good pet sitter

Step 1: Ask the pet owners for details.
    a. Visit the pet owner's home.
    b. Write down a list of important instructions.
    c. Find out when they'll leave and when they'll return.
    d. Ask how often you need to stop by and what you need to do.
    e. Get the keys so you can get in the house.
    f. Get emergency numbers.

Step 2: When it's time for your visit, call the pet by name.
    a. Give the pet some love and attention while you're there.

Step 3: Give the pet its food and water.

Step 4: If the owners requested it, take the pet for a walk.
    a. Make sure to take waste bags with you.
    b. Remember to put the pet on a leash.

Step 5: Repeat the above steps for as many times as the owners requested.
    a. Leave the owners a note to tell them how things went.

Result: The pet is well cared for, and the owners appreciate it!

Remember! Choose a graphic organizer to arrange steps in the order that they should be followed.

Reflect
Did I include enough steps on my Sequence Chain?

Prewriting Check the Scoring Guide

Information/Organization

Writing Strategy Check my graphic organizer against the scoring guide.

You won't have much time to revise during a writing test, so prewriting is more important than ever. Before I start writing, I'll check my Sequence Chain against the scoring guide in the writing prompt.

Topic: How to be a good pet sitter

Step 1: Ask the pet owners for details.
    a. Visit the pet owner's home.
    b. Write down a list of important instructions.
    c. Find out when they'll leave and when they'll return.
    d. Ask how often you need to stop by and what you need to do.
    e. Get the keys so you can get in the house.
    f. Get emergency numbers.

Step 2: When it's time for your visit, call the pet by name.
    a. Give the pet some love and attention while you're there.

Step 3: Give the pet its food and water.

Step 4: If the owners requested it, take the pet for a walk.
    a. Make sure to take waste bags with you.
    b. Remember to put the pet on a leash.

Step 5: Repeat the above steps for as many times as the owners requested.
    a. Leave the owners a note to tell them how things went.

Result: The pet is well cared for, and the owners appreciate it!

Information/Organization

- Be sure your writing is sequentially ordered.

I'll mention my topic in my introduction, and I'll use my Sequence Chain to help me write the body of my guide. This will help me keep things in order.

 Voice/Audience

- Be sure your writing contains a lot of explanative details that help the reader understand the process.

I'll explain the steps from my Sequence Chain in detail, and I'll talk about my own experiences, too.

 Content/Ideas

- Be sure your writing is supported with factual information.

I've already written some facts on my Sequence Chain, but I'll be sure to include even more in my guide.

 Word Choice/Clarity

- Be sure your writing has been checked for proper use of homophones.

As I write, I'll make sure to use the correct words.

 Sentence Fluency

- Be sure your writing flows smoothly.

I'll use different kinds of sentences to make one step flow to the next.

 Grammar/Mechanics

- Be sure your writing contains correct grammar, punctuation, capitalization, and spelling.

I'll pay close attention to this as I write. Then, I'll go back and edit my draft before turning it in.

Remember! Check your graphic organizer against the scoring guide before you start to write. This will help you remember what to do once you begin the writing process.

Reflect

My Sequence Chain has given me a good start. Do you think I'm missing anything?

Drafting Write a Draft

Voice/Audience

Writing Strategy Provide plenty of explanative details for the reader.

I used my Sequence Chain to outline the steps of my how-to guide, but the scoring guide says I also need to provide plenty of explanative details for the reader. As I write, I'll include the steps from my Sequence Chain, and I'll also include details that explain why each step is important. After all, the reader may not have taken care of a pet before!

[DRAFT]

How to Be a Good Pet Sitter

by Briana

Being a pet sitter is an important responsbility. I've done a lot of pet-sitting and have learned some important tips for taking care of other people's animals.

The first step is to get details and instructions from the pet owner. You should do this in person so that you can meet the pet and get a better idea of how things are done. You might also want to make a list of instructions such that you don't forget anything.

[explanative details]

First, you need to ask the pet owner when you'll be pet-sitting. Make sure you are free. Ask how often you need to come over. Find out what you need to do. Find out what the pet eats. Ask where the food is kept. Ask about any special needs the pet has, such as going outside after it eats or going on a walk. You'll also need to know where the leash is kept if you are going to take a dog for a walk, and you'll want to get the keys to the house so that you can get in. Its also important to get the vet's number, along with the phone number where the owner can be reached.

When you first go to the house to pet-sit, call out the pet's name so that it won't be scared. Then, pet or play with it. Then, give it some food and water.

[explanative details]

If you're supposed to let the animal out, now is a good time to do it. Be sure that you take waste bags with you if you have a dog to walk, and make sure the dog is on a leash.

Before you leave, give the animal one last bit of attention, and make sure that you haven't forgotten anything. Then, repeat the steps above as often as necessary, four as many times a day as needed.

On your last visit, leave the owners a note, summarizing what their pet did. Most pet owners really seem to appreshiate this!

Reflect

Did I include enough details? Do you think the reader will understand the process?

Remember! Provide explanations and details to help your readers understand the steps in your how-to guide.

Revising Extend Writing

Writing Strategy Add supporting facts.

After I completed my draft, I checked the scoring guide to see if I missed anything. It said to add supporting facts. Even though I had already included some facts, I still didn't think I had enough. For instance, if animals don't have water to drink, they can get really sick and dehydrated. This is one of the facts that I added to my guide.

[DRAFT]

[added supporting facts] ——→ Pets can get lonely when their owners are away, so it's nice to give them some attention when you are there.

When you first go to the house to pet-sit, call out the pet's name

so that it won't be scared. Then, pet or play with it. Then, give it

some food and water. It's really important for animals to have water to drink; otherwise, they can get sick and dehydrated.

> **Remember!** Be sure to include plenty of facts to support your explanation.

Revising Clarify Writing

The scoring guide says to check my paper for proper use of homophones, so I read it again to be sure I hadn't gotten any words confused with other words that sounded the same. When I found a mistake, I corrected it.

[DRAFT]

make sure that you haven't forgotten anything. Then, repeat the steps

above as often as necessary, ~~four~~ for as many times a day as needed.

[corrected a misused homophone]

Remember! It's easy to misuse homophones because they sound alike but mean different things. That's why you should carefully check to be sure you're using the right words.

Reflect

Have my revisions made my writing clearer? Are my word choices correct now?

Editing Check Sentences

Writing Strategy Combine short sentences to make the writing flow smoothly.

I read my paper again to be sure that my writing flows smoothly, just as the scoring guide says. I found an area where I had used a bunch of short sentences that didn't flow well, so I combined them to make the writing more fluid.

[DRAFT]

[combined short sentences]

First, you need to ask the pet owner when you'll be pet-sitting. , and then

Make sure you are free. Ask how often you need to come over. Find , and

out what you need to do. Find out what the pet eats. Ask where the , and

food is kept. Ask about any special needs the pet has, such as going

Remember! If your writing doesn't flow, try combining short sentences into long ones.

Editing Proofread Writing

Writing Strategy Check my grammar, punctuation, capitalization, and spelling.

There's one last step! The scoring guide says that I should check for correct grammar, punctuation, capitalization, and spelling. I'll reread my how-to guide to be sure my test is error-free. I always make sure I have enough time to check my grammar and mechanics, since it's a really important step!

How to Be a Good Pet Sitter

by Briana

Being a pet sitter is an important responsbility. responsibility I've done a lot of pet-sitting and have learned some important tips for taking care of other people's animals.

The first step is to get details and instructions from the pet owner. You should do this in person so that you can meet the pet and get a better idea of how things are done. You might also want to make a list of instructions such so that you don't forget anything.

First, you need to ask the pet owner when you'll be pet-sitting. , and then Make sure you are free. Ask how often you need to come over. , and Find out what you need to do. Find out what the pet eats. , and Ask where the

Remember! Don't forget to check grammar, punctuation, capitalization, and spelling every time you write for a test.

food is kept. Ask about any special needs the pet has, such as going outside after it eats or going on a walk. You'll also need to know where the leash is kept if you are going to take a dog for a walk, and you'll want to get the keys to the house so that you can get in. It's also important to get the vet's number, along with the phone number where the owner can be reached.

When you first go to the house to pet-sit, call out the pet's name ~ Pets can get lonely when their owners are away, so it's nice to give them some attention when you are there. so that it won't be scared. Then, pet or play with it. ~~Then~~ give it Now, the pet some food and water. It's really important for animals to have water to drink; otherwise, they can get sick and dehydrated.

If you're supposed to let the animal out, now is a good time to do it. Be sure that you take waste bags with you if you have a dog to walk, and make sure the dog is on a leash.

Before you leave, give the animal one last bit of attention, and make sure that you haven't forgotten anything. Then, repeat the steps above as often as necessary, ~~four~~ for as many times a day as needed.

On your last visit, leave the owners a note, summarizing what their while they were away pet did. Most pet owners really seem to ~~appreshiate~~ appreciate this!

Reflect

I'm ready to turn my test in, but before I do, I'll check it against the scoring guide one more time. Remember to use your writing prompt's scoring guide to check your writing anytime you take a test.

Well now, that wasn't so bad! Just remember to use the writing process when you take a writing test. The process is just a little different for a test, but if you keep in mind these important tips, I'm sure you'll do just fine!

TEST TiPS

1. **Study the writing prompt before you start to write.** Most writing prompts have three parts: the setup, the task, and the scoring guide. The parts probably won't be labeled. You'll have to figure them out for yourself!

2. **Make sure you understand the task before you start to write.**

   - Read all three parts of the writing prompt carefully.

   - Circle key words in the task part of the writing prompt that tell what kind of writing you need to do. The task might also identify your audience.

   - Make sure you know how you'll be graded.

   - Say the assignment in your own words to yourself.

3. **Keep an eye on the clock.** Decide how much time you will spend on each part of the writing process and try to stick to your schedule. Don't spend so much time on prewriting that you don't have enough time left to write!

4. **Reread your writing. Compare it to the scoring guide at least twice.** Remember the rubrics you've used? A scoring guide on a writing test is like a rubric. It can help you keep what's important in mind.

5. **Plan, plan, plan!** You don't get much time to revise during a test, so planning is more important than ever.

6. **Write neatly.** Remember, if the people who score your test can't read your writing, it doesn't matter how good your essay is!

PERSUASIVE writing convinces the reader of something.

Hi, my name is Luis. We're studying persuasive writing in school. I'm excited about trying to convince readers of my opinions. I can't wait to try it!

IN THIS UNIT

1 Editorial

2 TV Commercial Script

3 Persuasive Speech

4 Writing for a Test

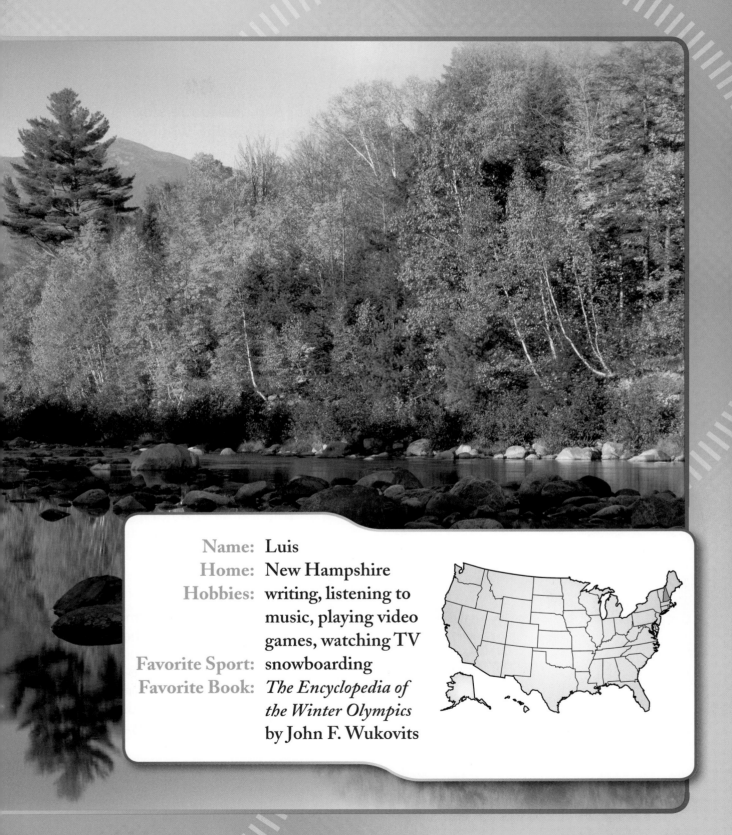

Name: Luis
Home: New Hampshire
Hobbies: writing, listening to music, playing video games, watching TV
Favorite Sport: snowboarding
Favorite Book: *The Encyclopedia of the Winter Olympics* by John F. Wukovits

What's an Editorial?

It's a type of persuasive writing that is published in newspapers or magazines. I have strong opinions, so I'm looking forward to writing about an issue that affects me.

What's in an Editorial?

Opinion
In an editorial, a writer expresses his or her opinion about an important problem. Then, it's up to the reader to decide if he or she agrees.

Problem and Solutions
This is the focus of an editorial. The writer states a problem and offers some possible solutions. Thinking about an issue that affects me is going to help me come up with possible solutions.

Pros and Cons
This is a good way to organize an editorial because there are usually two sides to every issue. When I argue my case, I'll state both the pros and the cons of each solution. That way, I'll be sure to address the reader's concerns.

Details
An editorial is opinion-based, which means it's really important for the writer to include details, facts, and examples that back up his or her beliefs. Without this kind of information, the reader might not trust the author's credibility.

Why write an Editorial?

There are all kinds of reasons for writing an editorial. I've listed some here, and I'll use these ideas to help me decide on a purpose for my own writing.

Education
The writer of an editorial can educate the reader with facts and details. In turn, the reader can decide what to do with the information.

Persuasion
Convincing readers to agree with an opinion or to take specific action is the focus of most editorials—and, in my opinion, the strongest reason for writing them.

Action
Sometimes, an editorial writer wants readers to do more than just agree with his or her opinions. Here, the author's purpose is to urge readers to take action.

Leadership
People sometimes look to folks in leadership positions for guidance on relevant issues. When a politician or a class council member writes an editorial, the reader receives that person's advice on an important issue or problem.

Editorial Writing Traits

I know that there are six traits of good writing. Here's a list of what makes a good editorial. I'll use it later to help me write.

Information/ Organization	The editorial is focused on a problem. The editorial is organized around several solutions.
Voice/ Audience	The editorial states a problem and offers some helpful solutions for the reader.
Content/ Ideas	Detail sentences accurately support topic sentences throughout.
Word Choice/ Clarity	All catch phrases are clarified with quotation marks.
Sentence Fluency	A variety of sentence patterns is included.
Grammar/ Mechanics	Spelling, punctuation, and capitalization are correct. Compound personal pronouns are used correctly.

I can use Julia Powell's editorial on the next page as a model for my own writing. Later, we'll check out how Julia used the traits to help her write.

The Fate of the Main Street Theater

by Julia Powell

Problem

In three weeks, the city of Springside is planning to tear down its oldest landmark, the Main Street Theater. First opened in 1927, this historical building has deteriorated to such a degree that it is too expensive to save. The theater, which stood empty for years, is situated in a prime location in the center of downtown. Two groups have their eye on that location and are fighting to gain support for their plans. One group wants a multilevel parking garage. The other wants a park with an amphitheater. Both groups want support from the people of Springside in the upcoming election. Therefore, we must educate ourselves about the pros and cons of both proposals.

Solutions

Pro
Details

First, let's look at the park proposal. The best thing about it is that it would give people some much-needed green space downtown. During the day, downtown workers would have a place to relax and eat lunch. Plays and concerts in the amphitheater would draw people downtown in the evening. This would provide business and income for the stores and restaurants in the area. The park itself would not make money for the city, but its existence would benefit the entire downtown area in other ways, both financially and ecologically.

Con

On the negative side, however, the costs of designing and building the park would come from our pockets, possibly from a tax levy. The additional cost to maintain the park would be covered by various garden clubs in Springside.

Pro

Now, let's look at the garage. What would be good about it? If people know they have a convenient place to park, they're much more likely to come downtown and frequent the businesses there. This would attract new businesses, which might consider Springside a good place to call home.

Con

What's the downside? Some people say a garage would be an eyesore, especially if it's not well maintained. Others say it would be a "crime magnet" that would invite trouble if not well guarded. Yes, hiring people to maintain and guard the garage would create a few jobs. However, I doubt that the hourly fees charged for parking would be enough to pay these workers and maintain the facility.

Personally, I'm in favor of using the site for a downtown park. How about you? Which side will you take when you vote? Choose carefully now! The vote you cast in the upcoming election will affect Springside for years.

Opinion

Editorial

Rubric

The traits of a good editorial from page 312 have been used to make the rubric below. By using 1, 2, 3, or 4 check marks to judge each trait, you can decide how well any editorial was written.

	Excelling ✓✓✓✓	Achieving ✓✓✓	Developing ✓✓	Beginning ✓
Information/ Organization	The editorial is focused on a problem and is organized around several solutions.	The editorial is mainly focused on a problem and is mostly organized.	The editorial is focused on more than one problem and is loosely organized.	The editorial should focus on one problem, and it should be more organized.
Voice/ Audience	The editorial states a problem and offers some helpful solutions for the reader.	The editorial states a problem and a solution for the reader.	The editorial states a problem for the reader.	The editorial needs to state a problem and offer some solutions for the reader.
Content/ Ideas	Detail sentences accurately support topic sentences throughout.	Detail sentences support topic sentences in many areas.	Detail sentences support topic sentences in some areas.	More detail sentences are needed to support topic sentences.
Word Choice/ Clarity	All catch phrases are clarified with quotation marks.	Some catch phrases are clarified with quotation marks.	A few catch phrases are clarified with quotation marks.	All catch phrases should be clarified with quotation marks.
Sentence Fluency	A variety of sentence patterns is included.	Many kinds of sentences are used.	A few kinds of sentences are used.	A variety of sentence patterns should be included.
Grammar/ Mechanics	Spelling, grammar, and compound personal pronouns are used correctly.	There are a few errors in spelling, grammar, and compound personal pronoun usage.	There are several errors in spelling, grammar, and compound personal pronoun usage.	There are many errors in spelling, grammar, and compound personal pronoun usage.

Using the Rubric to Study the Model

Editorial

Now, let's use the rubric to check Julia Powell's editorial, "The Fate of the Main Street Theater." How many check marks would you give her for each trait?

Information/Organization

- **The editorial is focused on a problem.**
- **The editorial is organized around several solutions.**

Julia focuses on a clear problem and organizes her editorial around possible solutions. She explores the first solution in the second and third paragraphs.

> **[from the writing model]**
>
> First, let's look at the park proposal. The best thing about it is that it would give people some much-needed green space downtown.

She explores the second solution in the fourth and fifth paragraphs.

> **[from the writing model]**
>
> Now, let's look at the garage. What would be good about it?

Voice/Audience

- **The editorial states a problem and offers some helpful solutions for the reader.**

Julia draws readers into her editorial by stating the problem in the first sentence. Then, she explains how two different groups have proposed to solve the problem.

> **[from the writing model]**
>
> Two groups have their eye on that location and are fighting to gain support for their plans. One group wants a multilevel parking garage. The other wants a park with an amphitheater.

Content/Ideas

- **Detail sentences accurately support topic sentences throughout.**

Julia uses detail sentences to support each topic sentence. In this paragraph, she begins with the following: "First, let's look at the park proposal." Then, she adds detail sentences that describe the advantages of putting a park downtown.

[from the writing model]

The best thing about it is that it would give people some much-needed green space downtown. During the day, downtown workers would have a place to relax and eat lunch. Plays and concerts in the amphitheater would draw people downtown in the evening.

Word Choice/Clarity

- **All catch phrases are clarified with quotation marks.**

Julia uses the catch phrase *crime magnet* in her editorial. Normally, I wouldn't know what she means by this, but she uses quotation marks to show that the phrase has become popularly associated with the issue of the Main Street Theater.

[from the writing model]

Some people say a garage would be an eyesore, especially if it's not well maintained. Others say it would be a "crime magnet" that would invite trouble if not well guarded.

Sentence Fluency

• A variety of sentence patterns is included.

Julia uses sentence patterns that vary in length, pattern, and type. This adds interest to the editorial, since it keeps readers from being lulled by repetition in tone and rhythm. Check out this paragraph to see what I mean.

[from the writing model]

Personally, I'm in favor of using the site for a downtown park. How about you? Which side will you take when you vote? Choose carefully now! The vote you cast in the upcoming election will affect Springside for years.

Grammar Mechanics

• Spelling, punctuation, and capitalization are correct. Compound personal pronouns are used correctly.

I know that a compound personal pronoun like *herself, themselves,* or *yourself* must refer to its antecedent. Julia makes sure each compound personal pronoun refers back to the subject of its sentence. This eliminates any confusion and makes the editorial easy to follow.

[from the writing model]

The park itself would not make money for the city, but its existence would benefit the entire downtown area in other ways, both financially and ecologically.

I'm going to write an editorial about something I feel strongly about. I'll follow the rubric and use good writing strategies. Read on to see how I do it!

Prewriting Gather Information

Information/Organization   The editorial is focused on a problem.

Writing Strategy   State the problem. List the pros and cons of several solutions.

I'm on the staff of our school newspaper. I contribute poems, articles, and editorials. So when my teacher said we were going to write an editorial about an important school or community problem, I knew exactly what to write about: Our administration is upset about the clothes some kids are wearing to school. They want us to start wearing uniforms.

To begin working on my editorial, I jotted down the issue. Next, I wrote down possible ways to solve it. Then, I started listing some positives and negatives (pros and cons) about each solution. I also gathered more information by interviewing a friend who has to wear a uniform to school. Several of my arguments came out of that interview.

Problem: Our administration is upset about the clothes that some students wear to school.

Why it's a problem: They feel that the students' clothing causes discipline problems.

Possible solutions:

1. School uniforms for all students

Pros

It's the "great equalizer."
You never have to wonder/worry about what to wear to school.
It saves parents money on kids' wardrobe and accessories.

Cons

Everyone looks the same every day.
Students can't express individuality through clothing.
You get singled out in public—and ridiculed!

2. Dress code that restricts certain clothing

Pros

It allows for individual expression, within limits.
Students can wear different outfits every day.
Parents don't waste money on new uniforms for their kids.

Cons

Dress code guidelines would be set per administration's personal opinions.
Some kids will try to test/abuse the rules.
Their rebellion could end up proving the administration's point.

Practice!

Now it's your turn. Think about a problem, along with several possible solutions. Gather information by jotting down the pros and cons of each solution.

Prewriting Organize Ideas

Information/Organization   The editorial is organized around several solutions.

Writing Strategy   Make a Problem-Solution Frame to organize the pros and cons of several solutions.

According to the rubric, my editorial should be organized around several solutions. I'll use a Problem-Solution Frame to organize the ideas from my list. This will allow me to make a side-by-side comparison of the pros and cons of a dress code versus school uniforms.

First, I'll write details about the problem in the problem box. Then, I'll write each solution in its own box. Finally, I'll list the pros and cons under their related solutions.

✏ Writer's Term

Problem-Solution Frame
You can use a **Problem-Solution Frame** to analyze a problem and its possible solutions. Then, after comparing and contrasting solutions, you can choose the best way to solve the problem.

Problem-Solution Frame

Problem Box

| What is the problem? | Our administration is upset about the clothes that some students wear to school. |
| Why is it a problem? | They feel that the students' clothing causes discipline problems. |

Solution Box

| Solution 1 | Solution 2 |
| School uniforms for all students | Dress code that restricts certain clothing |

Pros	Cons	Pros	Cons
It's the "great equalizer."	Everyone looks the same every day.	It allows for individual expression, within limits.	Dress code guidelines would be set per the administration's personal opinions.
You never have to wonder/worry about what to wear to school.	Students can't express individuality through clothing.	Students can wear different outfits every day.	Some kids will try to test/abuse the rules.
It saves parents money on kids' wardrobe and accessories.	You get singled out in public—and ridiculed!	Parents don't waste money on new uniforms for their kids.	Student rebellion could end up proving the administration's point.

Practice!

Now it's your turn. Make a Problem-Solution Frame to organize your ideas.

Reflect

How did I do? Do you think my Problem-Solution Frame will help me write a well-organized editorial?

Drafting Write a Draft

Voice/Audience

The editorial states a problem and offers some helpful solutions for the reader.

Writing Strategy

State a problem and offer some helpful solutions for the reader.

Now I'll use my Problem-Solution Frame to help me write my editorial. The rubric says I should state the problem and offer some possible solutions. Then, readers will know exactly what the issues are, which will help keep them interested. Right now, I'm only going to worry about getting my ideas down. I won't worry too much about spelling, grammar, and punctuation mistakes, since I can always go back and fix those later.

[DRAFT]

To Uniform or Not to Uniform?

[problem]

There's a debate raging at Oakbrook School. The administration is concerned about our clothing. They claim it is disrespectful and causing us to become rebellious. As a result, they are trying to impose school uniforms as soon as next semester. Needless to say, this has caused some students to speak out. Certainly, uniforms are one solution. But there are others. How about a restricted dress code, for instance?

[solution 1]

[solution 2]

First, let's look at uniforms. My strongest argument against them is that they impose upon students' right to express individuality. Fashion is a big part of a teenager's life. If we students look the same every day, how will we be allowed to express themselves? If we have to conform to the "fashion" of a uniform, the only way to express ourself will be through our hairstyles.

Another problem with uniforms is that although we will look the same in school, we'll stand out in public. Can you imagine? We'll feel like we're wearing costumes all the time!

Practice!

Now it's your turn. Write a draft that states a problem and some possible solutions.

Reflect

What do you think? Did I state the problem and solutions clearly? Will this keep the reader interested?

Revising Extend Writing

Content/Ideas

Detail sentences accurately support topic sentences throughout.

Writing Strategy

Add detail sentences that accurately support their topic sentences.

Writer's Term

Topic Sentences/Detail Sentences
A **topic sentence** states the main idea of a paragraph or a piece of writing. **Detail sentences** contain information that supports a topic sentence. This support can be in the form of facts, explanations, illustrations, or examples.

After I finished my draft, I checked the rubric. It says topic sentences should be accurately supported by detail sentences. A lot of the details in my editorial are based on the experiences of a friend, so I feel that most of my information is accurate. But I did find one paragraph in my draft that could use more detail.

[DRAFT]

There are a few advantages to wearing uniforms, however. The most important one is that uniforms are the "great equalizer."

The amount of money a family has is all but indistinguishable when everyone's clothing looks the same.

[added a detail sentence]

Practice!

Now it's your turn. Add accurate information to strengthen your topic sentences.

Revising Clarify Writing

Word Choice/ Clarity

All catch phrases are clarified with quotation marks.

Writing Strategy

Use quotation marks to clarify catch phrases.

I want to make sure my writing is clear, so I checked the rubric one more time. It says to use quotation marks to clarify catch phrases. I know that quotation marks can be used around a term or an expression to show that it has a specific meaning. I used a few catch phrases in my draft, so I'll be sure to add the proper punctuation now.

[DRAFT]

[clarified a catch phrase]

For example, T-shirts endorsing tobacco or alcohol products would be forbidden, as would shirts with "suggestive slogans."

Practice!

Now it's your turn. Review your draft to see if you have included any catch phrases. If you have, clarify them with quotation marks.

Reflect

Have my revisions made my writing clearer and more interesting?

Editing Check Sentences

Sentence Fluency   A variety of sentence patterns is included.

Writing Strategy   Use a variety of sentence patterns.

Now it's time to edit. I read my draft again and realized that many of my sentences were the same length and pattern. Then, I looked to the rubric for help. It says to include a variety of sentence patterns, so I rewrote some sentences to mix things up a little. Here's one example.

[DRAFT]

[formed a complex sentence for variety]

Because of their behavior,

This would be problematic. These teens just might prove the administration correct in saying that clothing causes disruptive behavior!

Practice!

Now it's your turn. Make your writing more interesting by using a variety of sentence patterns.

Editing Proofread Writing

Grammar/Mechanics Spelling, punctuation, and capitalization are correct. Compound personal pronouns are used correctly.

Writing Strategy Make sure each compound personal pronoun refers back to the subject of its sentence.

Writer's Term

Compound Personal Pronouns

A **compound personal pronoun** is a pronoun that ends in *–self* or *–selves*. A compound personal pronoun always refers back to the subject of the sentence, usually indicating that the subject is doing something to itself. Because of this, a compound personal pronoun must match its subject in number and gender.

Now it's time to proofread my editorial. I always check for spelling and punctuation errors, but the rubric reminds me to make sure each compound personal pronoun refers back to the subject of its sentence. I know I used some compound personal pronouns in my draft, so I'll make sure they're used correctly right now.

[DRAFT]

[corrected a compound personal pronoun error]

Nonetheless, I'd like to ask for your support in fighting for a

                                    ourselves
dress code. Let us prove ~~ourself~~ to the administration. Let us show

                    responsible
that we can be ~~responsable~~ and mature.

Practice!

Now it's your turn. Edit your draft for spelling, punctuation, and capitalization. Also, make sure that you've used compound personal pronouns correctly.

Grammar/Mechanics

For more practice with compound personal pronouns, use the exercises on the next two pages.

Reflect

I tried hard to add variety to my sentence patterns. Did this make my writing more interesting? How are my grammar and mechanics? Did you find any mistakes?

Compound Personal Pronouns

KNOW the RULE

A **compound personal pronoun** is a pronoun that ends in *–self* or *–selves*. It usually shows that the subject of a sentence is doing something to or for itself.

Example: I made **myself** a cup of tea.

Sometimes, a compound personal pronoun is used for emphasis.
Examples: Mrs. Jenkins built the table **herself**.
Carson changed the tire **himself**.

A compound personal pronoun always refers back to the subject of the sentence; therefore, it must match its subject in number and gender.

Practice the Rule

Number a separate piece of paper 1–6. For sentences 1–3, write the compound personal pronoun and the subject to which it refers. For sentences 4–6, write the compound personal pronoun that correctly completes each sentence.

1. I sat myself down last night to write an editorial for our school newspaper.
2. We have been talking among ourselves about the cafeteria food.
3. The cafeteria employees themselves are unhappy with it.
4. In an editorial, you can really express _____.
5. The students _____ have written many editorials.
6. Coach Decker can get _____ a lot of attention by writing an editorial.

Apply the Rule

Read the editorial below, noting any errors in compound personal pronouns. On a separate sheet of paper, rewrite the editorial correctly.

Avoiding Summer School

Winter glee turns to June gloom when schools have to make up snow days at the end of the year. Last June, kids found theirself in class until the last day of the month. The classrooms were hot, and many summer camps had already begun. Families delayed vacations, and teachers theirselves had to rearrange summer plans.

State laws require that students attend school for a certain amount of calendar days each year, and educators have proposed solutions for making up snow days. One idea is to begin school before Labor Day. Another is to lower the state attendance standards.

An earlier start would add 7–12 days to the beginning of the year. If kids have to make up lost time, they will do so at the beginning of school instead of at the end of June. I myselves am not used to starting school before September. But if others have adjusted to this change, we themselves can, too.

The other option, lowering attendance standards, would allow school administrators ourself to shorten the number of "make-up" days. Some critics believe this option would lower education standards. That's why this proposal would be difficult to attain. Changing the required number of days would necessitate the state legislature to pass a new law.

I herself think the earlier start is the best idea. It's a far better option than staring out the classroom window on a beautiful day in late June!

Publishing Share Writing

Publish my editorial in the school newspaper.

Now that I'm done, I need to publish my editorial. I could read it to a friend or display it on a class bulletin board. But I feel strongly about this issue, so I want to reach as many readers as possible. That's why I'm going to submit my editorial for publication in our school newspaper. Then, maybe we can all work together to convince the administration to adopt a dress code.

Before I submit my work, I'll read through it one last time to make sure it includes all of the items on my checklist.

My Checklist

✔ One problem is discussed.

✔ Several solutions are proposed.

✔ Detail sentences support topic sentences.

✔ Catch phrases are set off with quotation marks.

✔ Sentences are varied and interesting.

✔ Spelling, capitalization, and punctuation are all correct. Compound personal pronouns are used correctly.

Practice!

Now it's your turn. Make a checklist to check your editorial. Then, make a final draft to publish.

To Uniform or Not to Uniform?

by Luis

There's a debate raging at Oakbrook School. The administration is concerned about our clothing. They claim it is disrespectful and causing us to become rebellious. As a result, they are trying to impose school uniforms as soon as next semester. Needless to say, this has caused some students to speak out. Certainly, uniforms are one solution. But there are others. How about a restricted dress code, for instance?

First, let's look at uniforms. My strongest argument against them is that they impose upon students' right to express individuality. Fashion is a big part of a teenager's life. If we students look the same every day, how will we be allowed to express ourselves? If we have to conform to the "fashion" of a uniform, the only way to express ourselves will be through our hairstyles.

Another problem with uniforms is that although we will look the same in school, we'll stand out in public. Can you imagine? We'll feel like we're wearing costumes all the time!

There are a few advantages to wearing uniforms, however. The most important one is that uniforms are the "great equalizer." The amount of money a family has is all but indistinguishable when everyone's clothing looks the same. Uniforms are also time-savers. They take the guesswork out of what to wear. They are also cost-effective since they eliminate the need for elaborate wardrobes and accessories. I know of a girl who said her parents saved at least $300 in clothing costs because she wears a uniform to school!

Before I sound like I'm in favor of school uniforms, let me propose another solution: a dress code that prohibits certain clothing. This would let students know exactly which items are no-noes. This solution still allows students to express their individuality, but it sets certain limitations. For example, T-shirts endorsing tobacco or alcohol products would be forbidden, as would shirts with "suggestive" slogans.

Of course, this solution has a downside. Some students might abuse the dress code and try to test its limits. They might argue that what they're wearing does not violate the rules. This would be problematic. Because of their behavior, these teens just might prove the administration correct in saying that clothing causes disruptive behavior!

Nonetheless, I'd like to ask for your support in fighting for a dress code. Let us prove ourselves to the administration. Let us show that we can be responsible and mature. We can "dress for success" in this effort. We can win—and keep—our right to choose our own clothes!

Reflect

What do you think? Did I use all the traits of a good editorial in my writing? Check it against the rubric, and don't forget to use the rubric to check your own editorial.

Ways to Publish an Editorial

As you decide how to publish your work, it's a good idea to think about who might want to read it. That way, you can figure out the best way to share it. Here are some ideas for publishing your editorial.

 Present your editorial in a class debate.

 Post your work on a Web site where others have submitted opinions on the same subject.

 Include your editorial as part of a "Class Opinions" publication.

 Post your editorial, along with an editorial that takes the opposite view, on a "Pro and Con" class bulletin board.

Take your editorial home and share it with your family.

Writing Across the Content Areas
Editorial

Your school subjects can be a surprising source of writing ideas. Choose a subject and see how many related topics you can brainstorm. Check out these examples.

Science
- Should recycling be mandatory in your community? Take a stand on this issue.
- Write an editorial that agrees or disagrees with a scientific theory you have learned in school.

Social Studies
- Do teenagers watch too much TV? Should parents set TV limits? State your opinion in an editorial.
- Should all young people be required to serve in the military? Write an editorial that argues for or against an enforced draft.

Art and/or Music
- What can musicians do to enforce copyrights on their works? Propose a solution in an editorial.
- Should art and/or music remain part of the curriculum? Take a stand in an editorial.

What's a TV Commercial Script?

It's a type of persuasive writing that tries to convince viewers to buy something. I love TV, and I've always wondered what goes into writing a commercial. This should be a lot of fun!

What's in a TV Commercial Script?

Product
The product is the item or service that the seller wants viewers to buy. It's the main focus of a commercial script.

Sales Technique
Every commercial has a gimmick. Some ads use celebrities to pitch products; others play out a simple story, featuring the product. Sales techniques also include catchy songs, cartoons, and demonstrations.

Attention-Grabber
A commercial has to get viewers interested right away. It's important to use words and images that will grab people's attention at the beginning. One way to do this is to include short, snappy sentences.

Call to Action
Many commercials end by calling on viewers to act— to buy a product, attend a show, donate to a cause, etc. Often, this suggestion is introduced early in the commercial, but leaving viewers with a final thought also works well.

Why write a TV Commercial Script?

There are many reasons for writing a TV commercial. I'll list some here. This might give me an idea about what product I should sell.

Sell a Product

Whether you're selling sneakers, soft drinks, or spaghetti, TV is a great way to sell your product and reach your audience.

Sell a Service

Products aren't the only things on the market. Sometimes, the purpose of a commercial is to sell a service like a car wash, a camp, or computer repair help.

Education

They might be short, but TV commercials can provide a whole bunch of information over the airwaves. Public Service Announcements, or PSAs, educate viewers about health, safety, and other important issues.

Persuasion

If you watch TV, you've probably seen commercials that show "taste tests" or other techniques that compare the featured product with another, similar one. Here, writers have decided that the best way to sell something is to persuade viewers that their product is better than others.

TV Commercial Script Writing Traits

I know that there are six traits of good writing. Here's a list of the traits for a good TV commercial script. Later, I'll use this list to help me write.

Information/ Organization	The script is based on one product. Ideas are well sequenced.
Voice/ Audience	The script begins with words and images that grab the audience's attention.
Content/ Ideas	The script ends with a clear call to action.
Word Choice/ Clarity	All words and images are clear.
Sentence Fluency	Short, exclamatory sentences create a fast pace throughout.
Grammar/ Mechanics	Spelling, punctuation, and capitalization are correct. Pronouns and antecedents are used correctly.

I can use Lori Kaspar's TV commercial script on the next three pages as a model for my own writing. Later, we'll check out how Lori used the traits to help her write.

SuperMegaBlast

a TV Commercial by Lori Kaspar

1 *(Roger and Bill are hiking in the woods. They enter a clearing and decide to rest. Roger opens his backpack and pulls out some water. Bill opens his pack and pulls out a bottle of green liquid. He shakes it, opens it, and begins gulping the contents.)*

2

Attention-Grabber

Roger: Hey! Hold on there, buddy! What's that green stuff you're drinking? It looks like spinach juice.

Bill: Spinach juice? No way! This is SuperMegaBlast. It's much better than spinach!

Product

3 **Roger:** Better than spinach? How's that, Bill?

Bill: Well, you see, SuperMegaBlast is made with spirulina.

Roger: Spiru—what?

4 **Bill:** Spirulina. It's one of the oldest foods on the planet. It's blue-green algae, and it has fifty-eight times more iron than spinach!

Roger: Why, that's incredible!

5 **Bill:** Yes, it is. But iron isn't the only good thing in spirulina. It's also nature's richest source of vitamin B12. It's got so much, as a matter of fact, that Olympic athletes use it to improve their energy and endurance. It's also a great source of vitamin E and beta carotene, which are essential for healthy skin and eyes.

6 **Roger:** Wow, Bill! What else does SuperMegaBlast do?

Bill: Well, it helps relieve arthritis pain. And SuperMegaBlast with spirulina is so beneficial and nutritious that NASA might take it into space some day!

↖ Sales Technique

7 **Roger:** Space food, eh? I'll bet it tastes awful. It sure doesn't look very good.

Bill: Awful? No way! SuperMegaBlast is delicious. It contains fruit juices—strawberry and banana—so it's sweet and refreshing, especially when chilled.

Roger: Hmm. Say, Bill, would you happen to have another SuperMegaBlast in that backpack of yours?

8 **Bill:** Sure do, Rog.

(Bill takes another bottle from his backpack and hands it to Roger. Roger shakes the bottle, opens it, and takes a tiny sip. He smacks his lips and smiles. Then, he takes a much bigger sip.)

9 **Roger:** Hey! This SuperMegaBlast is really good stuff!

Bill: I thought you'd like it.

Roger: Like it? I love it!

10 *(Roger takes another long sip and looks at the bottle. Then, he suddenly jumps to his feet.)*

Bill: Whoa, Rog! Where are you going?

Roger: To the store! I want to get my own SuperMegaBlast before everyone buys it all. I'd hate to wait so long that the only place I can get it is in outer space!

11 *(Bill laughs. The two put on their backpacks and hike away briskly. As they do, the camera points above them and into the sky. A SuperMegaBlast bottle appears.)*

12 **Announcer's Voice:** SuperMegaBlast. It's out of this world. <u>Get it at your local grocer's . . . while supplies last.</u>

Call to Action ⤴

TV Commercial Script

Rubric

The traits of a good TV commercial from page 336 have been used to make the rubric below. By using 1, 2, 3, or 4 check marks to judge each trait, you can decide how well any TV commercial was written.

	Excelling ✓✓✓✓	Achieving ✓✓✓	Developing ✓✓	Beginning ✓
Information/ Organization	The script is based on one product; ideas are well sequenced.	Most of the script is based on one product; most ideas are sequential.	Some of the script is based on one product; some ideas are sequential.	The script should be based on one product; ideas should be sequential.
Voice/ Audience	The script begins with words and images that grab the audience's attention.	The script begins with interesting words and images.	The script begins with mildly interesting words and images.	The script should begin with words and images that grab the audience's attention.
Content/ Ideas	The script ends with a clear call to action.	The script ends with a call to action that is mostly clear.	The script contains a call to action, but not at the end.	The script should end with a clear call to action.
Word Choice/ Clarity	All words and images are clear.	Most words and images are clear.	Some words and images are clear.	All words and images should be clear.
Sentence Fluency	Short, exclamatory sentences create a fast pace throughout.	Short, exclamatory sentences are used in many areas.	Short, exclamatory sentences are used in some areas.	Short, exclamatory sentences should be used to create a fast pace throughout.
Grammar/ Mechanics	Spelling, grammar, pronouns, and antecedents are used correctly.	There are a few errors in spelling, grammar, and pronoun-antecedent usage.	There are several errors in spelling, grammar, and pronoun-antecedent usage.	There are many errors in spelling, grammar, and pronoun-antecedent usage.

TV Commercial Script

Using the Rubric to Study the Model

Let's use the rubric to check Lori Kaspar's TV commercial script, "SuperMegaBlast." How many check marks would you give her for each trait?

Information/ Organization

- **The script is based on one product.**
- **Ideas are well sequenced.**

Lori focuses her commercial on one product: SuperMegaBlast. She also does a good job of sequencing the script. First, Bill pulls out the product, sparking Roger's curiosity. Next, Roger and Bill have a conversation during which facts about the product are revealed. It's like the reader of the script is actually watching the commercial!

[from the writing model]

Roger: Better than spinach? How's that, Bill?

Bill: Well, you see, SuperMegaBlast is made with spirulina.

Voice/ Audience

- **The script begins with words and images that grab the audience's attention.**

Lori's script grabs the audience's attention right from the beginning. The opening scene paints a mental image for the reader.

[from the writing model]

(Roger and Bill are hiking in the woods. They enter a clearing and decide to rest. Roger opens his backpack and pulls out some water. Bill opens his pack and pulls out a bottle of green liquid. He shakes it, opens it, and begins gulping the contents.)

Content/Ideas

- **The script ends with a clear call to action.**

Lori includes a clear call to action at the end of her script. Leading up to this, Roger says he's hurrying off to buy some SuperMegaBlast before it's too late. This sets up the announcer's final words, which hold viewers' attention until the end.

[from the writing model]

Announcer's Voice: SuperMegaBlast. It's out of this world. Get it at your local grocer's . . . while supplies last.

Word Choice/Clarity

- **All words and images are clear.**

The commercial is descriptive and clear because Lori does not include any information that would confuse viewers. When Bill tells Roger about spirulina, he uses a lot of clear, precise details.

[from the writing model]

Bill: Spirulina. It's one of the oldest foods on the planet. It's blue-green algae, and it has fifty-eight times more iron than spinach!

Roger: Why, that's incredible!

Bill: Yes, it is. But iron isn't the only good thing in spirulina. It's also nature's richest source of vitamin B12. It's got so much, as a matter of fact, that Olympic athletes use it to improve their energy and endurance. It's also a great source of vitamin E and beta carotene, which are essential for healthy skin and eyes.

Sentence Fluency

- Short, exclamatory sentences create a fast pace throughout.

A commercial writer needs to get the point across in an extremely short amount of time. So it's good that Lori uses a lot of short exclamations to create a fast pace. Here's an example of what I mean.

[from the writing model]

Roger: Hey! This SuperMegaBlast is really good stuff!

Bill: I thought you'd like it.

Roger: Like it? I love it!

Grammar/Mechanics

- Spelling, punctuation, and capitalization are correct. Pronouns and antecedents are used correctly.

Lori's script seems to be free of errors. She also makes sure that each pronoun has a clear antecedent. In this excerpt, I can tell that the pronoun *it* replaces the word *bottle*.

[from the writing model]

(Bill takes another bottle from his backpack and hands it to Roger. Roger shakes the bottle, opens it, and takes a tiny sip. He smacks his lips and smiles. Then, he takes a much bigger sip.)

My Turn!

I'm going to write a TV commercial script about a fun product. I'll follow the rubric and use good writing strategies. Follow along to see how I do it!

Prewriting Gather Information

Information/Organization

The script is based on one product.

Writing Strategy

Choose a type of product to advertise. Search the Internet and take notes on the product.

I totally love snowboarding, so I always read up on the best new equipment. When I found out that I had to write a TV commercial, it didn't take me long to decide what kind of product to advertise. You really need the right kind of clothes to stay warm, dry, and safe on the slopes, so I decided to make my commercial about a made-up brand of snowboarding pants called ChillSnowriders.

The first thing I did was log onto the Internet and search for some Web sites that sell snowboarding clothes. I looked at the special features and fabrics of several styles of pants. After deciding what I wanted my product to be like, I wrote down my ideas.

Information About Snowboarding Pants

highback waist that keeps the snow out

large front pockets

need extra padding or fabric around knees and seat

reinforced knees

elastic cuffs

leg vents with zipper

General Notes:
- must be loose fitting and comfortable
- must be waterproof, windproof, and breathable
- outer shell: nylon
- lining: wicking mesh and taffeta

Practice!

Now it's your turn. Choose an interesting product or service to advertise. Then, do some basic research and take useful notes.

Prewriting Organize Ideas

Information/Organization   Ideas are well sequenced.

Writing Strategy   Choose a sales technique. Make a Storyboard to sequence ideas.

> **Writer's Term_____**
>
> **Sales Technique**
> A **sales technique** is the method used to persuade people to buy a product.

In order to sell my product, I need to choose the right sales technique. I'll use the chart on the next page to help me get started.

I'm selling snowboarding pants, so my audience will probably consist of kids like me. I know the "scientific approach" would be boring to them, so I won't use it. The "animated ad" could work, but that would be hard for me to produce. I think that I'd be a great salesperson, so I'm going to use the "testimonial," featuring me—the famous Luis Rios—as the expert on my product. After I write my script, I'll get to star in my own commercial!

Common Sales Techniques

The Bandwagon Ad	pictures a group of people using and enjoying a product. The message is usually "EVERYBODY'S using this product, and so should you! Join the crowd!"
The Testimonial	uses familiar faces—sports figures, actors, and other famous people—to endorse a product. The message is usually "You know me, and you can trust me. I use this product, and you should, too!"
The Good Times/ Good Friends Ad	pictures happy people enjoying themselves and each other's company. The setting for these ads is generally a warm, cozy environment or an exciting, exotic location where people are engaged in lively activities. The message is usually "If you use this product, you will have good times and good friends, too."
The Humorous Ad	includes jokes, funny situations, or catch phrases that entertain the audience. This is a "feel good" approach. Because the audience enjoys the advertisement, some viewers are likely to have positive thoughts about the product.
The Animated Ad	uses cartoonlike animals, people, or fictional creatures to sell a product. The audience is usually familiar with the animated character (from a movie, a comic strip, or other advertising). But sometimes a new character is introduced and used instead.
Scientific Approach	uses many scientific-sounding terms and charts to impress the audience. The message is usually "You can believe us because we have scientific evidence to back up our claims."

Now it's your turn. Read the sales techniques on this page. Then, pick the best one for your commercial.

Prewriting Organize Ideas

Information/Organization

Ideas are well sequenced.

Writing Strategy

Choose a sales technique. Make a Storyboard to sequence ideas.

✏️ **Writer's Term___**

Storyboard

A **Storyboard** can help you sequence the main points of a TV commercial. Each frame represents a new idea or event.

TV is visual, so I have to get an idea of what people will "see" when they hear the words in my script. First, I'll use a Storyboard to organize my ideas into six key scenes. Then, I'll draw a picture for each scene.

STORYBOARD

① At the start of the commercial, announcers introduce themselves along with Luis Rios, who is competing in a halfpipe event. The announcer says Rios is being sponsored by ChillSnowriders pants.

② Rios comes to a dramatic stop in front of the camera. The crowd is cheering wildly. A fan shouts, "Hey, dude! Nice ChillSnowriders!"

3 Rios steps out of his bindings and picks up his board. As he walks toward the camera, a TV announcer tells him that he's won and asks about the secret of his success.

4 Rios talks about how ChillSnowriders are essential to his performance. He praises their fit, their warmth, and their ability to wick away moisture.

5 He steps up to the center platform and receives his gold medal. The crowd begins cheering again. TV announcer: "Be unbeatable! Wear ChillSnowriders—the only choice of champions."

6 The camera zooms in on Rios. He smiles and holds up his board. A big ChillSnowriders logo appears on it. Freeze frame.

Practice!

Now it's your turn. Make a Storyboard to plan your commercial.

Reflect

What do you think of my sales technique? Is my Storyboard convincing?

Drafting Write a Draft

Voice/Audience

The script begins with words and images that grab the audience's attention.

Writing Strategy

Begin with words and images that grab the audience's attention.

I'm ready to write my script. The rubric says that I should begin with words and images that grab my audience's attention. I'll begin with an exciting setting—a snowboarding competition. Then, I'll have two sportscasters address the audience. To draw viewers in further, I'll use words that are common to the snowboarding scene.

While drafting, I'll use my Storyboard to keep my writing on track. I'll do my best with spelling and grammar, but I won't focus too much on mistakes right now. I can always go back and fix those later.

Proofreading Marks

⅃ Indent	ℓ Take out something
≡ Make a capital	⊙ Add a period
/ Make a small letter	⑤ℙ Spelling error
∧ Add something	¶ New paragraph

[DRAFT]

[attention-grabbing image]

ChillSnowriders

a TV Commercial by Luis Rios

First Sportscaster: A great good afternoon, Extreme fans! I'm Jim

Smith, and this is Carol Jones. We're here at the Annual Big Air

Competition in beautiful New Hampshire, and the crowd is really

stoked. Right now you're watching the current champion, Luis Rios,

shredding his way to a sure victory in the halfpipe competition.

As always, Rios is sponsored by ChillSnowriders, makers of the

world's finest snowboarding pants. [attention-grabbing words]

Second Sportscaster: Whoa! Rios caught some really big air there!

Did you see that amazing burger flip? This guy is unbelievable! I

think he's done it again, Jim!

(Rios comes to a dramatic stop right in front of the camera.)

Fan: Hey, dude! Nice ChillSnowriders!

(Rios nods to the fan, steps out of his bindings, picks up his board,

and begins walking toward the winners platform.)

Smith: Hey, Luis! You've won! What's the secret of your success?

Practice!

Now it's your turn. Write a draft
that begins with attention-grabbing
words and images.

Reflect

What do you think? Did I choose an
interesting setting? Will my words and
images draw the audience in?

Revising Extend Writing

 Content/ Ideas

The script ends with a clear call to action.

Writing Strategy   Add a clear call to action at the end of my script.

Writer's Term

Call to Action

A **call to action** is an appeal to the audience to buy, try, or use whatever is being advertised. A call to action contains strong words and images that persuade the audience.

According to the rubric, my commercial needs to end with a clear call to action. Earlier in the commercial, I used the words *champion* and *unbeatable* to describe the character of Luis. I think I'll use these words again in my call to action to convince my audience that if they wear ChillSnowriders, they can be unbeatable champions, too!

[DRAFT]

(The camera zooms in on Rios. Him looks into the camera, smiles broadly, and holds his board over his head. The ChillSnowriders logo appears across the board, and the frame freezes.)

Jones: You can be unbeatable, too! Wear ChillSnowriders. They're the only choice of champions!

[added a clear call to action]

Practice!

Now it's your turn. Add a clear call to action at the end of your script.

Reflect

Have my revisions made my commercial stronger?

Revising Clarify Writing

Word Choice/ Clarity

All words and images are clear.

Writing Strategy

Delete any unnecessary, irrelevant, or confusing words and images.

I read my draft to my classmate Jack. He liked it, but he was a little confused about one part that didn't seem to fit. The rubric says all my words and images should be clear, so I'll get rid of the unnecessary information now.

[DRAFT]

[deleted an unclear image]

Rios: Well, ChillSnowriders are loose fitting, which means that it allows great freedom of movement and the ability to layer in extreme weather conditions. ~~I remember getting caught in a blizzard once. Man, that was intense! It was so white out that I couldn't see my hand in front of my face.~~ ChillSnowriders are waterproof, windproof, and they have a special lining that wicks moisture away from my body.

Practice!

Now it's your turn. Review your draft to see if you have included any unnecessary or irrelevant parts that should be deleted.

Editing Check Sentences

Sentence Fluency

Short, exclamatory sentences create a fast pace throughout.

Writing Strategy

Use short, exclamatory sentences to create a fast pace.

Writer's Term

Exclamatory Sentences

Exclamatory sentences express strong feelings and end with an exclamation point. Normally, they are used sparingly. But in a commercial, many exclamatory sentences can be used to create a fast pace.

Commercials are short, so I know I have to be quick with information. The rubric says to use short, exclamatory sentences to create a fast pace, so here's how I rewrote one long sentence. I also saw a compound personal pronoun that I used incorrectly, so I fixed that, too.

[DRAFT]

[formed an exclamatory sentence]

My ChillSnowriders help, too, ~~because they really help keep me warm and dry when I'm snowboarding.~~! My team and I recommend them

ourselves
~~ourself~~. They're essential to our performance!

[corrected a compound personal pronoun error]

Practice!

It's your turn. Make your writing strong and lively by using short, exclamatory sentences.

Editing Proofread Writing

Writer's Term

Pronouns and Antecedents

A **pronoun** is a word that takes the place of a noun. Pronouns must have clear antecedents. An **antecedent** is the word that a pronoun refers to or replaces. A pronoun must agree with its antecedent in number (singular or plural), gender (male or female), and case (subject or object).

N ow it's time to proofread my script. I'll check for errors in spelling and punctuation, but the rubric also says to make sure that I've used pronouns correctly. I'll do all of this now.

[DRAFT]

[corrected a pronoun-antecedent error]

He

(The camera zooms in on Rios. H̶i̶m̶ looks into the camera, smiles broadly, and holds his board over his head. The ChillSnowriders logo appears across the board, and the frame freezes.)

Practice!

Now it's your turn. Edit your draft for spelling, punctuation, and capitalization. Also, make sure that pronouns and antecedents are used correctly.

Reflect

I worked hard at using exclamatory sentences, pronouns, and antecedents. Did this strengthen my writing? Is the pace of my commercial quick enough?

Pronouns and Antecedents

KNOW the RULE

A **pronoun** is a word that can take the place of a noun. It must have a clear **antecedent**. An antecedent is the word that a pronoun refers to or replaces. A pronoun must agree with its antecedent in number (singular or plural), gender (male or female), and case (subject or object).
Example: My aunt uses that shampoo. **She** says **it** works well.

Subject pronouns include *I, he, she, we,* and *they.* Use a subject pronoun as the subject of a clause or sentence.
Example: Jack and **I** like it, too.

Object pronouns include *me, him, her, us,* and *them.* Use an object pronoun after an action verb or preposition.
Example: Mom paid Tim and Todd. She paid **them** $10.

The pronouns *it* and *you* can be either subjects or objects.
Example: **You** bought **it**. **It** belongs to **you**.

Practice the Rule

On a separate sheet of paper, rewrite each of the following sentences. Then, circle the antecedent in each sentence and write the correct pronoun on the blank line.

1. My friends and I were in a restaurant, and _____ were eating lunch.

2. We heard this man behind us, and _____ had the greatest voice.

3. The man was telling a story, and _____ sounded like an announcer.

4. Christa and Peter thought _____ might know him.

5. His voice sounded familiar because _____ was rich and deep.

Apply the Rule

Read this script, noting any pronoun and antecedent errors. On a separate sheet of paper, rewrite the commercial correctly.

Tug-a-Bone
a TV Commercial

(The scene is a family room. The camera shows a dog, sad and bored, with its head on its paws. Then, the camera zooms out to show two girls.)

Jill: What's wrong with Molly? Is she sick?

Rose: No, it is just bored.

Jill: I know what Molly needs—a Tug-a-Bone!

(The camera shows Molly suddenly picking up his head, as if she understands the conversation.)

Rose: What's a Tug-a-Bone?

Jill: She is a new dog toy. I just got one for my dog Toby, and I forgot to take them out of my coat pocket.

(Jill holds up a Tug-a-Bone, which looks like a small, bone-shaped pillow. Rose grabs one end, and Jill tugs on the other. As the bone is tugged, he lights up in the middle. Molly leaps up and runs over, barking. Rose lets Molly tug on the toy.)

Rose: Here, Molly! Get the Tug-a-Bone! Hey, Jill, her really likes it!

Jill: I knew she would! Uh . . . Rose? Is him ever going to let go?

(Suddenly, Molly tugs the toy out of Rose's grasp and runs off.)

Rose: Molly! Come back here with that Tug-a-Bone!

Announcer: Get a new Tug-a-Bone today. Your dog might never let her go! Available wherever pet products are sold.

Publishing Share Writing

Perform the commercial for my class.

Now that I've finished my script, I want to publish it. I could include it in a class anthology or post it on a bulletin board, but that isn't lively enough. A TV commercial is meant to be viewed, so I'll perform mine for my class. I'll need to get some classmates to act in my commercial, and then I'll need to make copies of my script. I should also show everyone my Storyboard. We'll need to rehearse the lines and figure out what actions to use. Before all that, I'll read through my work one last time to make sure it includes all of the items on my checklist.

My Checklist

✓ The script "sells" one product.

✓ The opening grabs the audience's attention.

✓ There is a clear call to action at the end.

✓ All words and images are focused on the sales goal.

✓ Short, exclamatory sentences provide a fast, commercial-like pace.

✓ Spelling, capitalization, and punctuation are all correct. Pronouns and antecedents are used correctly.

Practice!

Now it's your turn. Make a checklist to check your TV commercial script. Then, make a final draft to publish.

ChillSnowriders

a TV Commercial by Luis Rios

1

First Sportscaster: A great good afternoon, Extreme fans! I'm Jim Smith, and this is Carol Jones. We're here at the Annual Big Air Competition in beautiful New Hampshire, and the crowd is really stoked. Right now you're watching the current champion, Luis Rios, shredding his way to a sure victory in the halfpipe competition. As always, Rios is sponsored by ChillSnowriders, makers of the world's finest snowboarding pants.

Second Sportscaster: Whoa! Rios caught some really big air there! Did you see that amazing burger flip? This guy is unbelievable! I think he's done it again, Jim!

2

(Rios comes to a dramatic stop right in front of the camera.)

Fan: Hey, dude! Nice ChillSnowriders!

(3)

(Rios nods to the fan, steps out of his bindings, picks up his board, and begins walking toward the winners' platform.)

Smith: Hey, Luis! You've won! What's the secret of your success?

Rios: Practice, skill, and determination. My ChillSnowriders help, too! My team and I recommend them ourselves. They're essential to our performance!

Jones: How so?

(4)

Rios: Well, ChillSnowriders are loose fitting, which means that they allow great freedom of movement and the ability to layer in extreme weather conditions. ChillSnowriders are waterproof, windproof, and they have a special lining that wicks moisture away from my body. They keep me warm and dry at all times. ChillSnowriders are unbeatable!

Smith: Just like you!

6

(The camera zooms in on Rios. He looks into the camera, smiles broadly, and holds his board over his head. The ChillSnowriders logo appears across the board, and the frame freezes.)

Jones: You can be unbeatable, too! Wear ChillSnowriders. They're the only choice of champions!

5

(Rios steps up to the center platform and receives his gold medal. Loud, pulsing music is playing in the background, and the crowd is cheering wildly.)

Reflect

What did you think? Did I use all the traits of a good TV commercial script? Check my writing against the rubric, and don't forget to use the rubric to check your own work, too.

Ways to Publish a TV Commercial Script

As you decide how to publish your work, it's a good idea to think about who might want to read it. Then, you can figure out the best way to share it. Here are some ideas for publishing your TV commercial.

✓ **Read your script to your school's business teacher. Then, discuss his or her feedback.**

✓ **Perform your script as a commercial break during a school assembly, variety show, or other performance.**

 Perform your commercial on videotape.

✓ **Include your commercial as part of a "Class Ads" publication.**

✓ **Take your script home and share it with your family.**

Writing Across the Content Areas
TV Commercial Script

Your school subjects can be a great source of writing ideas. Choose a subject and see how many related topics you can brainstorm. Check out these examples.

Math
- Write a commercial that compares the costs of two similar items, focusing on how much viewers will save if they buy one of them.

- Develop an idea for a math board game. Then, write a TV commercial about it.

Language Arts
- Do you have a favorite author? Write a script for a TV commercial that advertises his or her latest book.

- Write a TV commercial for computer software that promises to help viewers learn a foreign language.

Art and/or Music
- Advertise a concert by your favorite musical artist.

- Make up a new musical instrument. Then, write a TV commercial about it.

What's a **Persuasive Speech?**

It's a type of persuasive writing that tries to convince listeners to take a specific action. I'm not afraid to take a stand, so writing this speech should be interesting—as long as I pick an important topic!

What's in a **Persuasive Speech?**

Call to Action
This is the purpose of my speech—to get people to do something about the problem I describe in my writing. Getting people to act is going to take some persuasion!

Evidence
I'll use evidence to back up the opinions and arguments in my speech. I know it's the little things that win people over, so I'll include facts, examples, and details as evidence in my speech.

Convincing Tone
This is how I want my speech to sound. I want my audience to agree with me, but also to feel strongly enough to take action. To create a convincing tone, I'll make strong, calm statements that rely on evidence rather than hype or loaded words.

Questions and Answers
Often, speakers can persuade people by answering their questions. As I write, I'll think about the questions my audience might have. Then, I'll provide the answers in my speech.

Why write a Persuasive Speech?

There are a bunch of reasons for writing a persuasive speech. I'll list some reasons here, and I'll keep them in mind as I decide what to write about.

Information

A persuasive speech focuses on a problem and calls on listeners to act. But the audience might not have enough information to take a stand, so it's important to provide it for them.

Persuasion

In a persuasive speech, it's not enough to share your views. The speaker needs to convince the audience to agree with his or her ideas. Keeping this purpose in mind can help a person make decisions while writing.

Action

Often, a speaker wants an immediate response from listeners—a response that involves taking action to solve the problem described in the speech. Having this specific purpose can help a speechwriter maintain focus.

Decision-Making

Sometimes a writer can be clear about a problem but unsure about the best course of action. Writing a speech can be a good way to analyze the situation, come up with solutions, and decide on the best course of action.

Persuasive Speech Writing Traits

I know that there are six traits of good writing. Here's a list of what makes a good persuasive speech. I'll use it later to help me write my speech.

Information/ Organization	The speech is focused on one problem. The speech is organized around a call to action.
Voice/ Audience	A convincing tone is used to persuade the audience.
Content/ Ideas	Persuasive details are used throughout.
Word Choice/ Clarity	Neutral words are used to avoid bias throughout.
Sentence Fluency	The question-and-answer sentence pattern is used effectively throughout.
Grammar/ Mechanics	Spelling, punctuation, and capitalization are correct. Progressive tense verbs are used correctly.

I can use Nola Fabian's persuasive speech on the next page as a model for my own writing. Later, we'll check out how Nola used the traits to help her write.

Save Our Books

by Nola Fabian

Imagine an ordinary bookcase filled with your favorite books. Smell the worn pages? Are the titles beckoning you? See the crinkled jacket covers and ragged spines? Well, savor that thought because publishing companies are starting to post books on-line, which means that hand-held books might become obsolete. That's why I'm asking you to take action by demanding that publishers continue to develop and support "real" books. **← Call to Action**

Am I sounding a false alarm? I don't think so. Recently, publishers have made a startling number of titles available on-line, and growing numbers of authors are also allowing some form of on-line publication. **Questions and Answers**

Soon, publishers may even find ways to post books on the Internet after they go out of print. Just think of the devastating effect this will have on book collectors (and traders) worldwide. Many of these people have spent the better part of their lives collecting out-of-print titles and valuable old books.

So you may ask, what has led to this recent trend in publishing? In a word: technology. Word processing software makes it easy to manage massive amounts of text. The Internet has become a literate community, and advances in computer systems include a variety of portable gadgets.

OK, so it is possible to move the world of literature onto the Web. But is it probable? In some areas, it is becoming more profitable to publish solely on the Web. This summer, a handful of magazine publishers announced that they will be posting some issues exclusively on-line. **← Evidence**

So if publishing on-line is cheaper and easier, why fight it? Well, a book is more than a collection of words. Many readers enjoy the weight of the book, the texture of the cover, the smell of the ink, and the sound of the pages rustling. Hand-held books are often associated with meaningful memories of a person's journey into the literate world. Not to mention, some people cannot afford to access books on-line. While computers are readily available in most schools and libraries, not everyone owns a home PC. **← Convincing Tone**

For these reasons, we need to act now to keep books from being destroyed by the Internet. I have here a petition that calls on publishers to pledge their commitment to hand-held books. Please sign it before you leave, and don't forget to stop by your local bookstore on your way home and buy a hand-held book. You never know—it could be the last "real" book you ever buy! **← Call to Action**

Persuasive Speech

Rubric

The traits of a good persuasive speech from page 366 have been used to make the rubric below. By using 1, 2, 3, or 4 check marks to judge each trait, you can decide how well any persuasive speech was written.

	Excelling ✓✓✓✓	Achieving ✓✓✓	Developing ✓✓	Beginning ✓
Information/ Organization	The speech is focused on one problem and is organized around a call to action.	The speech is mainly focused on one problem and is mostly organized.	The speech is somewhat focused on one problem and is loosely organized.	The speech should be focused on one problem and should be more organized.
Voice/ Audience	A convincing tone is used to persuade the audience.	A convincing tone is used in many areas.	A convincing tone is used in some areas.	A convincing tone should be used more often.
Content/ Ideas	Persuasive details are used throughout.	Persuasive details are used in many areas.	Persuasive details are used in some areas.	More persuasive details are needed.
Word Choice/ Clarity	Neutral words are used to avoid bias throughout.	Neutral words are used in many areas.	Neutral words are used in some areas.	Neutral words should be used more often.
Sentence Fluency	The question-and-answer sentence pattern is used effectively throughout.	The question-and-answer sentence pattern is sometimes used effectively.	The question-and-answer sentence pattern is rarely used.	The question-and-answer sentence pattern should be used more often.
Grammar/ Mechanics	Spelling, grammar, and progressive tense verbs are used correctly.	There are a few errors in spelling, grammar, and progressive tense verb usage.	There are several errors in spelling, grammar, and progressive tense verb usage.	There are many errors in spelling, grammar, and progressive tense verb usage.

Using the Rubric to Study the Model

Now, let's use the rubric to check Nola Fabian's persuasive speech, "Save Our Books." How many check marks would you give Nola for each trait?

Information/Organization

- The speech is focused on one problem.
- The speech is organized around a call to action.

Nola introduces a problem early in her speech, and she remains focused on the issue throughout. She also introduces a call to action early on.

[from the writing model]

Well, savor that thought because publishing companies are starting to post books on-line, which means that hand-held books might become obsolete. That's why I'm asking you to take action by demanding that publishers continue to develop and support "real" books.

Voice/Audience

- A convincing tone is used to persuade the audience.

Nola persuades her audience with reasons and details. This contributes to a strong, convincing tone that doesn't sound wildly excited or desperate for support. See if you are convinced by the tone Nola uses in the following paragraph.

[from the writing model]

Soon, publishers may even find ways to post books on the Internet after they go out of print. Just think of the devastating effect this will have on book collectors (and traders) worldwide. Many of these people have spent the better part of their lives collecting out-of-print titles and valuable old books.

Persuasive Speech

• **Persuasive details are used throughout.**

Nola's speech is effective because she explains each reason with facts, examples, and other details that persuade her audience. In this example, she includes several persuasive details to explain why the audience should fight against on-line books.

[from the writing model]

Many readers enjoy the weight of the book, the texture of the cover, the smell of the ink, and the sound of the pages rustling. Hand-held books are often associated with meaningful memories of a person's journey into the literate world. Not to mention, some people cannot afford to access books on-line. While computers are readily available in most schools and libraries, not everyone owns a home PC.

• **Neutral words are used to avoid bias throughout.**

I appreciate how Nola uses persuasive reasoning without resorting to biased or loaded words. For example, in the lines below, she uses *profitable* instead of *lucrative*, which can sometimes imply greed. And she uses the neutral word *publishers* rather than *big corporations*, which can have a negative meaning.

[from the writing model]

In some areas, it is becoming more profitable to publish solely on the Web. This summer, a handful of magazine publishers announced that they will be posting some issues exclusively on-line.

Sentence Fluency

- The question-and-answer sentence pattern is used effectively throughout.

I like how Nola sharpens the focus of her speech by predicting her audience's questions about the topic. She spends most of her speech posing these questions and then answering them, creating effective question-and-answer patterns.

[from the writing model]

Am I sounding a false alarm? I don't think so. Recently, publishers have made a startling number of titles available on-line, and growing numbers of authors are also allowing some form of on-line publication.

Grammar/Mechanics

- Spelling, punctuation, and capitalization are correct. Progressive tense verbs are used correctly.

Nola's speech flows smoothly because there aren't any mistakes. When she shifts from one verb tense to another, she always gets it right. In the passage below, notice how she switches from the present tense *is possible* to the present progressive tense *is becoming* in one smooth transition.

[from the writing model]

OK, so it is possible to move the world of literature onto the Web. But is it probable? In some areas, it is becoming more profitable to publish solely on the Web.

My Turn!

I'm going to write a persuasive speech about something I feel strongly about. I'll follow the rubric and use good writing strategies. Read on to see how I do it!

Prewriting **Gather Information**

Information/Organization   The speech is focused on one problem.

Writing Strategy   Choose a problem that I feel strongly about. List a call to action, along with several reasons for the request.

I'm excited about writing a persuasive speech because I'm an opinionated person. I could write about the debate over the new shopping center in town, but Nola's speech made me think of a better topic: downloading music from the Internet. My dad is a musician, so we've talked a lot about this. I know that my position—copyrighted music should not be downloaded—is not very popular with my friends, so this should be interesting! I'll start by writing down my call to action. Then, I'll include some reasons for my position.

My Notes

Call to Action: Stop illegal downloads.

Reason 1: It violates copyright laws.

Reason 2: It teaches disrespect for the law.

Reason 3: It harms musicians.

Practice!

Now it's your turn. Choose an issue that you feel strongly about. Decide on a call to action, and jot down reasons for your position.

Prewriting Organize Ideas

Information/Organization

The speech is organized around a call to action.

Writing Strategy

Make a Persuasion Map to organize the reasons for my call to action.

A ccording to the rubric, my speech should be organized around a call to action. I can use my notes to make a Persuasion Map, which will help me plan my speech.

Writer's Term

Persuasion Map
A **Persuasion Map** organizes reasons, examples, and facts that support a call to action.

PERSUASION MAP

Call to Action: Stop illegal downloads.

Reason 1: It violates copyright laws.
- **Detail:** Songs composed after 1922 are protected by law.
- **Detail:** Royalty fees must be paid for songs.
- **Detail:** People have been punished for violating the United States Copyright Act.

Reason 2: It teaches disrespect for the law.
- **Detail:** Disrespect for the law is distressing.
- **Detail:** Disrespect is taught to younger siblings.
- **Detail:** Illegal downloads can be a "gateway" to breaking other laws.

Reason 3: It harms musicians.
- **Detail:** Royalties are musicians' livelihood.
- **Detail:** Musicians' wages are lost.
- **Detail:** Dad compares illegal downloading with stealing from an art gallery.

Practice!

Now it's your turn. Make a Persuasion Map to organize your speech.

Reflect

How did I do? Is my call to action clear? Did I include enough details to support it?

Drafting Write a Draft

Voice/Audience — A convincing tone is used to persuade the audience.

Writing Strategy — Use a convincing tone to persuade the audience.

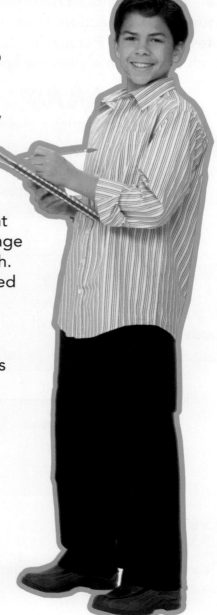

Now I'll use my Persuasion Map to help me write my speech. The rubric says I should use a convincing tone to persuade my audience. I already know that many of my readers (my classmates) are opposed to my view, so I will have to do a lot of convincing! I thought long and hard about what it takes for someone to convince me of something, and I decided that I will present my reasons, using strong language to explain details. I have to be careful, though. I know it will turn people off if I get too excited or emotional. So I'll focus on remaining calm but convincing throughout my speech.

I'll do my best with spelling, grammar, and punctuation, but I know that I can fix mistakes at any point in the writing process. For now, though, I'll pay close attention to my use of compound personal pronouns, since I know they sometimes give me trouble.

[DRAFT]

Stop Stealing Songs

by Luis

Last week, my friend and I is working on a history project together, and I borrowed his laptop for a minute to do some research. I work best with a little "study music," so he reccomended one of the songs in his music folder. When I opened the folder, however, I was shocked. It contained almost 3,000 songs. He told me that he himself had downloaded them for free.

[correct use of a compound personal pronoun]

Here's the problem: These songs aren't really free—they are copyrighted material that has been shared illegally. I know that my views on this issue are unpopular, and that downloading music has been such a wide spread practice that it has become a part of our modern culture. However, I think that if more people understand why this practice is wrong, they will stop. That's why I'm here today, asking each and every one of you to stop these illegal downloads.

[convincing tone]

Practice!

Now it's your turn. Write a draft using a convincing tone to persuade your audience.

Reflect

What do you think? Is my tone convincing? Will it help persuade my audience?

Revising Extend Writing

Content/Ideas   Persuasive details are used throughout.

Writing Strategy   Add persuasive details throughout.

After I finished my draft, I checked the rubric. It reminded me to use persuasive details throughout my speech. I knew that this would help explain my reasons in a convincing way, so I added some persuasive details to a part of my draft that sounded a little vague.

[DRAFT]

Because my dad is a musician, I know that any song composed by an American before 1922 is in the public domain. That means that it belongs to everyone and can be shared or performed freely. So when you download songs on the Internet, you are violating the United States Copyright Act.

[added persuasive details] → But music composed after 1922 cannot be used without permission. And even with permission, royalties must be paid.

Practice!

Now it's your turn. Add persuasive details to your draft to help convince readers of your opinions.

Revising Clarify Writing

Word Choice/ Clarity

Writing Strategy

Neutral words are used to avoid bias throughout.

Replace biased or loaded words with neutral words.

Writer's Term

Biased Words/Loaded Words
Loaded words and **biased words** express unfair judgment. For example, *shack* might be used as a biased or negatively loaded word for the more neutral term *house*.

I checked the rubric again and was reminded how important it is to avoid biased and loaded words. I want to persuade my audience with facts and details, not with tricky language. But when I reread my draft, I was surprised to see that I had included some biased words. Here's an example of how I changed them to neutral words. I also checked my use of pronouns since they've given me trouble in the past.

[DRAFT]

[used neutral words]

defendants

Many of these ~~criminals~~, some of whom are teenagers just like us,

[correct use of a pronoun]

are currently on trial. If convicted, they will have to pay hundreds of

thousands of dollars in fines. Now, you're probably thinking there's

file-sharers

no way that the government can prosecute all ~~thieves~~. But are you

really willing to take that chance?

Practice!

Now it's your turn. Review your draft to see if you used any biased or loaded words. If so, replace them with neutral words.

Reflect

Is my word choice persuasive but unbiased? Are my revisions convincing without being offensive?

Editing Check Sentences

Sentence Fluency

The question-and-answer sentence pattern is used effectively throughout.

Writing Strategy

Make use of the question-and-answer sentence pattern.

After once again comparing my speech to the rubric, I realized that I often used the question-and-answer sentence pattern to address my audience's concerns. However, I know that I can also use the question-and-answer sentence pattern to convince listeners to think further about the consequences of their actions. Here's a portion of my draft where I used the pattern for this purpose.

[DRAFT]

[used the question-and-answer sentence pattern]

Even though people might be "getting away with" illegal file-

sharing, it is really a broader issue. Many of us feel that it's

somehow OK to break the law.

Practice!

Now it's your turn. Strengthen your speech by using the question-and-answer sentence pattern.

Editing Proofread Writing

Grammar/Mechanics Spelling, punctuation, and capitalization are correct. Progressive tense verbs are used correctly.

Writing Strategy Make sure that progressive tense verbs are used correctly.

Writer's Term

Progressive Tense Verbs
Progressive tense verbs are verbs that show continuing action. To form the progressive tense, use the correct form of the verb *to be* before another verb ending in *–ing*.

It's finally time to proofread my speech. I always edit for errors in spelling and punctuation, but the rubric says to also make sure that progressive tense verbs are used correctly. Here's an example of some of my edits.

[DRAFT]

When a record label produces and sells an artist's music, the artist

is paid royalty fees for each copy sold. This is how artists make

money—its they're job. When you download an artist's music without

paying for it, you is stealing that person's livelihood.

[corrected a progressive tense verb error]

Practice!

Now it's your turn. Edit your draft for grammar and mechanics, making sure that progressive tense verbs are also used correctly.

Grammar/Mechanics

For more practice with progressive tense verbs, use the exercises on the next two pages.

Reflect

I worked hard to edit my draft. Do my edits enhance the writing?

Progressive Tense Verbs

KNOW the RULE

The **progressive tense** shows continuing action. To form the **present progressive tense,** add *am, is,* or *are* in front of a present participle verb (a verb ending in *–ing*).
Example: Joe **is walking** home.

To form the **past progressive tense,** add *was* or *were* in front of a present participle verb.
Example: Joe **was walking** home.

To form the **future progressive tense,** add *will be* in front of a present participle verb.
Example: Joe **will be walking** home tomorrow.

Practice the Rule

Number a separate sheet of paper 1–5. Read the sentences below. If a sentence contains a correctly used progressive tense verb, write the word *Correct*. If it contains an error, write the sentence correctly.

1. My friend Nicole is taking voice lessons after school.

2. Currently, her music school will holding auditions for teacher placements.

3. I were thinking about signing up for an audition.

4. Nicole said if I get the job, I will be teaching her class.

5. But last night, I am feeling nervous about it.

Apply the Rule

Read the following persuasive speech, looking for progressive tense verb errors. Then, rewrite the speech correctly on another sheet of paper.

Give Back Our Instruments

This year, we returned to school in September to discover that some changes had been made to our curriculum. Instead of having a full-time music teacher, we is sharing one with another school. Plus, instrumental music class has been dropped.

These cutbacks are upset to many students and parents, so we have started a petition drive. We were aiming to get the school committee to restore instrumental music in our schools, so please sign the petition.

Why is instrumental music important? Well, some young people will grow up to become great musicians, but many will miss their chance if they are not given the opportunity to discover an instrument. The time to be exposed to a wide variety of instrument choices is now, when we be developing our interests.

So what's wrong with learning an instrument outside of school? Some families do not have the resources to rent an instrument. Others don't know enough about music to guide their children in this area. Schools are cut this option and, as a result, creating unequal access to music education.

Let's act before these fresh cutbacks begin to harden and set. This is too important to leave up to a few government leaders. Get involved. Sign the petition, and tell the school committee to restore the cuts.

Publishing Share Writing

Present my speech to the class.

Now that I've finished my speech, I can decide how to publish it. I feel strongly about the issue of illegal music downloads, and I'm curious to see how my classmates will react to my views. So I think I'll present my speech to the class. Before that, I'll read through it one last time to make sure it includes all of the items on my checklist.

My Checklist

✔ The speech focuses on one problem.

✔ It includes a call to action.

✔ The tone is convincing.

✔ Persuasive details help convince the audience to act.

✔ Loaded and biased words have been replaced with neutral words.

✔ Spelling, capitalization, and punctuation are all correct. Progressive tense verbs are used correctly.

Practice!

Now it's your turn. Make a checklist to check your speech. Then, make a final draft to publish.

Stop Stealing Songs

by Luis

Last week, my friend and I were working on a history project together, and I borrowed his laptop for a minute to do some research. I work best with a little "study music," so he recommended one of the songs in his music folder. When I opened the folder, however, I was shocked. It contained almost 3,000 songs. He told me that he himself had downloaded them for free.

Here's the problem: These songs aren't really free—they are copyrighted material that has been shared illegally. I know that my views on this issue are unpopular, and that downloading music has been such a widespread practice that it has become a part of our modern culture. However, I think that if more people understand why this practice is wrong, they will stop. That's why I'm here today, asking each and every one of you to stop these illegal downloads.

Why do I feel so strongly about this issue? First of all, it violates copyright laws, which makes it illegal. Because my dad is a musician, I know that any song composed by an American before 1922 is in the public domain. That means that it belongs to everyone and can be shared or performed freely. But music composed after 1922 cannot be used without permission. And even with permission, royalties must be paid. So when you download songs on the Internet, you are violating the United States Copyright Act.

What are the consequences of breaking this law? Most people believe there are none. But tell that to the many people who are being prosecuted and punished. Many of these defendants, some of whom are teenagers just like us, are currently on trial. If convicted, they will have to pay hundreds of thousands of dollars in fines. Now, you're probably thinking there's no way that the government can prosecute all file-sharers. But are you really willing to take that chance?

Even though people might be "getting away with" illegal file-sharing, isn't it really a broader issue? Many of us feel that it's somehow OK to break the law. Even worse, when we download illegal music, we teach this lack of respect to our younger brothers and sisters. And some kids might learn a more dangerous lesson: If it's OK to break one law, maybe it's OK to break others. When you look at it this way, illegal file-sharing could be a "gateway" to breaking other laws.

But the most important reason to stop illegal downloads concerns the songwriters. Music is composed by artists who own the rights to their songs. When a record label produces and sells an artist's music, the artist is paid royalty fees for each copy sold. This is how artists make money—it's their job.

When you download an artist's music without paying for it, you are stealing that person's livelihood.

As I mentioned before, my dad is a musician. Maybe that's why I feel so strongly about this issue. He knows that people find it hard to understand how anyone can actually "own" a piece of music. Once a song is played, it's out there on the public airwaves for everyone to hear, and it's true that no one can stop you from singing or playing a song unless, of course, you charge admission. But my dad recently gave me this analogy: Pirating music is the same as going into a sculptor's studio, deciding which piece of artwork you like, and walking out the door without paying for it. You wouldn't do that, would you? Then you shouldn't download music for free, either.

I hope I've made you think about what you're doing when you download "free" tunes. It's not like you have to give up music entirely. There are a lot of ways to build a great music library without spending tons of money. Start investigating these alternatives. Talk to your friends. And please, stop downloading copyrighted music for free.

Reflect

What do you think? Did I use all the traits of a good persuasive speech in my writing? Check it against the rubric, and don't forget to use the rubric to check your own speech, too.

Ways to Publish a
Persuasive Speech

When it's time to publish your writing, you should think about your audience. That way, you can figure out the best way to share your work. Here are some ideas for publishing your speech.

 Present your work as part of a class lineup of speeches called "Can I Convince You?"

Record your speech on videotape. Then, share it with an appropriate audience.

Include your speech as part of a class booklet called "Persuasive Ideas."

Enter your work in a local speech contest for young people.

 Take your speech home and present it to your family.

Writing Across the Content Areas
Persuasive Speech

Your school subjects can be a great source of writing ideas. Choose a subject and see how many related topics you can brainstorm. Check out these examples.

Science
- Is there something your community can do to help the environment? Write a speech persuading your audience to think globally.

- Which medical procedures should be covered by insurance? Take a stand and promote it in a speech.

Language Arts
- Should students be required to do summer reading? State your case and present it in a speech.

- Should students be required to learn a foreign language in school? Write a speech convincing others of your position.

Art and/or Music
- Should artists and musicians be subsidized by the government? Write a speech that calls for some form of government funding.

- Think of a way to include more art in your community. Then, promote it in a speech.

PERSUASIVE test writing

Read the Writing Prompt

When you take a writing test, you will be given a writing prompt. Most writing prompts have three parts:

Setup This part of the writing prompt gives you the background information you need to get ready to write.

Task This part of the writing prompt tells you exactly what you are supposed to write: a persuasive essay.

Scoring Guide This section tells how your writing will be scored. To do well on the test, you should include everything on the list.

Remember the rubrics you've used in writing class this year? When you take a writing test, you don't always have all of the information that's on a rubric. But a scoring guide is a lot like a rubric. It lists everything you need to think about to write a good paper. Like the rubrics you've used, many scoring guides are based on the six traits of writing:

Your school is looking for new ways to raise money to support social programs, such as afterschool sports and band. Some schools accept money from businesses in exchange for placing advertisements around their school facilities. The Super Soda Company has offered to buy your school an expensive scoreboard, provided they can place an advertisement for Super Soda on it. Do you think this is a good idea?

Write a persuasive essay to read to the school board. Decide whether you think the school should accept or reject this offer. Then, give reasons to support your opinion.

Be sure your writing

- is well organized. You should state a point of view, give a new reason in each paragraph, and then restate your opinion.

- clearly states your opinion for your reader.

- includes facts and examples that support each reason.

- does not contain any unnecessary ideas.

- includes conditional sentences.

- contains correct grammar, punctuation, capitalization, and spelling.

Writing Traits
in the Scoring Guide

Take a look at the scoring guide in the writing prompt on page 389. Not every writing prompt will include each of the six writing traits, but this one does. You can use this chart to help you better understand the connection between the scoring guide and the writing traits in the rubrics you've used.

Information/Organization

- Be sure your writing is well organized. You should state a point of view, give a new reason in each paragraph, and then restate your opinion.

Voice/Audience

- Be sure your writing clearly states your opinion for your reader.

Content/Ideas

- Be sure your writing includes facts and examples that support each reason.

Word Choice/Clarity

- Be sure your writing does not contain any unnecessary ideas.

Sentence Fluency

- Be sure your writing includes conditional sentences.

Grammar/Mechanics

- Be sure your writing contains correct grammar, punctuation, capitalization, and spelling.

Look at Mika Peters' persuasive essay on the next page. Did she follow the scoring guide?

Say "No, Thanks"

by Mika Peters

I know that Super Soda's offer of a new scoreboard for our school seems like a worthwhile offer, but I think the school board should politely say "no, thanks."

Many middle-school students tend to go along with the crowd. Because they want to do what other kids are doing, some students often have trouble making up their minds about what to wear, how to act, and what to eat. These kids sometimes purchase brand-name clothing to "fit in" with their peers. They buy the same brands of snacks and drinks that everyone else buys, instead of thinking for themselves.

Now, Super Soda has offered to give our school a new scoreboard for the gym. I'm sure the basketball fans would love it. But the scoreboard would probably display a large Super Soda advertisement so that no one would miss it.

You might ask yourself, what's wrong with that? Well, we kids see so many ads for products like Super Soda that we often don't even consider anything else when choosing a product. It's like we've all been brainwashed. When we go to a store or a vending machine, we usually pass up the healthy options and buy the junk food instead. That's because we reach for the product in the familiar package—the one with the same name that everyone else is buying.

I realize that some people are saying that the money the school could get from Super Soda would be enough to support special programs. I'm also aware that the school received over $20,000 last year from beverage sales in the Super Soda vending machines. I understand that the school wouldn't have to pay anything for our new scoreboard if we accept this offer. But wouldn't you agree that students' health is more important? If the scoreboard were free, that would be great. But in my opinion, the cost of the new scoreboard is way too high.

We students are never going to learn to make up our own minds or make smart choices if we keep allowing advertisers to brainwash us. That's why I'm taking a stand (and hoping you'll join me) by saying "no, thanks" to Super Soda's offer!

Using the Scoring Guide to Study the Model

Now we'll use the scoring guide to check Mika's writing test, "Say 'No, Thanks.'" Let's see how well her essay meets each of the six writing traits.

 Information/ Organization

- The essay is well organized.
- It states a point of view, gives a new reason in each paragraph, and then restates the writer's opinion.

Mika begins by stating her opinion on the topic. Then, she gives new reasons in each paragraph to support her point of view. She concludes by restating her opinion.

> We students are never going to learn to make up our own minds or make smart choices if we keep allowing advertisers to brainwash us. That's why I'm taking a stand (and hoping you'll join me) by saying "no, thanks" to Super Soda's offer!

 Voice/ Audience

- The writer clearly states an opinion for the reader.

In the first paragraph, it is clear that Mika understands the argument over the school scoreboard issue. But she clearly states her own opinion: the school should say "no, thanks" to Super Soda's offer.

> I know that Super Soda's offer of a new scoreboard for our school seems like a worthwhile offer, but I think the school board should politely say "no, thanks."

Content/Ideas

- **The essay contains facts and examples that support each reason.**

Mika uses many facts and examples to support her reasons. In this paragraph, she fully explains kids' vulnerability to advertising, citing examples of how they buy clothes and snacks just to "fit in."

Many middle-school students tend to go along with the crowd. Because they want to do what other kids are doing, some students often have trouble making up their minds about what to wear, how to act, and what to eat. These kids sometimes purchase brand-name clothing to "fit in" with their peers. They buy the same brands of snacks and drinks that everyone else buys, instead of thinking for themselves.

Word Choice/Clarity

- **The paper does not contain any unnecessary ideas.**

Everything Mika includes in her essay is clear and easy to understand. In this passage, she relates everything to her idea of rejecting Super Soda's offer.

Well, we kids see so many ads for products like Super Soda that we often don't even consider anything else when choosing a product. It's like we've all been brainwashed. When we go to a store or a vending machine, we usually pass up the healthy options and buy the junk food instead. That's because we reach for the product in the familiar package—the one with the same name that everyone else is buying.

Using the Scoring Guide to Study the Model

- **The essay contains conditional sentences.**

Mika uses conditional sentences to present several convincing and persuasive "what if" scenarios to her reader. The second and third sentences in this passage present the idea that "if" the school accepts Super Soda's offer, it will "probably" have a large advertisement on it.

Now, Super Soda has offered to give our school a new scoreboard for the gym. I'm sure the basketball fans would love it. But the scoreboard would probably display a large Super Soda advertisement so that no one would miss it.

- **The paper contains correct grammar, punctuation, capitalization, and spelling.**

It looks like Mika used correct grammar, spelling, capitalization, and punctuation. I know it's important to check for these kinds of mistakes, so I'll be sure to keep that in mind as I write. Don't forget to check for proper grammar and mechanics in your writing, too. This can be done at every step of the writing process.

Planning My Time

Before giving us a writing prompt, my teacher always tells us how much time we'll have to complete the test. Since I'm already familiar with each step of the writing process, I can plan how much time I'll need for each one. Then, I'll be sure to have enough time to complete the entire process. If the test takes an hour, here's how I'll organize my time. Planning your time will help you, too!

Step 4:
Editing
10 minutes

Step 1:
Prewriting
25 minutes

Step 3:
Revising
10 minutes

Step 2:
Drafting
15 minutes

Prewriting Study the Writing Prompt

Writing Strategy Study the writing prompt to be sure
I know what to do.

When I take a writing test, I always study my writing prompt before I begin. It usually has three parts (the setup, task, and scoring guide), but they're not always labeled. You should look for (and label) these sections on your writing prompt, and you should circle key words that tell what kind of writing you will be doing and who your audience will be. I circled my topic in red below. I also used purple to circle what kind of writing I'll be doing (a persuasive essay) and who my audience will be (the people in my town).

My Writing Test Prompt

Setup

Your town owns some wooded land called the old Wingate property. Some people believe the land should be preserved for activities such as hiking and bird watching. Others think the town should sell the property to a real estate developer and use the money on schools and other municipal services.

Task

Write a persuasive essay for your townspeople, explaining whether you think the land should be sold or preserved. Explain your reasons.

Scoring Guide

Be sure your writing

- is well organized. You should state a point of view, give a new reason in each paragraph, and then restate your opinion.

- clearly states your opinion for the reader.

- includes facts and examples that support each reason.

- does not contain any unnecessary ideas.

- includes conditional sentences.

- contains correct grammar, punctuation, capitalization, and spelling.

Think about how the scoring guide relates to the six traits of good writing in the rubrics you've studied. Not all of the traits will be included in every scoring guide, but you'll still want to remember them all in order to write a good essay.

- **Be sure your writing is well organized. You should state a point of view, give a new reason in each paragraph, and then restate your opinion.**

I want my reader to understand my point of view and the reasons for it, so organization is important.

- **Be sure your writing clearly states your opinion for the reader.**

I'll make sure to clearly state my opinion.

- **Be sure your writing includes facts and examples that support each reason.**

I have to remember to provide plenty of facts and examples to help support my opinion.

- **Be sure your writing does not contain any unnecessary ideas.**

Unnecessary ideas will weaken my argument, so I'll only include what's really important.

- **Be sure your writing includes conditional sentences.**

I can be more persuasive if I use conditional sentences that describe the "what ifs."

- **Be sure your writing contains correct grammar, punctuation, capitalization, and spelling.**

I know to check my grammar and mechanics whenever I write.

Prewriting Gather Information

 Information/Organization

Writing Strategy Respond to the task.

Writers always gather information before they begin writing, so that's what I'll do. Let's take another look at the task, since that's the part of the writing prompt that explains what I'm supposed to write. When you write for a test, you don't have much time, so you need to decide how you'll respond to the task before you start writing.

I'm supposed to write a persuasive essay about what the town should do with the old Wingate property. I already know I want the land to be saved, so I'll begin by jotting down the reasons why I feel this way.

Task — Write a (persuasive essay for your townspeople,) explaining whether you think the land should be sold or preserved. Explain your reasons.

Notes

✓ Open land costs the town less than developed land.

✓ Both people and animals benefit from open land.

✓ People need a place to get away.

✓ There's not much open land left in my town.

Remember! Be sure to think about how you're going to respond to the task before you start to write. Gather information by jotting down some notes.

Writing Strategy Choose a graphic organizer.

I don't have a lot of time, so now I'll choose a graphic organizer. I already listed the reasons why I think the old Wingate property should be saved, so I think an Outline will help me organize facts and examples that support each of my reasons.

I'll write my opinion at the top of the Outline, and I'll use Roman numerals for each of my reasons. Then, I'll use capital letters for supporting facts and examples.

Opinion: The Wingate property should be preserved for the future of our town.

I. Open land costs the town less than developed land.
   A. If the land is used for homes, more tax money will be needed for schools.
   B. More homes require more services like fire and police protection.
II. Both people and animals benefit from open land.
   A. Animals would lose their habitats.
   B. Animals would come into people's yards and eat flowers and bushes.
III. People need a place to get away.
   A. We should get fresh air and sun outside, not inside a gym.
   B. Our moods are better when we find places with quiet space.
   C. I love to sit in a tree and read a book.
IV. There's not much open land left in our town.
   A. Only 20% of our town is undeveloped.
   B. We need to save open land while we can.

Reflect
Did I include enough reasons to help persuade my readers?

Remember! Choose a graphic organizer that will help you identify your main reasons and supporting details.

Prewriting Check the Scoring Guide

Information/Organization

Writing Strategy Check my graphic organizer against the scoring guide.

Without much time to revise during a test, prewriting is really important. Before I start to write, I'll check my Outline against the scoring guide in the writing prompt.

Opinion: The Wingate property should be preserved for the future of our town.

I. Open land costs the town less than developed land.
   A. If the land is used for homes, more tax money will be needed for schools.
   B. More homes require more services like fire and police protection.
II. Both people and animals benefit from open land.
   A. Animals would lose their habitats.
   B. Animals would come into people's yards and eat flowers and bushes.
III. People need a place to get away.
   A. We should get fresh air and sun outside, not inside a gym.
   B. Our moods are better when we find places with quiet space.
   C. I love to sit in a tree and read a book.
IV. There's not much open land left in our town.
   A. Only 20% of our town is undeveloped.
   B. We need to save open land while we can.

Information/Organization

- Be sure your writing is well organized. You should state a point of view, give a new reason in each paragraph, and then restate your opinion.

I'll just turn my Outline into an essay! I'll state my opinion in my introduction, and I'll use the reasons from each Roman numeral to make a new paragraph. Then, I'll wrap things up in my conclusion.

Voice/Audience

- Be sure your writing clearly states your opinion for the reader.

I'll use the opinion from the top of my Outline to form my lead paragraph.

Content/Ideas

- Be sure your writing includes facts and examples that support each reason.

I'll use the facts and examples from my Outline to support each reason.

Word Choice/Clarity

- Be sure your writing does not contain any unnecessary ideas.

I'll check on this later. I might need to get rid of unnecessary information when I revise my essay.

Sentence Fluency

- Be sure your writing includes conditional sentences.

My Outline already includes a few conditional sentences, but I'll be sure to use more of them as I write.

Grammar/Mechanics

- Be sure your writing contains correct grammar, punctuation, capitalization, and spelling.

I'll check for proper grammar and mechanics when I edit my essay.

Remember! Compare your graphic organizer with the scoring guide before you start to write. This way, you'll know what to do when you begin drafting.

Reflect

My Outline seems pretty complete. Can you think of anything it's missing?

Drafting Write a Draft

 Writing Strategy Clearly state my opinion for the reader.

Well, it's time to start writing. But as I look back at the scoring guide, I see that it's important to clearly state my opinion for the reader. I'm going to use my opening paragraph to do this. This way the reader will know my opinion right from the start.

[DRAFT]

Preserve Your Future

by Luis

Soon voters in our town will be asked to determine the future of the old Wingate property. Some think it should become a housing development. But I say this land must be preserved! ← [clear opinion]

First of all, keeping the land as open space will cost taxpayers less than developing it. If the land is used for houses or apartments, the children who move there will need schools. The residents will require costly services like Fire and Police Protection, as well as trash collection. My aunt is a Firefighter, and she earns a pretty good living.

Also, both people and animals benefit from open land. If forced off their own land, wild animals would look for other places to live. They would come into our backyards and eat our plants and bushes. Is this something we want?

Another important reason to keep Wingate as undeveloped land is that people need a place to get away. In my opinion we are much healthier if we exercise outdoors, where we can get fresh air and sun, instead of paying to belong to a gym. Not to mention, looking at trees and grass is relaxing! It relieves stress and eases the mind.

Finally, there's not alot of open land left in our town. Over three fourths of our city's land is already developed. Our quality of life depends on our ability to walk around freely enjoy trees and flowers, and have room to get away from noise and crowds. We will begin saving what little open space we have left.

In conclusion, there are many good reasons to keep Wingate as open land. It's cheaper, and it's healthier for people, animals, and plants. Surely these facts outway any reasons <u>not</u> to keep Wingate for public use.

Remember! Clearly state your opinion so the reader will know why you're writing.

Reflect

What do you think? Did I make a strong case for preserving the old Wingate property?

Revising Extend Writing

Writing Strategy Add facts and examples to support each reason.

The scoring guide says to include facts and examples that support each of my reasons. So I reread my essay to see if there were any places where I could add more support. My paragraph about people and animals seems OK as is, but I think I can add even more facts and details to persuade the reader about the dangers of developing wildlife land.

> Shrubs and gardens are not the only things that could get damaged. Deer, rabbits, and coyotes carry diseases such as Lyme disease, rabies, and rabbit fever. People could get sick from the close contact. ← [added facts]

Also, both people and animals benefit from open land. If forced off their own land, wild animals would look for other places to live. They would come into our backyards and eat our plants and bushes. Is this something we want?

> **Remember!** Don't just state your reasons; add facts and details that support them.

Once I added some new details, I reread my paper to make sure it made sense. The scoring guide says to leave out unnecessary details, which means all of my facts and examples should clearly support my reasons. But there was one sentence that seemed out of place. The fact that my aunt earns a good living has nothing to do with my argument, so I'll get rid of that sentence right now.

[DRAFT]

First of all, keeping the land as open space will cost taxpayers less than developing it. If the land is used for houses or apartments, the children who move there will need schools. The residents will require costly services like Fire and Police Protection, as well as trash collection. ~~My aunt is a Firefighter, and she earns a pretty good living.~~

[deleted an unnecessary idea]

Remember! Delete unnecessary details that weaken your argument.

Reflect

Do all of my details support my argument? Are there enough facts and examples to support each reason?

Editing Check Sentences

Writing Strategy Use conditional sentences.

I reread my paper one last time to make sure I included conditional sentences, just as the scoring guide suggests. There was one place in my draft where the existing sentence was kind of confusing to my argument, so I formed a conditional sentence there instead.

[DRAFT]

Finally, there's not alot of open land left in our town. Over three fourths of our city's land is already developed. Our quality of life depends on our ability to walk around freely enjoy trees and flowers, and have room to get away from noise and crowds. ~~We will~~ That's why we should begin saving what little open space we have left.

[formed a conditional sentence]

Remember! Use conditional sentences to strengthen your argument.

Editing Proofread Writing

Grammar Mechanics

Writing Strategy Check my grammar, punctuation, capitalization, and spelling.

I'm almost finished! The scoring guide says to use correct grammar, punctuation, capitalization, and spelling. I always leave plenty of time to check for errors in these important areas.

Preserve Your Future
by Luis

Soon voters in our town will be asked to determine the future of the old Wingate property. Some think it should become a housing development. But I say this land must be preserved!

First of all, keeping the land as open space will cost taxpayers less than developing it. If the land is used for houses or apartments, the children who move there will need schools. The residents will require costly services like ~~F~~ire and ~~P~~olice ~~P~~rotection, as well as trash collection. ~~My aunt is a Firefighter, and she earns a pretty good living~~.

Remember! Check your grammar, punctuation, capitalization, and spelling every time you write for a test.

[**FINAL DRAFT**]

Shrubs and gardens are not the only things that could get damaged. Deer, rabbits, and coyotes carry diseases such as Lyme disease, rabies, and rabbit fever. People could get sick from the close contact.

Also, both people and animals benefit from open land. If forced off their own land, wild animals would look for other places to live. They would come into our backyards and eat our plants and bushes. Is this something we want?

Another important reason to keep Wingate as undeveloped land is that people need a place to get away. In my opinion, we are much healthier if we exercise outdoors, where we can get fresh air and sun, instead of paying to belong to a gym. Not to mention, looking at trees and grass is relaxing! It relieves stress and eases the mind.

Finally, there's not a lot of open land left in our town. Over three fourths of our city's land is already developed. Our quality of life depends on our ability to walk around freely, enjoy trees and flowers, and have room to get away from noise and crowds. That's why we should ~~We will~~ begin saving what little open space we have left.

In conclusion, there are many good reasons to keep Wingate as open land. It's cheaper, and it's healthier for people, animals, and plants. Surely these facts ~~outway~~ outweigh any reasons <u>not</u> to keep Wingate for public use.

Reflect

I don't think I missed anything, but I'll check my essay against the scoring guide one more time before I turn it in. Use your writing prompt's scoring guide to check your writing anytime you take a test.

I'm finished! That wasn't so bad. The main thing to remember when you take a writing test is that you use the writing process. The process is a little different when you take a test, but if you keep in mind these important tips, you'll do OK.

TEST TIPS

1. **Study the writing prompt before you start to write.** Most writing prompts have three parts: the setup, the task, and the scoring guide. The parts probably won't be labeled. You'll have to figure them out for yourself!

2. **Make sure you understand the task before you start to write.**

    - Read all three parts of the writing prompt carefully.
    - Circle key words in the task part of the writing prompt that tell what kind of writing you need to do. The task might also identify your audience.
    - Make sure you know how you'll be graded.
    - Say the assignment in your own words to yourself.

3. **Keep an eye on the clock.** Decide how much time you will spend on each part of the writing process and try to stick to your schedule. Don't spend so much time on prewriting that you don't have enough time left to write.

4. **Reread your writing. Check it against the scoring guide at least twice.** Remember the rubrics you've used? A scoring guide on a writing test is like a rubric. It can help you keep what's important in mind.

5. **Plan, plan, plan!** You don't get much time to revise during a test, so planning is more important than ever.

6. **Write neatly.** Remember, if the people who score your test can't read your writing, it doesn't matter how good your essay is!

WRITER'S HANDBOOK

The Writer's Handbook will give you more help and some great hints for making your writing the best it can be. Use the Writer's Handbook any time you have more questions or just need a little extra help.

Table of Contents

Writer's Terms 412

Grammar/Mechanics
    Sentence Structure 414

    Quotations 414

    Punctuation 415

    Parts of Speech 415

Writer's Terms

Active Voice shows that the subject of a sentence is doing the action.

Biased Words are words that show favor for one person or point of view over another.

Call to Action is an appeal to the audience to buy, try, or use a product.

Cause-and-Effect Links can be used to show the relation between cause and effect.

Citing Sources is the act of telling readers where you found certain information.

Clichés are boring and overused expressions such as *white as snow* and *black as night*.

Details are facts, examples, and anecdotes used to support main ideas.

Diagrams are pictures that show how something works, how it's made, or how it's done.

Dialogue is the conversation between characters in a story.

Examples are pieces of information that support a topic, a statement, an idea, or an opinion.

Figurative Language is an expression in which words are used to create a mental picture for the reader.

Historical Details are facts about a particular time, place, or historical event.

Jargon is the specialized language of a particular business or trade.

Loaded Words cause the reader to have a strong positive or negative reaction.

Main-Idea Table can be used to show how a main idea is supported by details.

Metaphor is a comparison that calls one thing another.

Note Cards contain organized information about a topic.

Outline can be used to show the main idea and supporting details of a piece of writing.

Overused Words are used so often that they sound stale.

Paraphrase is a restatement of another person's words or ideas as one's own.

Participial Phrase is a phrase containing a participle, or verb form that ends in *–ed* or *–ing*. The participle in the phrase acts as an adjective because it describes the subject of the sentence.

Passive Voice shows that the subject of a sentence is not doing the action.

Personification is the writing technique of applying human qualities to an animal, object, or idea.

Persuasion Map can be used to show how examples and facts support the reasons in a piece of writing.

Plagiarizing is the act of copying another's words and presenting them as one's own.

Primary Source is a person or book that provides firsthand information about a topic.

Pro-and-Con Chart can be used to organize the positive and negative aspects of an argument.

Problem-Solution Frame can be used to define a problem and organize information to solve it.

Purpose is the author's reason for writing.

Sales Technique is the method used to make people want to buy a product.

Sequence Chain can be used to show the order of steps in a complex process.

Setting is the time and place in which a story takes place.

Simile is a comparison using the word *like* or *as*.

Storyboard can be used to plot the chronological order of a story's main events.

Story Frame can be used to organize the key events in a story, frame by frame.

Story Map can be used to organize the setting, characters, plot, major events, and outcome of a story.

Theme is the message about life that the author wants to convey.

Thesaurus is a reference book containing an alphabetical list of synonyms and antonyms.

Three W's Chart can be used to organize what you already know, what you want to know, and where you can look for further information about a topic.

Timeline can be used to sequence key events.

Tone is the way that the writing sounds.

Vague Words are words that aren't clear or distinct.

Web can be used to organize information about one main topic.

Works Consulted is a list containing the bibliographic information for the sources used in a piece of writing.

Grammar / Mechanics

Sentence Structure

Complex Sentence consists of an independent clause and a dependent clause. The dependent clause begins with a subordinating conjunction such as *although* or *because*.

Compound Sentence consists of two related independent clauses. The clauses can be joined by a semicolon or a comma and a coordinating conjunction such as *or, and,* or *but*.

Declarative Sentence is a sentence that states a fact or an opinion.

Exclamatory Sentence is a sentence that has a sense of urgency and ends with an exclamation mark.

Run-on Sentence is an incorrectly written sentence containing simple sentences that are run together without the proper adjoining punctuation and/or conjunction.

Sentence Fragment is an incomplete sentence that begins with a capital letter and ends with final punctuation.

Subject-Verb Agreement is when the subject and verb of a sentence agree with each other in number and tense. The verb in each sentence should agree with its subject and not with an object of a preposition that comes before the verb.

Quotations

Direct Quotation consists of the exact words of a speaker.
- Begin and end a direct quotation with quotation marks.
- If a direct quotation stands alone as a sentence, begin it with a capital letter.
- If the quotation does not stand alone as a sentence, do not begin it with a capital letter.
- Place the punctuation that ends a quote inside the closing quotation marks.
- Use a comma to set off a phrase that identifies the speaker.
- If a quotation is divided by such a phrase, enclose both parts within quotation marks.

Indirect Quotation consists of a retelling of the speaker's words.
- Do not use quotation marks around an indirect quotation.
- The speaker's words in an indirect quotation are often preceded by the word *that*.

Punctuation

Colon is a type of punctuation used

- when the second clause states a direct result of or further explains the first.
- to introduce a list or series.
- after the greeting in a business letter.
- to separate hours and minutes in an expression of time.
- between the city of publication and the publisher in a bibliographic reference.

Hyphen is a type of punctuation used

- to separate syllables when you break a word at the end of a line.
- to link the parts of certain compound words.
- to link two or more words that precede a noun and act as an adjective.
- to link certain spelled-out numbers.

Parts of Speech

Verbs

Verbs have three simple tenses: present, past, and future.

- The present tense states what currently happens.
- The past tense states what happened in the past. To form the past tense, add *–ed* to the end of most present tense verbs.
- The future tense states what will happen in the future. To form the future tense, add *will* in front of a present tense verb.

Perfect Tense Verbs also have three forms: present, past, and future.

- The present perfect tense states what began in the past and may still be happening. To form the present perfect tense, add *has* or *have* in front of a past tense verb.
- The past perfect tense states what began in the past and was completed. To form the past perfect tense, add *had* in front of a past tense verb.
- The future perfect tense states what will begin in the future and end in the future. To form the future perfect tense, add *will* in front of a present perfect tense verb.

Present Participle Verbs show continuing action. To form the present participle form of a verb, add *–ing* to the end of most present tense verbs.

Progressive Tense Verbs also have three forms: present, past, and future.

- The present progressive tense also states continuing action. To form the present progressive tense, add *am, is,* or *are* in front of a present participle verb.

Grammar / Mechanics continued

- The past progressive tense states action that continually happened in the past. To form the past progressive tense, add *was* or *were* in front of a present participle verb.
- The future progressive tense states action that will continually happen in the future. To form the future progressive tense, add *will be* in front of a present participle verb.

Introductory Verbal Phrase comes at the beginning of a sentence and describes the subject. It contains a verbal that acts like a noun, adjective, or adverb.

Pronouns

Subject Pronouns such as *I, we, she,* and *they* should be used as the subjects of sentences.

Object Pronouns such as *me, us, you, him, her, it,* and *them* should be used as objects following verbs and as objects of prepositions.

Indefinite Pronouns such as *everyone, nobody, nothing, something,* and *anything* are all considered singular.

Possessive Pronouns such as *my, mine, our, ours, your, yours, his, her, hers, its, their,* and *theirs* show ownership or possession but do not contain apostrophes.

Compound Personal Pronouns always end in *–self* or *–selves (himself, yourself, themselves).*

Antecedent is the noun that a pronoun replaces.
- Each pronoun must have a clear antecedent.
- Pronouns must agree with their antecedents in number and gender.

Adjectives/Adverbs

Comparative Form compares two people, places, things, or actions.
- Add *–er* to short adjectives and adverbs to create comparative forms.
- Use the word *more* before long adjectives and adverbs to create comparative forms.

Superlative Form compares three or more people, places, things, or actions.
- Add *–est* to create superlative forms.
- Use the word *most* before long adjectives and adverbs to create superlative forms.

Appositives

Appositive is a word or phrase following a noun that describes the noun.